# THE SCREENER

# SCREENING

## Adoptive and Foster Parents

### A GUIDE
### FOR STUDENTS AND PROFESSIONALS

### James L. Dickerson

### Mardi Allen, Ph.D.

SARTORIS
LITERARY
GROUP

SARTORIS LITERARY GROUP
Metro-Jackson, Mississippi
www.sartorisliterary.com

James L. Dickerson dedicates this book
to David and Debra Rice,
treasured friends who have devoted
their lives to making the world a better place.


Mardi Allen dedicates this book to her parents,
Frances and the late Earl Allen, who patiently spent
endless hours teaching every kid in
the community to water ski

# TABLE OF CONTENTS

**Preface**

**PART I**

## In Theory: Adoptive and Foster Parent Screening

Chapter 1: In the Beginning . . . (A History) ... 25

Chapter 2: Who Are Screeners and What Do They Do? ... 33

Chapter 3: Adoption Agencies: Private vs. Public ... 45

Chapter 4: Identifying Adoption Issues ... 54

Chapter 5: Understanding the Foster Parent Syndrome ... 64

Chapter 6: Screening Single and Gay Applicants ... 71

Chapter 7: Screening Male Child Predators ... 80

Chapter 8: What You Need to Know About Infants ... 87

Chapter 9: What You Need to Know About Older Children ... 100

**PART II**

## In Practice: Adoptive and Foster Parent Screening

Chapter 10: Home Study Interview Techniques ... 111

Chapter 11: First Interview with Adoptive Applicants ... 119

Chapter 12: First Interview with Foster Parent Applicants ... 130

Chapter 13: Follow-up Interviews with Foster and Adoptive Applicants ,,, 140

Chapter 14: Health and Background Interviews ... 152

Chapter 15: Marital and Relationship Interviews ... 166

Chapter 16: Exploring Parenting Issues ... 179

Chapter 17: Screener Recommendations for Adoptive and Foster Parents ... 195

Chapter 18: Finalizing the Adoption ...204

# PART III

## Psychological Assessment:

## A Means to Resolve Complicated Evaluation Issues

Chapter 19: The Referral Question: An Overview of Testing Possibilities ... 219

Chapter 20: Evaluating Mood and Anxiety Problems ... 234

Chapter 21: Ruling Out Major Pathology ... 246

Chapter 22: Measuring Levels of Cognitive Function ... 262

Chapter 23: Identifying Personal and Family Conflicts ... 268

Chapter 24: Assessing Parenting Skills ... 280

**ENDNOTES**

**BIBLIOGRAPHY**

# Acknowledgements

James L. Dickerson would like to thank the late R. S. Fenemore, the late Jean Gardner, the late Florene Brownell, Grant Fair; AND Sharon Gary, whose friendship and counsel is greatly valued.

Mardi Allen would like to thank former DMH Executive Director, Randy Hendrix, who has always supported my professional pursuits; librarian, Margueritte Ransom, who diligently searched for books and articles for this project; Christy Miller, who assumed the responsibility of research assistance with great enthusiasm; my family who always believes in me far beyond my abilities; Susan S. Holt, who showed me how precious adoption can be; and Austin, Matthew and Brandon who thought it was cool for me to write a book.

# PREFACE

Adoption and foster care is a life-altering experience for the children and adults who are directly involved—a realization that weighs heavily on those professionals responsible for guiding them through the process. Adoption and foster home workers are asked to play God with life's most vulnerable creations, yet, incredibly, they have access to little in the way of specialized training to prepare them for that task.

The training that adoption and foster home workers receive at institutions of higher learning, when it occurs at all, puts the focus on therapeutic interview techniques, the direct opposite of what is needed to screen adoptive and foster parents.

As part of our research for this book, we surveyed twenty schools of social work in the United States and Canada in 2004 and 2005 and asked if they offered a course in screening adoptive or foster home applicants. The results of the survey were surprising. Only one of the schools surveyed, Brigham Young University, offered courses in adoptive and foster parent screening, and only three schools offered courses in adoption and foster care (University of Georgia, University of North Carolina at Charlotte, and Temple University). The other schools surveyed were:

| | |
|---|---|
| University of Wyoming | Jackson State University |
| Miami University | University of Hawaii |
| University of Vermont | Tulane University |
| University of Oklahoma | University of Arkansas |
| Michigan State University | New York University |
| University of Montana | Florida State University |
| McGill University | Auburn University |
| Virginia Commonwealth University | |
| San Francisco State University | |

The University of Oklahoma offers a course titled "Interviewing Skills for Generalist Practice" for its BSW, but no interviewing course for its MSW, and San Francisco State University offers "Interviewing Skills in Social Work" for third-year BSW candidates, but nothing specific to adoption or foster homes. In the recent past, McGill University offered a course at the master's level that looked at the range of issues involved in foster care and adoption, including instruction on how to conduct home studies, but apparently the course has been dropped from the curriculum.

We initially planned to survey every school of social work in the United States and Canada, but once it became apparent that additional data would not alter the results evidenced in the first sample, we dropped the survey to avoid a "piling on" effect. Our first sample told us all we needed to know.

What the survey results suggest is that social workers by the thousands are being produced each year by an educational system that does not offer the specialized training required to screen adoptive and foster parents. With no courses designed specifically for that purpose, it is obvious that there is a need for a book like *The Screener* **to** be incorporated into course requirements and used by working social workers and psychologists who are involved with adoption and foster parent screening.

Most state departments of social and family services require adoption and foster home workers to attend social work schools before they can be hired, yet almost no schools of social work offer courses on adoption and foster parent screening. If the only way to become an adoption or foster home worker is to obtain a social work degree—and if schools of social work do not offer specialized training—how is it possible for anyone to be properly trained? The answer is that very few adoption and foster home workers are being properly trained. For the most part, they are hired without any specialized training and provided with in-house instruction under a supervisor who may have limited specialized training in that field.

Despite its long history, adoptive and foster parent screening, as a profession, is still in its infancy. There is very little empirical research on the subject upon which to base a screening guide and that is why our personal experiences were essential for the writing of this book.

*The Screener* is divided into three distinct parts:

**Part I** offers the theoretical and background information that students and practitioners need to become good screeners. Based on the conviction that we won't know where we are going until we understand where we have been, "In the Beginning . . . (A History)" puts adoption and foster parenting in historical perspective and looks at two areas where adoption has changed radically in recent years (open and subsidized adoptions), while "Who Are Screeners and What Do They Do?" defines the job title and explains why screening should exist as an entirely separate course in social work and psychology curriculums.

**Part I** continues with a chapter that points out the differences between private and public adoption agencies, helpful information for students considering a career in adoption. "Identifying Adoption Issues" discusses the attitudes of applicants as they reflect upon parenting issues that have a bearing on successful parenting. "Understanding the Foster Parent Syndrome" provides interviewers with a philosophical basis for understanding why foster-parent applicants have motivations for taking in children that are different from the motivations usually displayed by adoptive applicants. With "Screening Single and Gay Applicants" and "Screening Child Predators" we present the research and ground rules for interviews in those areas. Two chapters, "What You Need to Know About Infants" and "What You Need to Know About Older Children," offer growth-and-development information that screeners need to understand to be able to make informed decisions about an applicant's capacity to parent a child at different stages of the child's life.

**Part II** is the practical, "how-to" portion of the book and offers step-by-step instruction to students and practitioners on how to interview adoptive and foster-parent applicants for the purpose of writing a comprehensive home study. "Home Study Interview Techniques" provides instruction on how to conduct interviews in general, while the next three chapters offer specific questions and guidance on how to structure first, second and subsequent interviews. "Health and Background Interviews" guides screeners on methods to obtain important information about an applicant's health, educational and employment history, along with tips on obtaining references.

**Part II** continues with guidance on conducting what are usually the most challenging interviews: those that focus on the applicant's relationship history. "Exploring Parenting Issues" helps screeners make determinations about an applicant's potential to be a good parent to an adopted or foster child. This section continues with suggestions on how to make recommendations for the approval or rejection of applications, and advice on how to deal with applicants whose applications have been turned down. The final chapter in this section, "Finalizing the Adoption," walks the screener through placement, visitation and the finalization of the adoption.

An important ingredient of this book is the merger of social work and psychology. Those different perspectives will be celebrated and emphasized throughout the book. Often social workers and psychologists find themselves on opposing sides of an issue. Social workers consider their profession an art that is based on communicative skills and an understanding of human behavior, while psychologists consider their profession a science based on the evaluation of complex social systems. The book will essentially take the best of social work and psychology and merge it into a coherent approach to adoptive and foster parent screening.

**Part III** was written to provide screeners with options for dealing with problems that were unresolved during the interview process. The focus of this section is on advising screeners about when a referral to a psychologist for an assessment might be in order. Each chapter, such as "Ruling Out Major Pathology" and "Assessing Parenting Skills," lists individual standardized tests that psychologists can use to gather information in specific areas about which agencies have concerns.

The merger of social work and psychology is a logical reflection of our professional backgrounds. As a social worker, I worked in a public agency in Ontario, Canada, where I was a screener in charge of foster homes and adoptions, placing literally hundreds of children over a seven-year period—and, later, at a private agency in Memphis, Tennessee, where the focus was on international adoptions. Additionally, I worked as a crisis worker for children in need of protection; I worked as a consultant on a variety of child-related issues to a private practice of psychologists; and, for a time, I operated the Food Stamp office for the poorest county in America. I have written about foster and adoptive parents for professional journals such as the *Ontario Journal of Children's Aid Societies,* and I have written about children's issues for popular magazines such as <u>Good Housekeeping.</u>

My co-author, Dr. Mardi Allen, approaches this subject from the perspective of a psychologist. She earned her doctorate in psychology at the University of Southern Mississippi with an emphasis in Child, Developmental and School Psychology. During her internship at Primary Children's Medical Center, University of Utah, Dr. Allen conducted parent-training sessions, social skills groups for youth and was a therapist for both the outpatient and inpatient patients. She gained experience in working with neurologically involved patients during her post-doctoral residency at the Neurology, Learning and Behavior Center in Salt Lake City, Utah.

Dr. Allen is the former Clinical Services Liaison with Mississippi Department of Mental Health and a past president of the Association of State and Provincial Psychology Boards (2002-2003), an alliance of state, provincial and territorial agencies responsible for the licensure and discipline of all psychologists throughout the United States and Canada, with other affiliate members throughout the world.

Early in her professional career, Dr. Allen taught elementary school where she was honored as Outstanding Young Educator of the year. Later, she served as consulting psychologist to a university infant evaluation team and made television appearances to discuss issues affecting children. She has written numerous staff training manuals and produced training videos. Dr. Allen has assisted in writing several psychology documents related to the regulation of psychologists, including *Guidelines for*

*Prescriptive Authority for Psychology and History and Guidelines for Continuing Psychology Education.*

Dr. Allen has been a member of the National Reading Readiness Committee, Raising Resilient Children Advisory Committee, Task Force on Technology, Task Force on Impaired Psychologists, and a standing Grant Review Committee for U. S. Centers for Mental Health Services. The American Psychological Association honored Dr. Allen with the Heizer Award for outstanding leadership in facilitating the passage of state and federal mental health legislation. In 1997, she was selected for the American Association for the Advancement of Science Congressional Fellowship Program. As a Fellow, she served in Washington, DC for a year, where she worked as a legislative assistant and provided expertise in policy development. In addition to her many other responsibilities, Dr. Allen maintains a private practice.

Social work and psychology have undergone some interesting transformations since Dr. Allen and I entered our respective professions in the 1960s and 1980s. Social work has changed from a profession that stressed "people" skills to one that today often is more concerned with public policy and financial assistance issues. Psychology has evolved from a profession that dealt primarily with personality issues to one that today deals with a wide range of mental problems, family dysfunction, and social issues, and, most recently, a drive to seek prescriptive authority.

Lost among those changes are the thousands of children who enter child welfare agencies each year in need of foster and adoptive homes. Their needs are immediate and much too critical to be entrusted to screeners who have learned the profession by trial and error through in-staff training programs that typically have no theoretical foundation.

We wrote this book for social work schools and psychology departments that have an interest in training students to become effective screeners before they begin practice because we feel that the quality of their training has a profound impact on all the other layers of issues with which social workers and psychologists grapple on a daily basis.

Because it is the screener who determines whether foster and adoptive children will be placed in safe, nurturing environments, it is the screener who makes it possible for the caseworker or psychologist providing therapy to dysfunctional families that have entered the child-welfare system to have a level playing field on which to deal with policy and treatment issues. Few adults have the focus to respond to treatment as long as their children are in crisis, and the knowledge that their children are being properly cared for while they work out their problems is critical to the success of any therapy.

If a screener's first obligation is to provide safe homes for foster and adoptive children, the second obligation is to do no harm in the process. Few children survive bad foster and adoptive home placements without permanent scarring, a daunting reminder that a screener's margin of error is deceptively slight. Competent screeners are key players in the child welfare system and until they are provided with every training resource available the system will never be all that it can become.

**JAMES L. DICKERSON**
**(2022)**

# PART I

# In Theory

## ADOPTIVE
## AND
## FOSTER PARENT
## SCREENING

# Chapter 1

## In the beginning . . . (A History)

Foster care and adoption have been around for as long as mammals have inhabited the planet. You might say it is among the species' most endearing and enduring survival characteristic, unlike the every-species-for-itself mandate that cold-blooded creatures and plants have inherited in the Darwin evolutionary loop.

Mammals have a long history of taking in orphaned offspring for the purpose of suckling them and nurturing them to adulthood, so it is not surprising that practice would evolve into a cultural mandate for *Homo sapiens* intent on the survival of the species. In the beginning, foster home and adoption placements were arranged by tribal elders, who assigned motherless children to women deemed to have nurturing abilities.

Over the centuries, as families evolved into separate social jurisdictions within the tribe, individual family patriarchs assumed the child-placement duties formerly held by tribal leaders. If a daughter or grand-daughter died in childbirth, the patriarch took it upon himself to find a suitable home for the surviving child. If the child was female, he approached family members or neighbors and asked them to raise the child. If the child was male, the patriarch was more likely to take the child himself as a means of acquiring labor for his trade, agricultural, or business enterprises.

The first written adoption laws can be found in the Code of Hammurabi, dated around 2800 B.C., which described the relationship between birth and adoptive parents, and established procedures for resolving adoption conflicts, especially those involving birth and adoptive parents. The Roman Empire, with its emphasis on patriarchal rule, modified the Code of Hammurabi to emphasis the power of males to terminate a birth mother's rights in adoption. Foster and adoptive care proceeded along those lines for much of recorded history, with cultural evolution dictating that male family heads make all the decisions regarding the care of orphaned children.

That didn't change in a significant way until the arrival of the Industrial Revolution, which caused extended families in North America to be dispersed over a wider geographical area in search of economic opportunities. The more distance that coming-of-age women put between themselves and the patriarchs, the more freedom they demanded for self-determination—and that opened the door on an entirely new class of foster and adoption placements that were created by out-of-wedlock births.

With the decline of the patriarchal family in North America, it became obvious that society had to set up a system to find homes for children that otherwise might be abandoned by their extended families. Distraught mothers placed their children into adoptive homes with the approval of a legal system that viewed adoption as a property transfer in which adoptive parents filed a deed with the court similar to those used in real estate transactions. There were no minimum standards to be foster or adoptive parents.

In North America the first laws regarding adoption were enacted by Massachusetts in 1851, when for the first time in history, courts were asked to oversee adoptions. A reaction to changing roles of women in society, the new adoption laws were not written to protect children so much as they were to shift decision-making about adoption away from mothers and back to males, who dominated the court system.

Children's rights didn't enter the picture until much later, when individual Canadian provinces started enacting legislation in the 1870s to protect apprenticed children from industrial corporations that put a high premium on child labor. By the turn of the century, that basic protective concept mushroomed into a network of children's aid societies in Ontario that offered protective services to children, counseling to unwed mothers, and adoption for children that became wards of the state.

Over the next several decades, individual American states followed the lead set by Canada and established a network of child welfare agencies that evolved into the nationwide system that we have today in which each individual state's foster home and adoption policies are more similar than dissimilar. Unlike Canada, which has essentially remained true to its original concept of social work as a protective service for children victimized by physical, emotional or sexual abuse despite recent trends favoring preventative services, the United States has come to view social work more as an adult-oriented profession keyed toward financial and preventative services for a wide range of social problems associated with issues such as substance abuse and AIDS.

That shift in emphasis can be seen in the curriculums of social work schools that stress courses on public policy issues, administrative skills, social gerontology, addiction and AIDS counseling, etc., at the expense of courses that teach the fundamentals of foster care and adoption, or courses that teach social workers how to counsel children that have been emotionally, physically or sexually abused by their caregivers. That academic foundation of social work would seem to run counter to the U.S. Adoptions and Safe Families Act of 1997[i] that mandated that child welfare agencies "move children in foster care more quickly into permanent homes" as an expression of "paramount concern" for the health and safety of children in their care.

Of course, the irony is that despite the fact that precious few schools of social work today are training students how to screen foster and adoptive parents, the child welfare system is almost totally dependent on foster and adoptive parents for the care of children who are in need of protective services.

Today there are about 500,000 children in foster care in the United States, with about 126,000 of them awaiting adoption. Public and private adoption workers will find permanent homes for about 48,000 of them— and they will screen adoptive parents for an additional 18,000 children brought into the country from abroad—but that still leaves 78,000 children in foster care that need adoptive parents.

27

# Open Adoptions:
# A Reaction to the Secrecy of the Past

Once adoption became institutionalized, the guiding philosophy became one of confidentiality. Foster parents were not told where their children were going. Adoptive parents were told only what was absolutely necessary about the child and her background. And the adopted child was prevented from ever obtaining any information about her birth parents. At the time, the consensus was that there were good reasons for maintaining such a high level of secrecy:

- Foster parents who tried to sabotage adoptions when they realized they were too emotionally attached to a child.
- Birth parents that harassed adoptive parents and tried to destroy their child's new relationship with her adoptive parents.
- Instances of suicide among unwed mothers who could not live with the "shame" of having a child out of wedlock.
- Discrimination against adopted children in the community.

For the above reasons and more, it was deemed in the best interest of everyone involved to keep all records sealed and to pretend that the adoptive parents were indeed the birth parents. The truth was usually not considered a viable option.

For many years, child welfare agencies considered parental contact with an adopted child to be one of the greatest risks to a successful adoption—and they steadfastly refused to budge on that principle. It took years for child welfare agencies to feel comfortable recommending that adoptive parents tell their children that they were adopted. Today adoption "telling" is accepted practice and most professionals recommend that adoptive parents start discussing adoption with their children at age five.

There was not another major change in attitudes until the late 1980s and early 1990s, when a shrinking pool of adoptable children due to the availability of abortion and relaxed public attitudes about unmarried mothers keeping their children, changed the balance of power, so to speak. Unmarried mothers suddenly found themselves being courted as individuals whose opinions mattered.

With time, as the confidentiality of adoption was eroded by changing lifestyles and expectations, more cracks appeared in the confidentiality façade. As more and more adopted children reached adulthood and requested information about their birth parents—and as more and more birth parents requested information about their children, child welfare agencies in increasing numbers approved new policies that allowed contact with birth parents on the condition that everyone's identity would be protected. Birth parents were given updates on their child's school progress, activities and health, which inevitably lead to a sharing of letters, photographs and other important information.

Today there is a trend to maintain communication between all persons involved through a type of adoption termed the "open adoption." Under this system, birth parents often are involved in the selection of the adoptive parents and maintain contact with the child and the adoptive parents after the adoption takes place. It is a time-share style of adoption in which both birth and adoptive parents raise the child together.

The advantages of open adoptions are: Adoptive parents have a sense of partnership with the birth parents, which means that they don't have to live in fear that the child someday will discover the identity of his birth parents and reject them as parents; important medical information can be shared and that could be important to the diagnosis of life-threatening diseases; and the child can grow up knowing her biological parents, aunts, and grandparents.

The disadvantages of open adoptions are: stress and emotional uncertainty that arises when birth and adoptive parents discover that they have nothing in common other than the child and find that they are unable to successfully share the child; stress and emotional uncertainty for the child who has a difficult time trying to please two sets of parents; and the legal uncertainty that accompanies a botched open adoption can result in years of legal wrangling. The potential for legal difficulties are a major disadvantage of open adoptions. Minor-age birth mothers may change their minds when they become adults and petition the court for the return of the child. Fathers thought not to be an issue may appear years later and demand custody of the child, claiming that they were never informed of the pregnancy. Understandings between a birth mother and an adoptive couple may seem secure at the time of placement, but may change radically with the passing of time.

Since open adoptions are not right for everyone, it is important for public and private agencies to provide unwed mothers with a choice of whether their children will be placed in a traditional or an open adoption home. Confidentiality sometimes is an important consideration to many unwed mothers and if they are not offered that choice during their pregnancy many will opt for abortion instead of adoption. That is especially important in cases involving rape, incest, or mothers younger than eighteen years of age.

It is important for adoptive parents to understand all the possibilities associated with open adoption. What may sound like a great idea on paper is sometimes less than great in reality. If the birth mother is similar to the parent in age, ethnic background or intelligence, the adoption will have a greater chance for success than if she is substantially different from the adoptive parent—for example, if the birth mother is fourteen, the victim of incest, below average intelligence, or of an ethnic group that has strong political and religious opinions about the role women should play in society.

Proponents of open adoption often point to the benefits that type of adoption has on the birth mother. Two supporters of open adoption, Annette Baran and Reuben Pannor (Los Angeles-based social workers in private practice), participated in a 1978 study (Sorosky, Baran and Pannor) that demonstrated that "for most birthmothers, relinquishment and adoptive placement was a traumatic experience that remained with them throughout their life."[ii] Wrote Baran and Pannor: "Once the adoption proceedings have been completed, the birthparents seem to become the forgotten or hidden parents around whom the adoptee and adoptive parents have been able to weave fantasies of a positive or negative nature."[iii]

Social workers and psychologists who work with birthparents can perhaps be forgiven for wanting to ease the pain of their loss since there is no doubt that it affects birthparents in a negative way for the remainder of their lives. However, screeners have only one ethical way of viewing open adoptions and that is through the eyes of the child. What works for the birth parents does not always work best for the child.

The screener's responsibility is to find the best home possible for the child, not to make decisions that will be therapeutic for the birth parents, however compassionate and personally satisfying that might be. Sometimes open adoption will be the best solution for a placement. Other times it will not be a good solution. Screeners may find themselves in trouble if they try to please everyone by juggling the competing emotional needs of birthparents, adoptive parents and the child. When that happens it is important to take a time out and focus on the person who counts on you the most—the child.

# Subsidized Adoptions: A Viable Option In Some Cases

Subsidized foster homes have long been viewed as critical (and respected) components of the child welfare system, but not until recently have subsidized adoptive homes been considered appropriate for child placements. As the number of adoptable infants has decreased, agencies have realized that financial incentives are an appropriate incentive for adoptive homes in which certain classes of children are placed—those that are mentally and physically challenged, those that have diseases such as AIDS that will require long-term care, or those who are likely to have emotional problems that will require costly long-term care.

Adoption subsidy payments are not a salary. Their purpose is to help pay some of the medical costs associated with raising a child with "special needs"—that is, children with chronic physical, learning, or emotional problems that require special attention on an ongoing basis. Without adoption subsidy payments, some children would remain in foster homes or institutions until adulthood.

Adoption applicants rarely approach the agency with a suggestion that they be considered for subsidy payments. The subject usually arises when the screener detects an ability and desire on the part of adoptive applicants to care for special need children and determines that they do not have the financial resources to take on the responsibility. In that situation, the screener will ask, "How would you feel about adopting a special needs child if the agency contributed to her care?" If the answer is positive, the financial aspects of agency involvement will add an extra dimension to the screening process.

# Chapter 2

## Who Are Screeners
## and
## What Do They Do?

With so much work to be done, who is being trained to do it?

Foster home-finding and adoption placement are two separate but similar tasks, but since few institutions of higher learning have curriculums to prepare social workers for either of those positions, the individuals who do the work typically are trained in-staff by supervisors who may or may not have ever done the work themselves.

For the sake of clarity, we will refer to anyone who interviews foster parent and adoptive applicants, for the purpose of approving them for children, with a descriptive term that has universal application and acceptance—**screener.**

If you went from agency to agency in search of data about screeners, you would find some with degrees in social work, others with degrees in psychology, and some without degrees of any kind. Unless their supervisor is a former screener and moved up the ranks within the agency, they are unlikely to ever receive authoritative instruction on how to screen foster care and adoptive applicants.

As a result, standards vary considerably from agency to agency, with levels of excellence typically set by individual supervisors without regard to uniform applications of accepted practice. The only common denominator is an expectation, false as it often turns out, that foster and adoptive home studies will follow an established outline for providing required information about the applicants.

# Foster Parent Screeners

There was a time when foster parent screeners saw their work in black-and-white terms: They either found enough homes for the children that needed them—or they didn't. There was not much in the way of a gray area and success was measured with a calculator, without much regard to quality. Heads rolled if quotas were not met.

Those days have been gone for a long time.

Today quality is more important than quantity, and screeners who cannot maintain that priority can expect to experience uncertain job security. The shift in emphasis from quantity to quality occurred because of mounting evidence that increasing numbers of foster parent programs were being tainted by emotional, physical and sexual abuse directed toward foster children who typically were too frightened and intimidated to report the abuse to their child care workers.

News media stories of foster-home abuse, especially those involving accounts of physical and sexual abuse, bondage and starvation, have created public skepticism about the safety of foster home care. Stories such as the account of a man in New York who served as a foster parent to as many as fifty children before his past as a convicted rapist was discovered strike the public as inconceivable.

The challenge for today's foster parent screener is to recruit and approve enough foster parents to care for the approximately 400,000 children each year who depend on foster homes for survival, while weeding out potential abusers and others with questionable motivations for wanting to become foster parents. It is a daunting task that is made all the more so because of a lack of agreement within the profession about the definition of a good foster parent. It is one thing to screen foster parents for negative qualities that everyone agrees are unacceptable, but it's something else to screen for positive qualities that are often elusive and difficult to define.

Interest in research into this area reached a peak in the early to mid-1960s, as birthrates for children born to unmarried mothers skyrocketed as a result of the so-called "sexual revolution" that flooded child welfare agencies with children available for adoption. Those were the days before abortion was a legal alternative to birth and before birth-control pills came into widespread use. Very few infants were adopted from the hospital in those days, which meant that child-welfare agencies were required to find foster parents to care for infants during the usual 3-6 months they were in care of an agency prior to adoption.

The first comprehensive study of foster parents was undertaken by Martin Wolins, an associate professor at the School of Social Work of the University of California at Berkeley.[iv] Wolins's study, which was published in 1963, came on the heels of a national survey in 1960 that found that there were close to a quarter of a million children in the United States in foster homes with social agency ties. Previous studies (Sophie Van Theis' 1942 effort, *How Foster Children Turn Out*[v], and Henry Maas and Richard Engler's 1960 effort, *Children in Need of Parents*[vi]) have proved inconclusive and raised more questions than they answered. Mass and Engler sent shock waves through the social worker community by reporting that in six of nine communities studied "a quarter or more of the children in foster care had had four or more placements," an important finding in view of those authors' opinion that "instability in relationships fosters personality disturbances."[vii] They predicted that half of the children they studied would remain in foster homes for most of their childhoods.

Wolins's study, which was funded by the National Institute of Mental Health and the U.S. Public Health Service, targeted 907 families whose foster parent applications were pending after at least one interview with a social worker. The major goal of the research was to predict social workers' decisions regarding the applicants:

> **Is it a product of the imagination and practice applied in the field? Is it clear enough, specific enough, operational enough—is it right enough to be useful? These questions are unavoidable. What is wanted from a foster family, and how is it expressed? Who is chosen and who is rejected? How well do we professionals**

> **agree on standards? How true are we to our own dictates? These are the issues of our study.**[viii]

Wolins was unable to satisfactorily answer all of his own questions, but his study did advance the body of knowledge with new insights into the screening process. "A decision must be made that is usually irreversible and that—when a home is used—is subject to verification," he wrote. "The making of such a decision undoubtedly places the worker under considerable strain . . . The direction in which the worker or the agency is prepared to err varies according to the number of children needing placement and the supply of clearly good homes. When an imbalance exists, as is nearly always the case, it has a decided influence on the selection procedure. When the ratio is favorable, when many more good homes are available than there are children to place in them (as used to be the case in adoption programs), the selection process can be a form of 'skimming': the range of choice simply begins from the 'very best' end of the continuum, and it need never enter the risk area. When the ratio of applicants to children is low (as in foster care), the agency is forced closer to the threshold and must often invade the risk area of the continuum, where poor homes may be numerous. The emphasis then changes from completely eliminating risk to reducing it as much as possible . . . The direction of choice shifts: the process becomes one of elimination rather than of choice. The worker tires to eliminate as many unsuitable homes as possible."[ix]

What Wolins discovered about the selection process was that foster parent screeners seemed to agree on the characteristics that define applicants with the highest potential for being foster parents, but then acted out of agency need when demand outstripped supply. The applicants who had the greatest chance of approval were those who met enough of the following characteristics:

- The father of the family regards children as distinct individuals (1).

- The mother is farm-reared and is not excessively planful, ambitious, possessive or self-sacrificing (2-5).
- Both parents are fairly flexible in their notion of means and the pursuit of goals (6).
- The have several children of their own, are reasonably well-educated, and are not too old (7-9).

Wolins found that if applicants possess all nine of the above positives they had an 80 percent chance of acceptance, with eight producing a 73 percent acceptance rate, and six yielding a 57 percent acceptance rate. Wolins was not surprised at the findings since they confirmed the common-sense conclusion that screeners tend to approve applicants who follow a conservative, middle-of-the-road approach to childrearing and life in general.

The second major study that examined foster parents was undertaken in 1965 by David Fanshel, a professor in the Columbia University School of Social work and the former director of research for the Child Welfare League of America.[x] Fanshel used a smaller sample (101 foster families at one agency, the Family and Children's Services at Pittsburgh, Pennsylvania) and he took a different approach that attempted to clarify motive among approved foster parents. He also was interested in a foster parent's capacity to love children and then to give them up, and their ability to care for children with different types of problems.

Fanshel's study is of particular interest because of his decision to involve foster fathers in his evaluation. The history of foster parenting is that agencies often have assigned a second-class status to foster fathers in the belief that they are more passive players in child care than mothers. Some of Fanshel's findings were striking:

- Nine out of 10 of the foster fathers felt that foster family care was a good system for rearing children who could not live in their own homes, and they felt it to be superior to institutional care for these youngsters[xi].

- Seven out of 10 of the foster fathers believed that foster parents could adequately make up to a child for the loss of his own natural parents or their inadequacy.
- Seven out of 10 felt that the role of foster parents was just as important to them as it was to their wives.
- Two out of 3 indicated that they expected their homes to be used "indefinitely" for the care of foster children.

Fanshel also scored foster mothers and foster fathers on the sources of their satisfaction in caring for foster children. The top three sources of satisfaction for foster fathers were: 1) "I like helping the unfortunate, downtrodden people;" 2) "Since this makes my spouse happy, I am satisfied;" and 3)"I like being able to put my skills as a homemaker into action (or doing things only a father can do). The top three sources of satisfaction for foster mothers were: 1) "I am fascinated watching children grow up;" 2) "I enjoy the presence of a cuddly little baby in our home;" and 3) "I like putting my religious beliefs into action."[xii]

Fanshel's comparisons are important because they highlight gender differences when it comes to motivation for caring for foster children. Anecdotal evidence supports Fanshel's data that suggests that a foster father's motive for taking in foster children is more altruistic than his wife's and more likely to take her feelings into consideration. The foster mother's motives, on the other hand, tend to focus more on self-gratification and less on altruistic or relationship-related motives. As we will see later, these are important distinctions that can have a major impact on the ultimate success of a foster home.

One of the areas of Fanshel's study that we found particularly interesting was his investigation of the precipitating factors in the decision to become foster parents. The subjects were asked whether there had been any unusual circumstances in the year before they decided to become foster parents. When the thirty-eight foster mothers who reported an uneventful year were compared to the sixty-three who reported having to make unusual adjustments during the year, it was found that foster mothers who reported crises of one kind or another scored higher positives with caseworkers than those reporting uneventful years. "This was a surprising finding, since it had been anticipated that those who responded to a crisis by applying to the agency might well evidence more pathology as a group because of the stress they were experiencing," wrote Fanshel[xiii]. "One explanation of this finding suggests itself: those who reported uneventful periods in their lives before becoming foster parents may have kept their motivations hidden because of a somewhat pathological component."

# Adoption Screeners

The history of screeners is such that they often serve at different stages of their careers as both foster home screeners and adoption screeners. That has resulted in some misconceptions about the screening process as it affects foster and adoptive parents: the most notable one being that the same criteria is applied to both groups.

Foster and adoptive parents represent two separate sets of challenges to the screener, beginning with the fact that adoptive applicants typically are in their twenties or thirties, while foster applicants are typically in their forties, fifties or sixties; adoptive applicants are generally just beginning or headed toward the peaks of their careers, while foster applicants are usually past their career peaks; adoptive applicants seldom have a track record in child-rearing, while foster applicants often have birth children in the home or they have raised birth children to adulthood; and the ability of adoptive applicants to sustain a relationship with a significant other is usually a question mark, while the ability of foster applicants in that area is usually supported by a history of relationships of moderate or long duration. Other key areas where there is a marked difference between foster parents and adoptive parents include: parenting skills, motivation, frustration levels, temperament, and expectations for success.

When adoption applicants present themselves to the screener for their first encounter with the agency, it is not typically in response to a news story, pulpit message or peer pressure, but rather to address an assortment of personal needs that have accumulated over a period of time. If it is a married couple—and one of the partners is infertile—the need may be to build a family. Single applicants may possess a similar need to extend their family beyond its current narrow definition. Rarely the applicant may have a need to "help the world" by providing a permanent home to a child in need.

Typical explanations include:

"We feel it is time to build a family."

"We have plenty of love to give to a child."

"I have wanted a child for as long as I can remember."

"I want to make a difference in the world."

Once the applicants have explained why they have presented themselves to the agency, the screener's first task is to determine their true motivation (which will illuminate the specific needs that they are seeking to meet), while also assessing their potential as parents. Common motivations include: a belief that children in the home will save a faltering marriage; a reaction to childhood sexual, physical or emotional abuse; a need to "undo" the bad parenting they experienced as a child; a need to compensate for the loss of a loved one, especially a mother or father; a lack of sexual intimacy in the marriage; sexual attraction to children; to compensate for not having a desire for a career; to compensate for a career that has not proved to be satisfying; meeting the expectations of domineering parents; peer pressure from family or work associates; to compensate for a lifelong affection deficit; a need to help the less fortunate; a need of one partner to make the other partner happy because of a perception that they are disappointing the partner in other areas; and a need to express social awareness, especially as it applies to children who have suffered abroad because of war, famine, flood or disease.

When it comes to motivational needs, adoptive and foster parents differ in some significant areas. The short-term needs that a foster parent can meet by caring for a child are not adequate for an adoptive parent who envisions adoption as a long-term event. A foster mother whose motivation for caring for a child is based on a need to have something important in her life that is off limits to her partner's influence can be a successful foster parent under the right circumstances, but that type of motivation would be wholly unacceptable for an adoptive parent for obvious reasons.

# Motivations Associated With Adoptive Parents

ACCEPTABLE

- To help the less fortunate
- A need to build and share a family with a loved one
- To satisfy strong maternal or paternal drive
- To express general warmth for children

UNACCEPTABLE

- A belief that children in the home will save a faltering marriage
- To satisfy a sexual attraction to children
- A reaction to childhood sexual, physical or emotional abuse
- Peer pressure from family or work associates
- A lack of sexual intimacy in the marriage
- A need of one partner to make the other partner happy because of a perception that they are disappointing the partner
- To meet the expectations of domineering parents
- A need to control and direct others
- A reaction to recent trauma such as rape, assault, the loss of a job, etc.

41

| CONDITIONALLY ACCEPTABLE |
| --- |
| • A need to "undo" bad parenting experienced as a child<br>• A need to compensate for the loss of a loved one, especially a mother or father<br>• To express social awareness, especially as it applies to children who have suffered abroad because of war, famine, flood or disease.<br>• To compensate for a career that has not proved to be satisfying<br>• To compensate for not having a career<br>• To compensate for a lifelong affection deficit |

# Recognizing Adoptive Parenting Roles

Adoption parents not only differ from foster parents because of their motivation for taking on the task, but also because of their parenting approaches and skills. When you are screening foster parents you want individuals who can provide intensive short-term care to children with a minimal emotional investment—parents who can relinquish the children after a month, six months or six years without being devastated by the loss.

That is not a characteristic you want to find when you are screening adoptive parents. On the contrary, you want parents whose emotional investment in a child will increase with each passing day. Good adoptive parents make poor foster parents and vice versa. The process of making that judgment becomes complicated with couples when one partner is considerably more passive than the other in the emotional investment they are able to make to a child. Historically, foster fathers have proved to be more passive than foster mothers when it comes to parenting foster children. There are many exceptions, of course, in which foster fathers play very active roles, but our experience tells us that foster fathers who are more active than their partners are an infrequent occurrence. Most agencies will find that acceptable in situations where the foster mother is very nurturing and dominant in parenting issues, but there is a sliding scale that must be taken into consideration. A dominant mother/passive father would be within acceptable limits for placements involving infants and pre-school-age children, but less so for school-age children and totally unacceptable for teens.

There is also a sliding scale for adoptive parents, but it does not offer much wiggle room when it comes to making allowances for passive fathers. As a screener, one of the first determinations you have to make is which partner exerts dominance in the relationship. If it is the wife, then you will know from the start that the husband will exert more passivity than the wife in most of the parenting categories that will be of interest to you—and you can adjust your evaluation accordingly. A slightly passive adoptive father, when paired with an active mother, offers possibilities for acceptance that would not be possible with a moderately passive father and a slightly passive mother, even if she maintains overall dominance in the relationship.

If it is the husband who is dominant in most issues, then you will know to put more importance on any and all passive attitudes he displays on parenting issues since that could be a harbinger of potential problems over the long term. A dominant father who has parenting attitudes that are more active than the mother's does not offer the same potential for success that a dominant father with passive attitudes toward parenting would offer when paired with a mother with only moderately passive attitudes.

This may strike you as cultural heresy of one form or another, but when it comes to adoption or foster parenting you will have better odds of success in your placements if it is the mother who is the most motivated and dominant partner in the relationships, and if she has paired herself with a partner who is only moderately passive (or better) on parenting issues. The worst scenario will always be a dominant father/passive mother combination. Unfortunately, most adoption applicants fall between those two extremes, and that puts pressure on screeners to weigh multiple positives and negatives to arrive at a determination that can have predictive value.

The best way to lay a foundation for making a decision is to ask each partner during his or her individual interview who the dominant partner is. Most of the time there will be agreement, which will allow you to move on to the next level to determine how their dominance affects their parenting attitudes. The easiest way to handle that is to discuss each area of concern during the individual interviews and then follow up with a series of direct questions during the joint interview.

Sample questions that can be asked as statements that require agreement or disagreement from the applicants, include:

**"A child should have the right to say what she thinks."**
**"Children are children—they are all pretty much alike."**
**"It's all right for children to spend time alone if they want to."**
**"A parent's main pleasure in life is doing things for his children."**
**"It's important for a child to learn to obey her parents."**
**"Spanking is all right as long as you don't curse when you do it."**

Obviously, some answers are more important than others, but the purpose of the questions is to measure the applicants' agreement on a variety of parenting issues. Their answers are of lesser interest for their content than whether they agree with each other on the answers. You will have more confidence making decisions about dominant male/passive female applicants if they demonstrate a strong pattern of agreement on parenting issues, as reflected by the frequency of their agreement on the specific questions you pose to them.

# Chapter 3

## Adoption Agencies: Private vs. Public

One of the most disheartening lessons you will learn as a screener is that not all adoption agencies are created equal. Different agencies have different policies, different expectations, and different procedures. There are some constants that remain consistent within the profession from agency to agency, such as concerns about determining the potential for emotional, physical or sexual child abuse at the hands of adoptive applicants, but agreement among agencies in other areas related to adoption can vary from slight to non-existent.

There are two types of adoption agencies that require the services of screeners: public and private, with the private agencies further divided into categories of for-profit, not-for-profit, secular or religious. The agency classification has a great deal to do with the type of home study you are expected to write.

## Public Agencies

Generally speaking, public agencies have more experienced adoption workers than can be found in private agencies. A survey conducted in 2000 by the American Public Human Services Association, the Child Welfare League of America and the Alliance for Children and Families found that personnel turnover rates at private agencies were more than double those at state agencies—40 percent versus 19.9 percent.[xiv]

The authors of the survey suggested that one reason for the disparity may be because salaries are lower at private agencies than at public agencies (workers in state agencies averaged $33,436, while workers in private agencies averaged $28,646), but we think another reason may have to do with philosophical differences.

Screeners at public agencies are expected, at all times, to represent the interests of the children that are in the agency's care. It is a challenging responsibility that provides great inner satisfaction. Since the screener's primary obligation is to the child—and not to the applicants—he is encouraged to leave no stone unturned in the home study process. If his probing questions annoy applicants, he can feel confident that his supervisor will back him up if problems arise with applicants who try to exert political influence on the selection process. In such an atmosphere, the screener feels comfortable writing his assessments of the more intimate details of a couple's relationship without fear that confidentialities will be broken and the contents of the home study shared with the applicants. The exception to that occurs in rare instances in which the screener is asked to do a home study for an international adoption. In those situations, the home study is made available to a wide range of individuals in non-social work professions such as immigration, law enforcement and the courts.

Another difference that has an impact on the screener's work is the availability of infants for adoption. Abortion and growing community acceptance of unmarried mothers has greatly reduced the number of infants available for adoption through public agencies. The children that are available at public agencies tend to be school-age or late pre-school-age and sometimes have chronic health, physical, or emotional problems that require long-term follow-up care by adoptive parents.

Screening adoptive applicants for older children, especially if they are challenged in some way, is more time consuming, complicated and stressful than screening applicants for infants—and the margin for error is much greater. Even so, many screeners find it professionally satisfying, to the extent that it has an impact on where they choose to work.

# Private Agencies

There are two types of private adoption agencies—non-profit and for-profit. The difference between them is that non-profit agencies charge fees for adoption so that they can pay salaries and expenses, and for-profit agencies charge fees for the purpose of making a profit. Typically, non-profit agencies are affiliated with religious or philanthropic organizations that have set up adoption agencies for altruistic reasons.

Many adoption applicants are attracted to private agencies because they feel they will be more tolerant of their shortcomings and try harder to find them a child because they are paying for the agency's services. Sometimes that is the case, but it has been our experience that most private agencies do not approach adoptions that way and strive to provide services in a professional and ethical manner consistent with the service levels expected of public agencies.

The private agency's approach to adoption differs from that of a public agency in two major areas: child acquisition and the home study process. Concerning acquisitions, private agencies obtain children from a variety of sources—mothers who voluntarily relinquish their children to them, orphanages located abroad, etc.—but in no instance is the child ever in their physical custody under a court-ordered guardianship, as is always the case with public agencies that often place children on adoption that have been taken away from birth parents because of abuse or neglect. The only "selling" that a screener for a public agency has to do involves introducing the child to the adoptive applicants. By contrast, a screener for a private agency often finds himself in the awkward position of "selling" the adoptive applicants he has approved to the individual or institution that has guardianship of the child.

Since home studies that are written for private agencies are made available to individuals outside the agency, including the applicants, attorneys, immigration officials, court officers in foreign countries, etc., the screener must be selective in the information that he puts into the home study for reasons of confidentiality. Competent screeners for public and private agencies will discuss the intimate details of an individual's sex life with the same thoroughness, but the screener for the private agency will be less likely to include that information in his report than will a screener for a public agency for fear that its publication would violate the applicant's privacy rights. As a result, home studies compiled by private agencies are often viewed as "light weight" documents that sometimes avoid serious issues that could affect the success of a placement.

Those who argue that home studies should be open documents and available to anyone who wants to read them has never interviewed an applicant who has confessed prior sexual mistakes of an embarrassing nature, such as a pre-marriage affair with a spouse's sibling—or listened as a wife confided about her husband, "Bob is the worst sexual partner I have ever had, but it would kill him if he ever knew that I felt that way. I have adjusted to that and I am fine with it. If he knew I felt that way, he would leave me in a heart beat." Both of those examples are worthy of discussion with the screener's supervisor, but if they are not written into the home study for fear that they will be read by the wrong persons that is not likely to happen.

Additional ways private agencies differ from public agencies:

- Private agencies must be licensed by state government, but they are not directly accountable to state legislatures and governors and that translates to less paperwork.

- Private agencies are more likely than public agencies to have infants available for adoption because mothers that give their children up for adoption sometimes feel more comfortable dealing with private agencies.

- Children adopted through private agencies were obtained because the mother made a studied decision to give the child up, whereas the children obtained by public agencies often are available only because a judge has declared their mothers or fathers to be unfit parents. The birth parents are usually unwilling participants in the adoption.

- Public agencies usually have a wide variety of professionals on staff, including nurses, behavioral experts, relationship experts, etc., so if a problem in the placement arises, the public agency is in a position to provide a variety of supportive services. Private agencies seldom have the financial resources to provide in-depth supportive services.

- Since private agencies have no investigative authority, the information they gather from the birth parents is voluntary. The agency may have adequate information about the child's medical history since birth, but little information about the parents' medical history or lifestyle choices prior to the child's birth.

# Religion-Based Adoption Agencies

There are a significant percentage of adoption applicants with strong religious convictions who distrust public adoption agencies. Those individuals prefer to adopt through private agencies operated by religious organizations with which they feel a strong spiritual connection. Some feel that a religious organization, by definition, will be more compassionate toward them as potential parents. Others feel that if an agency embraces the same religious beliefs it is more likely to agree with them about childrearing practices and religious instruction.

Religion-based agencies have a long history of making adoption placements and today there are agencies that represent just about every religious affiliation imaginable. The advantages to adopting though a religion-based agency are: They typically have the same level of professional competence that can be found at public and for-profit agencies; they are more likely to place a child born to a mother of a particular religion with adoptive parents of the same religion; and applicants are more likely to feel that the adoption will be blessed by a higher power.

The biggest disadvantage of adopting through a religion-based agency is the possibility of bias if the applicants are not of the same religion. Bethany Christian Services, a national organization with offices in Jackson, Mississippi, attracted national media attention in 2005 when the Mississippi office rejected a Roman Catholic couple as adoptive parents because their religion conflicted with the agency's "Statement of Faith."

Disclaimers aside, common sense argues that if applicants are of one religion and apply to an agency that embraces a different religion, they probably will not receive the same thoughtful consideration they would receive if they were of the same religion. The agency may have a public policy against religious discrimination, but that does not necessarily guarantee that screeners will observe the policy.

Screeners that would feel uncomfortable injecting religion into the adoption process, or participating in prayer with applicants or other agency personnel, would obviously not be a good match for a religion-based agency.

# Adoption Facilitators

Facilitators have always played a role in child placement, but their importance has increased in recent years with the growing popularity of international adoptions. A facilitator is non-adoption professional—usually a physician, lawyer, mid-wife, business executive, etc.—who uses his or her contacts to arrangement child placements. The nature of international adoption is such that it is difficult to proceed without the help of facilitators who are familiar with the laws and customs of the host country.

Adoption screeners come into contact with facilitators on those occasions when they are asked to do home studies for international or domestic private adoptions. When it comes to domestic adoptions, there are few pluses to adoptions arranged by facilitators such as physicians and lawyers. Those types of adoptions have always been of concern to professional adoption workers because they involve individuals who have had no training in evaluating individuals as adoptive parents.

Physicians and lawyers have important roles to play in the adoption process, but they act beyond their capabilities when they make decisions about placements that bypass psychosocial assessments undertaken by professionals. Unfortunately, in the case of domestic private adoptions, by the time the screener is called in to do a home study the placement has already taken place and removal of the child is traumatic for everyone involved if the screener uncovers information that would disqualify the adoptive parents.

Facilitators involved in international adoptions seldom participate in the actual selection process and that isolates them from the evaluative decisions that must be made by screeners during the home study process. For that reason, they seldom pose problems for screeners of the type that sometimes are caused by domestic facilitators.

# The Interstate Compact

The Interstate Compact, also known as the Interstate Compact on the Placement of Children, is an administrative organization that was formed to oversee reciprocal laws on adoption enacted in the fifty states, the District of Columbia and the Virgin Islands.

Since there are no federal laws regulating adoption, each state has its own separate set of rules and regulations. The Interstate Compact, which was given the task of developing a uniform procedure for dealing with those differences, enters the picture whenever a child born in one state is adopted by individuals in another state.

In addition to the requirements set by the states, the Interstate Compact requires applicants to complete the following[xv]:

- The completion, in duplicate, of the Compact Request (Form 100A)

- Three copies of a family history on both birth parents. A family history is not the same as a home study, although it includes much the same information that goes into a home study. The family history must include information such as age, religion, appearance, employment history, educational background, race, information on physical and mental health problems, and special interests or creative talents.

- A notarized statement from the birth parent or legal guardian that it is the intent of the birth parent or guardian to place the child with the prospective parents named in the Compact Request.

- A notarized statement signed by the birth parents or guardian that they have been provided personal information about the adoptive applicants, including their name, address, ages, religion, race employment and health history, as well as similar information about any individual living in the home with the applicants.
- A statement indicating how the financial and medical needs of the children are being met in a pre-placement home or facility.
- Written authorization from the birth parents or guardian for the adoptive parents to obtain medical treatment for the child while the adoption in pending before the court.
- A statement identifying the names of the lawyers involved in the case.

The Interstate Compact is a bureaucracy, not a social services agency, so the only services it provides to applicants are administrative. It seems to be the most effective when public agencies are involved in the adoption and the least affective in adoptions involving private agencies or private placements involving facilitators. That is because state laws differ more widely for those types of adoptions than they do for agency adoptions and that has made it necessary for the Interstate Compact to formulate more complicated procedures for dealing with those situations.

Adoption screeners asked to provide home studies for adoptions under the oversight of the Interstate Compact should keep in mind that their reports will be read by numerous individuals acting in various capacities. Since confidentiality is not always the highest priority to those receiving the reports, you must exercise caution in reporting comments given to you in the strictest confidence and you must at all times be protective of the privacy of the individuals you have interviewed for the reports.

As a result of the complexity of the paperwork involved, there have been many calls for reform of the Interstate Compact; but that seems unlikely as long as it is subject to fifty different sets of state laws.[xvi] Until the compact is changed, you must deal with it as it is. Adoption applicants have attempted creative legal maneuvers to circumvent the compact's authority—such as having the pregnant mother move to the applicants' state to have the baby—but they have thus far not met with much success. Failure to comply with the compact's regulations is a serious violation of the law and could result in the child being returned to the state of origination.

# Chapter 4

## Identifying Adoptive Parent Issues

Since each of us grows into adulthood with certain attitudes about how children should be raised (based on our own experiences) it is not surprising that men and women enter marriage with divergent views on the subject of parenting. The question of whether to have children or not may be an important one in mate selection for some individuals, but unfortunately specific parenting beliefs are seldom determining factors in shaping the ultimate assessment of the relationship's potential—and couples are sometimes surprised to learn that they are incompatible when it comes to parenting.

The screener's task is to undertake the type of evaluation that every couple should undergo before committing to marriage. When it comes to adoption, the question for the screener is not whether the individuals sitting across from him are good people, but rather whether they agree on enough parenting issues to be good parents. Adoptive applicants often are surprised at their partner's responses on parenting issues. A common comment is, "I didn't know you felt that way!" Of course, you would not expect them to agree on all issues—just enough issues to provide the foundation for effective parenting.

As a screener, here are some of the issues that will concern you:

**Discipline.** What are the issues that each prospective parent feels are important enough to merit an uncompromising attitude? In other words, where does each person draw the line? Is it talking back to adults? Is it stealing? Is it being disrespectful of authority? Is it striking other children? Is it excessive crying? Is it not going to bed when told? What methods of discipline are acceptable? Spanking? Hand slapping? Withdrawal of privileges? Isolation (being sent to their room)? Time out? Repetitive writing (as in fifty copies of "I promise not to hit my sister again")? Do the applicants feel that one parent should be the major dispenser of discipline or should they take turns? How do they feel about non-parent authority figures, such as teachers, disciplining their child?

There are two areas that society historically has set aside for fathers: discipline and play time. Mothers feed and nurture the children, activities that involve a minimum interaction by the children with the physical environment, while fathers serve as gatekeepers to all things beyond the mother's loving arms. Discipline and play are closely related in the eyes of children because they involve a change in the life rhythms they experience with their mother.

For infants, dad is the person who makes lots of noise coming into the room; the person who is always smiling and making eye contact. Sometimes he leans over and sticks his giant finger into the infant's tiny fist and stimulates his grasping reflex. Other times he lifts the infant into the air and swings him to and fro, sometimes taking the infant's breath away. Dad is always fun.

By contrast, mom always seems to come quietly into the room, so as not to awaken baby. She speaks in a soothing manner and tells baby how pretty he or she is. She makes eye contact when her purpose is non-nurturing in nature, but most of her time is spent feeding, bathing and changing baby, tasks that usually require her to gaze someplace other than the infant's eyes. Inadvertently, she frowns or gently chastises baby when he kicks soapy water into her eyes during his bath, or when he makes an unusually pungent mess in his diapers. Mom is only human; she reacts to her environment, just as baby does. For those reasons—and more—mom is not always fun.

For older children, those of pre-school age and older, dad is the parent who tosses balls with them, roughhouses with them, gets down on his hands and knees and pretends to be a horse, and the one who gleefully announces, "Everyone get ready—we're going to the circus!" For boys, the play activities they experience with dad are crucial for their long-term emotional and social development.

For adolescents, playtime with dad takes on more of a competitive edge. The skills he learned from dad as a youngster are used during adolescence as weapons with which to be competitive with dad and his peers. Moms tend to see competition as events in which someone is hurt by being the loser; dads see competition as a means of solving problems while negotiating for dominance. Moms don't want to see their sons get their feelings hurt; dads want to see their sons get their feelings hurt so that they will learn to adapt to a world in which winning is more important than avoiding hurt feelings.

Dad is not insensitive to his son's feelings; rather he wants him to learn to live with pain instead of avoiding it. Interestingly, dad's attitude toward his daughter will be exactly the opposite; he will fight to protect her from hurt or disappointment, while the mom takes the opposite position, the same one that he took with their son. Typically, mom and dad will see no inconsistency in their opposing positions.

Of course, not all fathers are good playtime teachers. If they grew up as sons without fathers—and had difficulty learning how to play because they didn't have a father in the home—they will find it difficult to give their sons proper instruction. Even if they did grow up with a father in the home, they may have been taught by fathers that were overly critical of their efforts or prone to verbal abuse.

Psychologists Dan Kindlon and Michael Thompson touched on that in their book, Raising Cain[xvii]: "The problem-solving strategies that boys bring to adolescent and adult social situations are directly traceable to the lessons learned from dads on playing fields and in family dens. For instance, research shows that young boys who are aggressive and are low in prosocial behaviors—meaning they don't share—have fathers who are more likely to engage in angry exchanges with them, such as yelling back at a son who yells at them."

When fathers teach sons to play, hopefully it is to play fair and to let their actions, not their tempers, speak for them. The nightly news offers frequent reminders of what happens when fathers teach their sons the wrong lessons. We have all seen video footage of fathers charging out onto the playing field, screaming obscenities—or, even worse, fighting with other adults over calls made by game officials.

For better or worse, dads program their sons to be good players or bad players.

# The Play-Discipline Connection

The furious mother stormed into the caseworker's office, tossed her purse onto a nearby table, then sat down hard in the chair across from the desk and rolled her eyes skyward. "My husband drives me crazy," she said, sighing after every other word. "All he does is play silly games with Johnny. I am the one who takes him to the doctor and to school—and he gets to be the hero and have all the fun. He should be doing something important with his son. You know, teaching him something!"

What the irate mother didn't understand was that her son's father is filling a very important role in their son's development. It is through games that boys learn enough self-control to respond in a positive manner to parental discipline.

Dad's "silly" games all have rules. "Three strikes and you're out!" "If you cross this line, you're out of bounds!" "You are down when your knee touches the ground!" "Don't touch his arm or you'll get a foul!" "You have two men on the field!" "You threw it too high to be a strike!" "You dropped the ball!" "The ball landed past the line!" "That's an illegal tackle—you've got to pay a penalty!" And so it goes.

Boys learn cause and effect from their dads. They learn that when they break the rules, they must be penalized—and that means they are at greater risk to lose! When they play a game with dad—and dad wins—that means they lose. Little boys like to win. Moms sometimes have a more difficult time disciplining boys because they are not the parent who taught them about winning and losing.

Athletics are important for boys, not so much for the physical exercise (though with children today becoming increasingly obese, the importance of exercise increases), or because of the teamwork it requires (or the competitiveness it engenders), but because of the gamesmanship involved. Non-athletic games, such as card or board games (or even computer games) accomplish the same function as sports.

What may appear "silly" to the mother is an important building block in her son's development. When people describe a child as a "problem child," one who will not obey adults, what they are really saying is that he does not exhibit good self-control. No child wants to be punished for misbehavior. There is nothing about punishment that a child enjoys. He indulges in forbidden behavior because he does not have the self-control necessary to put on the brakes. Boys who are good at playing games with other people are usually good at accepting discipline.

Men and women sometimes have opposing approaches to discipline. Mothers soon learn that the best way to avoid the need for discipline is to allow their son to watch television for hours at a time. The biggest problem with that, aside from subjecting them to dubious programming, is the fact that children who spend all their time watching television do not learn the play skills they need.

Sometimes mothers complain that their sons, who have just spent four hours watching television, are suddenly difficult to discipline once they tire of that activity. Watching television is not a substitute for play activity; it teaches children nothing about self-control or negotiating with their playmates for what they want. If watching television is a good activity, why do parents invariably end up sending their children to their rooms for punishment for some misdeed once the television programming has ended?

Mothers sometimes use television as a defense against discipline. They think that they can avoid discipline by keeping the child busy. When that doesn't work they threaten to take away privileges or they threaten to tell daddy when he gets home. They spank them as a last resort, primarily because it upsets them to strike their children.

Fathers are just the opposite. They urge the child to "go outside and play," instead of watching television. Admittedly, there may be selfish motivation involved, especially if there is a sports event he wants to watch on television. Fathers seldom threaten to punish; they usually do it on the spot. That is what boys expect because that is what they have been taught while playing games with their dad. It's not three strikes you're out later. It's three strikes you're out *right then*. Fathers spank their sons as a means of demonstrating physical dominance, something that becomes increasingly importance as boys head into adolescence.

We refer to spanking here only to explain what happens in typical families. We don't recommend striking children at any age for any reason. Whatever advantages we are tempted to see in mothers and fathers paddling children for bad behavior are erased by our experience with parents who physically abuse their children. We've seen mothers who spanked infants (only to have them placed in a foster home) and fathers who have beaten sons or daughters so severely that the children had to be hospitalized.

The reason so many parents spank their children is because it is often an effective short-term remedy to bad behavior. The problem with that, even when done lightly and sparingly, is that the parent is also teaching lessons while administering punishment. They are teaching that violence is all right in some situations. They are teaching that one acceptable result of anger is violence. And they are associating violence with authority.

**Empathy**. Research data indicates that fathers teach children characteristics that often are not taught by mothers—self-control and empathy, math skills, and respect for females. Studies show that males who grow up in families with an involved father do not have the same need to dominate women or create exclusionary, all-male activities.

Empathy is one of the most important survival skills a child can possess. It allows children to not only care about what others are feeling, but to make accurate judgments in a wide range of social situations.

Without empathy, children would be unable to determine if people are uneasy, despondent, horrified, bored, cautious, playful, irritated, relieved, shy, hostile, dangerous, annoyed or preoccupied. A child without empathy is a disaster waiting to happen.

Biblical or philosophical definitions aside, what we call morality is actually the ability to make decisions based on a discernment of whether our actions will help or hurt other people. Often our only clue is based on a reading of body language and facial expressions. If a child does not have that ability, he will have a difficult time judging the appropriateness of his actions. One definition of a psychopath is someone who is without empathy for others. The empathy-free masked gunman who robs a convenience store, puts his pistol in the face of the clerk, and then pulls the trigger, has no concept of what his victim is feeling. His emotions are focused entirely on himself.

A mother can possess tons of empathy, but for some reason she cannot transfer significant amounts to her children. For reasons no one completely understands, only a father can do that. When he fails to do so, the child suffers the consequences. He becomes aggressive, impulsive and prone to risky behavior. In a report on violence, the National Research Council named several factors that their researchers found that correlated with aggressive behavior in children: "harsh and erratic discipline, lack of parental nurturance, physical abuse and neglect, poor supervision, and early separation of children from parents."

Sociologist David Popenoe, citing a twenty-six-year longitudinal study that found that the most important childhood factor for the development of empathy is "paternal involvement in child care," feels that it is not clear why fathers are so important to the process. "Perhaps merely being with their children provides a model for compassion," he wrote in *Life Without Father*[xviii]. "Perhaps it has to do with their style of play or mode of reasoning. Perhaps it is somehow related to the fact that fathers typically are the family's main arbiter with the outside world. Or perhaps it is because when mothers receive help from fathers and are thus freed from some of the instrumental demands of child-rearing, they are more able themselves to promote empathic concerns. Whatever the reason, it is hard to think of a more important contribution that fathers can make to their children."

**Education.** How important is education to each applicant? Do they expect their child to go to college? What are their feelings about public versus private schools? Does either applicant worry that teachers may influence their children in negative ways? What do the applicants see as the end result of an educational experience?

**Religious instruction.** Do the applicants have the same religious affiliation? If not, how do they intend to handle the child's religious instruction? How important is religion to each applicant's family members?

**Sports.** Once the child is school age, how do they feel about organized sports? Is it important for the child's development, or is it a harmful diversion? How much time should a child devote to sports? Are both applicants willing to attend sporting events on a regular basis to show support for the child? Would either applicant ever encourage the child to pursue a career in professional sports? How do the applicants feel about spending scheduled time with the child paying basketball, baseball, etc.?

**The arts.** Do the applicants have strong beliefs about the value of the arts in a child's development? Do they think that music lessons are a good idea? Do they think that creativity should be encouraged, whether it involves music, painting or writing, or do they think that it is a waste of time? Does either applicant have artistic abilities they hope to teach to the child?

**Cultural (if biracial).** If the applicants are different races, how do they see that having an impact on the child? If the wife is white and the husband is black, or vice versa, are they in agreement about adopting a mixed race child, or do they think that the child should be one race or the other? Do they have any negative attitudes about people of a different race? Has either applicant ever been charged with a racially motivated crime? Did the applicants have friends of a different race while growing up? Has either applicant ever had a negative experience with a person of a different race? If they express an interest in adopting an aboriginal child, do they feel that it is important to provide the child with opportunities to learn about his or her native culture?

**Open adoption.** What are their feelings about open adoption? Would they be able to share parenting duties with the birth parents? How would they handle disagreements with a birth parent on issues such as discipline and religious instruction? How would they handle disagreements if the birth parents are racist or hostile to certain religions? If a birth parent is in prison, how would they feel about the child visiting the parent? What are their coping mechanisms to deal with the possibility of the birth parent suing for custody of the child, despite prior approval of the adoption?

**Adoption telling.** What are their plans when it comes to telling the child that he or she is adopted? At what age do they think the child is ready to hear references to the "A" word? Does either applicant have reservations about talking to the child about adoption?

**Behavioral problems.** Since behavioral characteristics are the main determinant of adjustment—and research shows that behavior is influenced equally, if not more, by genetics than by environment—what capacity does the adoptive couple have to deal with behavioral problems on an ongoing basis? Are they capable of giving more love than they receive? Can they raise a difficult child and be satisfied with the possibility that the emotional "payoff" will not be immediate and may require years of patience?

Research shows that adopted children have a statistical edge on behavioral problems when compared to the non-adopted population. Adopted children make up about 2 percent of the population in the United States, yet they represent nearly 5 percent of the children referred to outpatient mental health facilities and up to 15 percent of the children in residential care facilities.[xix]

When it comes to problems associated with acting out (stealing, lying, aggression, oppositional behavior), and learning difficulties, adopted children are more likely than their non-adopted counterpart to require parental guidance.[xx] One study found that a higher proportion of adopted children from hospitalized schizophrenic women developed schizophrenia than from a comparative group of offspring from non-schizophrenic women.[xxi] When it comes to personality development, adoption studies have found modest positive correlations between adopted children and their biological parents, but almost no correlation between adopted children and their adoptive parents.[xxii]

Remi J. Cadoreta, a psychiatry professor at the University of Iowa School of Medicine, concludes that the major finding in most studies is that "shared environment contributes very little to adult personality. However, genetic effects, while demonstrable, do not appear to be all controlling and other factors such as special unique experiences or gene-environment interaction might figure significantly in personality development."[xxiii]

Rutgers psychology professor David M. Brodzinsky feels that the common thread running through adjustment problems experienced by adopted children is the stressfulness of adoption for all involved. "Simply put, adopted children, once they come to realize the implications of being adopted, not only experience a loss of their biological parents and origins, but also a loss of stability in the relationship to their adoptive parents," he concludes. "In addition, there is a loss of self . . . These various losses often leave the adoptee feeling incomplete, alienated, disconnected, abandoned or unwanted."[xxiv]

As a screener, your concern should be about an adoptive applicant's range of acceptance, not only of personality and intellectual differences between the adoptee and the parent, but also of adoptee behavior that could be interpreted as aggressive or even rejecting. In other words, how sensitive will the adoptive applicant be to adoptee behavior that runs counter to his or her view of how a family should look and act? Put in advertising terms, can they "take a lickin' and keep on tickin'?"

# Chapter 5

## Understanding

## The Foster Parent Syndrome

Men and women become foster parents for a variety of reasons, but at the core of their motivation is a desire to satisfy one or more well-defined needs. It is the screener's job to identify those needs during the home study process and determine whether they fall within the limits of acceptable motivations.

The first task for the screener is to separate an individual's reason for applying to be a foster parent from his or her motivation for wanting to be a foster parent. Common reasons for applying include: a response to news stories or public speakers that solicit foster parents as an expression of community service; a response to ministers, priests, rabbis, etc., who urge individuals to take in foster children as an expression of religious doctrine; expectations for increased income; to acquire a playmate for a birth child already in the home; the death of a child or close relative;

If the "reason" is why the applicant approaches the agency, it is the "motivation" that determines whether he or she will be a good foster parent. Common motivations for men and women include: a belief that children in the home will save a faltering marriage; a reaction to childhood sexual, physical or emotional abuse; a need to "undo" the bad parenting they experienced as a child; a guilt need to compensate for perceived injustices to a loved one such as a deceased child or close relative; a lack of sexual intimacy in the marriage; poor social skills with adults; sexual attraction to children; a need to feel young; and a need to find an outlet for what some applicants call "nervous" energy.

64

Gender-specific motivations include: For women, the need to have "something of my own" within the marriage; the need to have close physical contact with "cuddly" babies; fascination with watching children grow up; meeting the expectations of domineering parents; and peer pressure from neighbors or work associates.

Gender-specific motivations for men include: a need to give the wife "something of her own;" a need to help the less fortunate; a need for affection; a need to make their wife happy because they feel they are disappointing her in other areas, especially in the bedroom; and a need to be seen as a leader in the community, which can be viewed as a need for dominance among other males.

Typically, foster parents present themselves to the screener with an explanation that they "love" children or want to "give back" to their community because of "blessings" they have received in life. When pressed, they will attribute their "reasons" to one of the explanations given above, the most common being in response to a news story or public speaker who has focused on the need for foster parents in the community.

Once the screener has ascertained the applicants' explanations and reasons for wanting foster children, he can begin to determine and evaluate their actual motivation. We have thus far referred to foster parents in the plural because married couples are the preferred standard, but the acceptance in recent years of single parents by many agencies has added a new dimension to foster parent programs. That is a difference that will have a bearing on child-rearing potential, as we will discuss later, but it has little or no bearing on the process for determining motivation. In that respect, married and single applicants should be held to the same standards when it comes to establishing motivation.

The findings of the Fanshel and Wolins studies were of great interest to James L. Dickerson, the co-author of this book, because their publication was preceded by his employment as a foster and adoptive parent screener at a children's services agency in Canada by only a couple of years and he viewed the research as fresh and innovative. After four years of adapting the research compiled by Wolins and Fanshel into practical applications for the screening of foster and adoptive parents, he published an article in the *Journal of the Ontario Association of Children's Aid Societies* in October 1972 entitled "A Casework Approach to Foster Homes" in which he first introduced the concept of the "foster parent syndrome":[xxv]

> **With little research, the information that was available seemed to suggest that foster homes could be utilized as neutral territories for the child, freeing the social worker to venture into battle to combat poverty, injustice and a host of assorted psycho-social maladies. Since foster homes were considered to be 'cool' situations, casework was usually directed entirely toward the 'hot' situations as defined by protection caseloads. As a result, child care workers, usually the only workers to have contact with the foster parents, were each assigned dozens of children and encouraged, if not forced by their caseloads, to devote little of their time to the foster family as a unit . . . My experience has led me to think that there is in existence a foster parent syndrome which can be identified and documented as falling within the boundaries of distinct behavioral patterns. If these patterns are identified and catalogued prior to the placement of a foster child, the home accepted as existing within a framework of special needs, and the placement of a child into the home viewed as a problem instead of a solution, then the success probabilities of such a placement can be greatly**

**extended, as long as there is constant
casework being directed toward the family
as a unit.**

The Foster Parent Syndrome is a motivational marker that allows screeners to group applicants in acceptable or unacceptable categories based on the needs that they seek to address by becoming foster parents. The satisfaction of some needs is consistent with being a good foster parent, while the satisfaction of other needs is not acceptable for a variety of reasons. The first challenge for the screener is to cleanse his intellectual palate of any notion that the applicants he is interviewing will prove to be neutral co-partners in the agency's mission to care for children in need. That will never happen. Foster parents are individuals with special needs and the measure of their effectiveness will be determined by whether those needs are addressed by having foster children in the home. The screener's job is to: 1) identify those needs; 2) determine if they are of a type that pose an acceptable risk for the agency—and 3) formulate a casework approach to working with the foster family once they have a child in their care.

## Case History

Mary B. was one of our favorite foster mothers. In her mid-50s, she and her husband, Bob, had raised two children of their own. A third child, Bob Jr., had died of cancer at the age of three. Mary and Bob blamed themselves for Bob Jr.'s death, convinced that they should have been able to prevent their son from getting cancer.

After Bob Jr.'s death, the tensions between husband and wife grew so strong that they separated for six months after the funeral. They reunited once they realized that their two surviving children needed them to work together as a family. Once Bob and Mary focused on their other children, they were able to rediscover the common bond that had defined their marriage.

The timing of Mary and Bob's application to be foster parents coincided with the departure from the home of their youngest child, who enrolled in an out-of-state college. By that point, Mary and Bob had reconciled their differences and come to understand that they were happier together than they were apart. They loved each other, but they were not in love with each other, as they had been when they began their family.

Mary and Bob were transparent in their motivation. Mary had a need to give hands-on care to a child that she could hold and cuddle and whisper sweet nothings to—a child that she could give a second chance for life, and Bob had a need to make up for his abandonment of his wife and children at their time of greatest need. Bob also had a need to please Mary and a need to prove his belief in her on a daily basis.

Mary and Bob were not a good risk for older children for several reasons. The screener felt that they would become attached to the point of dysfunction to older children that stayed longer than six months in their home and he felt that they would experience parenting disagreements based on unresolved conflicts rooted in the loss of their son. However, the screener did feel that they would make good foster parents for infants that would be in their home no longer than three to six months and they were approved for infants only. The results were spectacular.

Mary was a rosy-cheeked woman who beamed whenever she saw an infant. Her initial interaction with them was a fascinating thing to witness. Each time the screener entered her home with an infant, her eyes locked onto the child with laser efficiency and her arms automatically extended to take the child. At that moment there was no one else on the planet except that child.

The warmth that the screener could see in Mary's face was felt by each infant that entered her home. She cared for three to four infants a year for a period of ten years and gave each child a wonderful new start in life. She cried with sadness each time the infants left her home and she cried with happiness each time a new one came into her life. It was a type of stress that she and Bob could live with.

Mary and Bob were successful foster parents because the screener was able to get an accurate reading on their motivation, which made it possible for him to address their needs in a manner that posed minimum risk to the foster child and the agency. Equally important was the screener's ability to set perimeters for their use as foster parents by establishing a casework approach to their supervision.

# Motivations Associated With the Foster Parent Syndrome

ACCEPTABLE

- A need to feel young
- A need to have close physical contact with "cuddly" babies
- A need for affection
- A need to help the less fortunate
- A fascination with watching children grow up
- For men, a need to give their wife "something of her own"
- For men, a need to be seen as a leader in the community, which can be viewed as a need for dominance among other males
- For women, the need to have "something of my own" within the marriage

UNACCEPTABLE

- Sexual attraction to children

- A reaction to childhood sexual, physical or emotional abuse
- A belief that children in the home will save a faltering marriage
- A lack of sexual intimacy in the marriage
- A need to make their wife happy because they feel they are disappointing her in other areas, especially in the bedroom
- Peer pressure from neighbors or work associates

## CONDITIONALLY ACCEPTABLE

- A guilt need to compensate for perceived injustices to a loved one such as a deceased child or close relative
- A need to "undo" the bad parenting they experienced as a child
- Poor social skills with adults
- A need to find an outlet for what some applicants call "nervous" energy
- A need to meet the expectations of domineering parents

# Chapter 6

## Screening Single and Gay Applicants

In 1970 less than 1 percent of the adoptions in the United States involved single parents, but today single-parent adoptions are legal in all fifty states and the percentage varies between 8 to 33 percent, depending on the state. Even so, public and private adoption agencies still give a preference to married couples, public agencies more so than private agencies. That should not come as a great surprise since the mission of child welfare agencies is to take each child's long-term care into consideration and the statistics of child-rearing makes it clear that a child with two parents has better odds of success in life than a child with one parent.

In recent years adoption agencies have elevated the desirability of single-parent applicants for older and special-needs children because couples have not responded as well as hoped for with those harder-to-place children. However, if the choice is between temporary care in multiple foster homes versus permanent care with a single parent, it is the single parent who offers the better odds. As a result, most of the adoptions that take place with single parents are with older and special-needs children that were in foster care prior to adoption. On the rare occasions when single parents adopt infants it almost always is the result of an international adoption.

There are many areas in which the screening of single adoptive applicants overlaps the screening of married adoptive applicants, just as there is overlap in the screening of heterosexual and gay and lesbian applicants. Strong parenting skills in a variety of areas are desirable whether the applicants are married, single, or gay or lesbian. The same thing goes for attitudes about discipline, education, religious instruction and open adoption. But that is not to say that there are not important differences between couples and single applicants that should be addressed during the screening process.

Adoption screeners should hold single-parent applicants to the same overall standard that they hold couples, but there are four special areas that should receive special emphasis during the interview process:

**Past and present relationships.** What is the applicant's history when it comes to maintaining a romantic relationship with a significant other? How long did each relationship last? Was harassment, abuse or violence ever an issue? Has the applicant ever been charged with a crime against a significant other? What is the nature of the current relationship? Does the applicant live with the significant other or do they maintain separate households? Is the significant other supportive of adoption? What role has the absence of children played in the relationship? Has the applicant ever undergone relationship counseling with the significant other? If so, what were the results?

Pet relationships should also be of interest. If the applicant has never had a pet why is that the case? If the applicant has a history of having cats or dogs in the home, how did that work out for the applicant? Was the applicant able to provide a support network for the care of the pets when it was necessary to leave town? Is pet care an issue with the applicant's current employer, insofar as taking time off from work is concerned? If so, how was that conflict resolved with the employer?

**Finances.** The most fundamental financial question is whether the applicant earns enough money to care for a child without borrowing. Equally important is the issue of health and life insurance. It is essential for the applicant to provide coverage in both areas. What are the applicant's plans to financially provide for the child in the event of his or her death? Are there family members who will assume that responsibility?

The purpose of financial planning is to prepare for when things go wrong. Does the applicant have enough life insurance to support the child into adulthood in the event of the applicant's death? Does the applicant have a will or trust that will provide for the child's care and education?

**Health issues.** In times of illness couples have each other to fall back on for support. Does the single applicant have someone who can be counted on in the event of a serious illness? Does the single applicant have any serious illnesses such as cancer that will limit his or her longevity and put a child's long-term care at risk? Does the applicant have any diseases that might require him to be bed-ridden before the child is grown? Does the applicant see a child as a potential caregiver later in life?

**Gender awareness.** Children must have male and female role models if they are to grow into healthy adults. Other than food and shelter, the most primary need that children have is for opposite-sex role models. What plans has the applicant made to provide opposite-sex role models for an adopted child? Whether the applicant is male or female, it is important for them to provide opposite-sex role models for their child by networking with friends and relatives willing to spend time with the child.

If the applicant is female and she adopts a boy, it is important that she offer him strong male role models—and the same is true of males who adopt girls. Making the right decisions in this area will affect the child's health, academic performance, social development and ability to maintain adult relationships with the opposite sex.

Sometimes mothers try to bypass the male role-model issue by having their mothers move into the household with them, thinking that two female role models will somehow compensate for the lack of a male role model.

There is evidence that two-mother family structures do no harm for young children and may, in fact, contribute to the well-being of the family by providing the mother more time to play with her children. However, studies have shown that teenagers raised in mother/grandmother homes fare worse than those raised by mothers alone. Sociologists Sara

McLanahan and Gary Sandefur report that children raised in mother-grandmother homes produce children that are twice as likely to drop out of school.[xxvi]

Mother-grandmother pairings probably do no harm with younger children because they consider the grandmother to be the "daddy." Grandmother, because she is older and more experienced, invariably offers advice to the mother in the presence of the child regarding what clothes should be worn, what food should be eaten, etc.

That makes sense to a six-year-old, since the grandmother looks older and is usually physically larger than the mother, but teens see through that facade. They understand that the grandmother is not a substitute for their father and it disturbs them at a primal level to see their mother bossed around by her mother. After all, that is one of the great fears expressed by teens—the possibility that their mother will always be telling them what to do—often expressed by the phrase, "Oh, Mother, just leave me alone!"

Teenage sons are also affected by what they see when they are in public with their mother and grandmother. They both may be the boss at home, but if the son sees male strangers open doors for them, or otherwise extend courtesies to them, he interprets those gestures as acknowledgments that his mother and grandmother are submissive to males. We've seen heterosexual mothers and grandmothers cut their hair short and dress like men in a deliberate effort to appear more masculine and fulfill a fatherly role, but that never works with bright teens that invariably see through the ruse and end up suffering extreme embarrassment among their peers.

No matter how hard they try, mothers and grandmothers cannot become fathers. The harder they try to fill that role, the more damage they do. However, there are positive things they can do. They can respect the distance their son and grandson need from them in areas such as sports. They can encourage his interests in any activities in which he can express his identity as a male. And they can make an effort to find him suitable male role models to help guide him through the trauma of adolescence.

Mother-grandmother families have a great deal to offer, as long as the mother and grandmother do not offer confusing role models to the boys in the family, especially teens who are confused about their own place in society. Teenage boys have to deal with surging hormones that often make them question their own sanity. The last thing they need to worry about is their mother's sanity.

Among some social workers and psychologists there is a line of thinking that rejects gender differences between men and women. It maintains that men can do anything that women can do, and vice versa. That philosophy, which has been labeled the "New Father model" and the "androgynous parent," can be expressed as follows:

**There is very little about the gender of the parent that seems to be distinctly important.**

In his book *Fatherless America,* David Blankenhorn argues against the concept of the "New Father" standard: "The essence of the New Father model is a repudiation of gendered social roles. But fatherhood, by definition, is a gendered social role. To un-gender fatherhood—to deny males any gender-based role in family life—is to deny fatherhood as a social activity. What remains may be New. But there is no more Father."[xxvii]

Psychologists Henry Biller and Mark Reuter once did a study on 172 college men to determine how often their fathers were at home when they were children, and how nurturing their fathers had been when they spent time with their sons. They found that well-adjusted students were likely to see themselves as dependable, trusting, practical and friendly, while poorly adjusted students were more likely to label themselves as aloof, anxious, inhibited and unfriendly. The most poorly adjusted students in their study had fathers who were home very little and were very nurturing, or were home a lot and were aloof and non-nurturing. The well-adjusted students had fathers who were at least moderate in both nurturance and availability.

"If you are not home much and are really affectionate and play with your child when you are home, he may feel very frustrated that you are frequently absent, and it may affect his personal adjustment; he may wonder why, if you appear to love him so much, you do not spend more time with him," Biller wrote.[xxviii] "Conversely, if you are home a lot but are cold and distant, your child may feel that he is inadequate in your eyes, and he will feel very insecure. It would probably be better for a child with a cold, distant father to have him be home very little. At least the child would not be exposed to such consistently negative experience with a male."

It is unclear how much play Biller and Reuter included in their definition of nurturing, or whether the play included both physical and mental exercises, but their findings do indicate the fragile nature of a father's influence on his son. It is not enough for the father to simply be present in the home; to have a positive effect on his son he must engage him in physical or mental play. Biller and Reuter concluded that moderation in availability and nurturance offered the most beneficial balance.

A 1971 study, conducted by psychologists Peggy Ban and Michael Lewis at the Educational Testing Service in Princeton, New Jersey, found that fathers spent only about fifteen to twenty minutes a day playing with their one-year-old children.[xxix] There are probably a lot of reasons for that: Fathers often feel embarrassed talking to or playing goo-goo with infants; they don't feel competent handling small children; and they don't see such behavior as being compatible with their self-image as a male.

The older children get, the more time dad is likely to spend playing with them, especially if they are boys. Whatever their nurturing instincts as fathers, they are not as likely to spend a great deal of time playing with their daughters. Growing public awareness of the subtleties of child sexual abuse may have something to do with that. Men worry that their attentiveness to their daughters could be misconstrued and they worry that spending too much time with their daughters could affect their own masculinity, at least in the eyes of other men. Fathers don't have those same fears when they play with their sons.

Obviously, the twenty-minutes-per-day average cited by the above-mentioned study is not optimal. The amount of time that is adequate depends on the age of the child and the quality of the play that the father offers to the child. Pre-schoolers require more time than school-age children, as do adolescents, though getting them to make a time commitment is sometimes difficult. Quality also influences the determination of how much time should be spent with a child. A father is not playing with his son if he watches a football game while he rolls his son's favorite truck around his foot.

By the time a boy is ten or twelve he will have selected a male figure that he admires and wants to pattern his life after. If that male figure is not a member of his immediate family he will look elsewhere. It could be a coach or a teacher, or, more likely, a much older boy. The problem with that is that coaches and teachers have dozens, sometimes hundreds, of boys to supervise. They seldom have time to give more than passing attention to any single boy. They probably would not even know that they have been chosen. As a result, they will almost certainly disappoint the child, creating more problems for the parent. Coaches and teachers can be effective role models, within limits, but only if they do the choosing.

An attachment to an older boy could be a parent's worst nightmare, especially if the child is a son without a father. Adolescent boys don't have finely-honed moral compasses. Since they are a work in progress, they are easily influenced by their peers and they often have unresolved issues with their fathers. It is through these types of attachments that school-age boys are drawn into drug use, religious cults, white nationalist organizations, and street gangs. Boys who choose older boys as role models, instead of adult males, often end up either as victims of peer abuse or as bullies to younger children.

# Gay and Lesbian Applicants

With so many children in need of adoptive homes, many adoption agencies have turned to gay and lesbian couples to provide homes to the "special needs" children that heterosexual couples have declined to adopt because of their age, ethnic backgrounds or health problems. The 2000 National Census revealed about 600,000 same-sex partner households in America (about 1 percent of the total), a five-fold increase over 1990. That is a significant pool of potential foster and adoptive applicants, one that would have child-welfare agencies jumping with joy if it were not for public opposition to gay and lesbian adoptions, which in some states has limited their widespread acceptance.

Gay parents face the same challenges that single parents face, but there are important variations of which screeners should be aware. For example, if a gay or lesbian applicant does not have a history of good relationships with the opposite sex, it will be difficult for them to provide for a child's basic emotional needs. If the applicant is male he will need the influence of a female role model in his child's life, whether the child is male or female—and the same situation exists for female applicants insofar as finding male role models is concerned. If the applicant has been unable throughout his or her life to form close friendships with the opposite sex, there is little chance that the applicant will be able to teach the child to have close relationships with the opposite sex.

A promise to provide a child with an opposite-sex role model is not good enough. The applicant must have a history of successful relationships with the opposite sex. If that is not the case, the applicants should be encouraged to postpone their adoption plans until they can demonstrate they can provide an appropriate opposite-sex role model for a child.

Once they start school, children may be teased for a variety of reasons, regardless of whether their parents are heterosexual or homosexual. They may be overweight or have a mixed race heritage, or they may be physically or mentally challenged. Children adopted by gay parents face all of the same risks as children adopted by straight parents, but they also risk being taunted for having a "queer" parent. Children are not known for their tolerance for differences. That may place an unbearable burden on a child who is adopted by a gay or lesbian and feels compelled to take up for his parent with peers who may consider the parent an oddity. Since it is important for prospective gay adoptive parents to come to terms with those possibilities before being approved for adoption, screeners should question applicants about those issues during the home study process.

Heterosexual parents often have a difficult time accepting homosexuality among their children. If the parent reacts badly when told by a son or daughter that they are gay or lesbian, the reaction may not be so much to the gay issue as to the realization that the child will not be a carbon copy of themselves. Duplication is an issue that goes to the core of parenthood, which is why screeners should address it with gay or lesbian applicants. How will they feel if their son or daughter tells them they are heterosexual? Will they be disappointed not to be duplicated by their child and will they be able to accept the child's decision? How they deal with that issue will define them as parents.

Another issue that screener's should address is the applicant's self-image as a gay or lesbian person. Are they ashamed, proud, indifferent, troubled, or burdened by their sexual orientation? Are they defensive or combative about it? Is it a subject that caused them pain growing up? Do they feel discriminated against in the work place? Do they feel anger over their situation in life? Basically, as the screener, you want to understand how successfully they have dealt with problems associated with their sexual orientation.

# Chapter 7

## Screening Male Child Predators

Child predators cannot be weeded out based on a preconceived idea of how they look. In fact, they often look like the man next door because they are the man next door. They have responsible jobs and families of their own. More often than not, they are married and may be perceived as leaders in their communities. With that in mind, we have prepared a list of red-flag warning signs and problem areas that are consistent with pedophilic leanings in adult males.

**The absence of a significant other**. Pedophiles gravitate to children because they have a history of failed relationships with adults. They idealize children by anointing them with the innocence they feel they lost in their own lives. Of course, there are millions of men in America who are temporarily without significant others. That does not make them pedophiles, but the absence of a significant other should raise questions about the nature of past relationships. Does the applicant have a history of failed, short-term relationships, or does he have a history of satisfying, long-term relationships? If most of the relationships were short-term, why did they fail? Were there problems with sexual or emotional compatibility?

**A history of sexual abuse.** One of the more insidious aspects of child abuse is the fact that abused children often grow up to become abusers themselves. For that reason, it is important to determine if an applicant experienced sexual abuse as a child. If indirect questioning does not produce a clear understanding of that issue, the screener should ask the applicant outright if he was ever been abused as a child.

**The display of inappropriate symbols**. Men who wear neckties with cartoon characters; men who have stuffed animals in their home; or men who have photographs on their walls of children to whom they are not related should come under increased scrutiny. Pedophiles use those symbols of childhood to attract victims and to make them feel at ease. It is not so much the cartoon characters or stuffed toys, as it is the circumstance under which they are displayed that should be of concern.

**Inappropriate behavior**. It is one thing for a biological father to run his fingers through his son's hair, to tickle him and roll on the floor with him, or to engage in playful behavior such as squirting him with a water hose or wrestling with him, but that same behavior would be inappropriate for a male to display toward neighborhood children and it should raise questions about his motivation for instigating the behavior. Screeners should ask single males to give detailed examples of things they like to do with children when interacting with them.

**Discomfort discussing brothers and sisters.** This is a key area of concern. Men who have been abused as children—or have abused children as adults—often are reluctant to discuss their siblings. They have a difficult time remembering their names and ages; they seem at a loss to tell you where they live or what they do for a living; and they often try to change the subject when pressed for more information. Men who have sexually abused their siblings, even if it occurred twenty or thirty years ago, will not want you contacting them about their adoption application for fear the truth will come out. To prevent that they will manufacture memory lapses to cover their tracks.

**Involvement as a pastor, youth minister, or church music director.** Pedophiles are attracted to church youth-group organizations because they feel it offers them a degree of immunity from detection since it provides them with a "man of God" image. The vast majority of men involved in youth ministries are there for the right reasons, but as news stories remind us each year there are a significant percentage of men who pursue those affiliations as a cover for child abuse. Screeners should be concerned about men affiliated with youth ministries who do not have a significant other or a history of satisfying relationships with adults.

**Panic attacks that occur while discussing children.** Panic attacks can occur when heterosexual men engage in conversation with a woman they find attractive, and they can occur when homosexual men talk to men they find attractive. The same type of phenomenon can occur when pedophiles discuss children. During an interview, you will not be able to detect all the physical symptoms of a panic attack—increased heart rate and respiration, for example—but you can be alert to increased sweating and increased hand movements to the face, along with apparent blushing.

The most telling symptom will be the individual's sudden need for flight. He may stand up while you are sitting down, and he may pace about the room and then busy himself watering a plant or lighting a cigarette or nervously peering out the window, all done to avoid eye contact with you. In other instances, he may request permission to briefly leave the room to go to the restroom or make a telephone call.

## CASE HISTORY

Malcolm and his wife Sarah came into the agency to apply for adoption, even though they had two birth children of their own. They said that they understood that couples that were unable to have birth children would have priority for infants, so they decided to apply for an older child, in particular a girl aged three to five.

Malcolm and Sarah, both in their mid-thirties, made a good first impression. They were an attractive couple, friendly and outgoing. Malcolm worked as a police officer and Sarah was the owner of a day-care center for pre-school age children. The screener used the first interview as an opportunity to explain agency policies and to probe the couple about their motivation for adoption.

"I just love children," explained Sarah.

"Kids that age are just so cute, we'd like to have more now that our children are in school," added Malcolm.

The screener scheduled the next interview for the office, with Malcolm soloing for his individual interview. He seemed more nervous for his individual interview than he had been for the first joint interview. The screener didn't think too much about it since that sometimes happens with over-anxious couples.

The screener explained to Malcolm that he was going to talk about his childhood so that he could write up a family history for the home study. The screener used this approach to build a rapport with Malcolm. With his head down, avoiding eye contact that could be perceived as threatening, the screener wrote down detail after detail about Malcolm's early family life—early memories, school experiences, questions that did not break the rhythm of the interview. It was when the screener asked him for the names and birthdates of his siblings that the interview slammed into a brick wall.

Malcolm said he had six sisters, but he couldn't remember their names. Asked if he could put them in birth order, youngest to oldest, and recall any of their birthdates, he answered that he could not.

"We just weren't real close," he explained. "I don't even know where any of them live."

Questioned about his memory—whether he had problems recalling other details about his childhood or recent events—he was adamant that he had no memory problems. To prove that he had a good memory, Malcolm told the screener about two little girls that his wife had babysat ten years ago, during their first year of marriage. "They were beautiful little girls," he gushed. "Their names were Bette and Marcie. One was three, born on April 15, and the other was five, born on December 2."

That episode raised red flags for the screener. Male pedophiles that are attracted to females often have bad relationships with their sisters.

Often their sexual experimentation begins at an early age with their younger sisters. Malcolm was correct about one thing—there was nothing wrong with his memory, as his detailed descriptions of Bette and Marcia proved. The screener also was bothered that Malcolm became so animated when he discussed the little girls.

Alerted to the possibility that he might be interviewing a pedophile, the screener became more aggressive with his questioning. His technique was to ask a series of innocuous questions, dutifully writing down his answers on a legal pad. He did that for ten minutes, avoiding eye contact with Malcolm, building up Malcolm's confidence that he was controlling the interview. Then, abruptly, he put down his pen and looked Malcolm directly in the eye, shattering his composure with the question. "Do you know if any of your sisters were ever sexually abused?"

Malcolm was stunned. After a few awkward moments, during which he started and stopped a series of sentences, he asked if he could be excused to go to the bathroom. The screener excused him. As he was walking out the door, Malcolm turned around and smiled. "I'll answer that question when I get back."

Ten minutes later, Malcolm returned to the interview room, his face no longer showing the perspiration it had displayed when he left—an indication that he had washed his face. When he sat back down, he was composed. "To answer your question," he said. "No—sex was never discussed in my family."

Again, the screener asked a series of innocent questions, allowing Malcolm to relax. Then, as he had done before, he looked him directly in the eye and asked, "How have you prepared your daughters to deal with sexual abuse?"

Malcolm stared back at the screener, trying to break his gaze, but the screener held firm, looking him squarely in the eye. It was at that point that Malcolm experienced a panic attack. He rose to his feet and paced about the room, muttering, "Well, now . . . let me see." His newly washed face suddenly grew shiny. He sighed several times in rapid succession and then said, "I would tell them to beware of strangers."

After the interview, the screener went into his supervisor's office and told her that he had serious doubts about Malcolm's ability to be an adoptive parent. Said the screener, "I think he is a pedophile."

The supervisor asked why he felt that way, and he hit the high points of the interview. Noted the supervisor, "It sounds like he is afraid we will contact his sisters."

The screener agreed. Together, the interviewer and the supervisor decided to structure an aggressive interview for Sarah when she came in for her individual interview. As it happened, Sarah's interview never took place.

The following week, the agency learned that Malcolm had been arrested and charged with molesting two of the little girls enrolled in Sarah's day-care center. The agency further learned that the adoption application had been a ploy devised by Malcolm's lawyer, who thought that getting them approved for adoption would establish the agency as a source for "expert" witness testimony. He had coached Malcolm on how to respond in the interview and he had instructed him to list out-of-state references that would have no knowledge of his arrest.

This story ended with the agency preserving its integrity and protecting its adoptive children—and with Malcolm pleading guilty to child molestation.

## SEX ABUSE STATISTICS SCREENERS SHOULD KNOW

- The typical child sex offender molests an average of 117 children, most of whom do not report the offence.[xxx]
- About 60 percent of male survivors surveyed report at least one of their molesters to be female.[xxxi]
- Young girls who are abused are three times more likely to develop psychiatric disorders or abuse alcohol and drugs as adults than girls who are not sexually abused.[xxxii]
- Female survivors of child sexual abuse are four times more likely than non-survivors to have worked as a prostitute; male survivors are eight times as likely. Survivors are 40 percent more likely to have sex with someone they don't know.[xxxiii]
- Despite the fact that immediate family members have the most access to children, fewer than half of the sexual abuse perpetrators are family members or close relatives. Strangers make up only 10 to 30 percent of the cases, with the remainder identified as mothers' boyfriends, neighbors, teachers, coaches, religious leaders, and peers.[xxxiv]

# Chapter 8

## What You Need to Know About Infants

"Is my child all right?"

It is the first question that a concerned birth parent asks after delivery—and the last question a parent asks on his or her way out of life. Unfortunately for parents, it is only during the first eighteen years or so of their child's life that their decisions and actions can affect the type of person that the child ultimately becomes.

A parent can offer love, understanding, and financial support to their child for a lifetime, but they have a relatively short time during which to affect his or her growth and development. That eighteen-year period is shaped like a funnel, with the years between birth and school age representing the wide end of the funnel.

A parent's influence is greatest in the first few years of life, up until the child begins school. After that, it decreases on a steady basis until the child reaches adulthood. From that point on, parental influence is exerted primarily in the child's perception of the relationship the parents have with each other—and in the quality of the relationship each parent has with the adult son and daughter.

Adoptive parents who understand how children develop—and can distinguish what is considered normal from what is considered abnormal—will be better prepared to deal with the inevitable problems that lie ahead. With each unexpected challenge, a parent may feel overwhelmed, especially if they are single and facing all the decisions alone. Often they feel under extreme pressure when navigating through the rough waters of parenting; sometimes problems that are perceived to be catastrophic are simply normal phases of development.

Prior to the seventeenth century, children held little, if any, status in the community, or even in their own families. A large proportion of children died at birth or soon after. Those that survived delivery were of little value to their parents until they could help support the family. Often by the age of seven, children held jobs or worked as apprentices to learn a specific trade. Their pattern of development was not considered a topic of much concern or interest.

That changed in the 1600s and 1700s when philosophers John Locke and Jean Jacques Rousseau began arguing that children had needs that were different from their parents' needs. Locke proposed the idea that, at birth, the child's mind is a *"tabula rara,"* or a "blank slate," on which ideas are only recorded through experience. He suggested that children, because of their limited experience, needed the more experienced adults to teach them life's survival skills. Rousseau suggested that children could be "perfected" through a process of observation and education based on their emerging needs. Locke and Rousseau were radical thinkers for their time.

By the nineteenth and twentieth centuries, society began recognizing the uniqueness of childhood. Scientific observation, experimentation and better documentation lead to changes in attitudes and treatment of the early years. In the years since then, increasing interest in the role of parents in the "making of a child" has dominated child development literature.

Development, by definition, suggests an unfolding sequence of changes, acquisitions or growth. This process can usually be grouped within three major developmental categories: physical, mental and social. These categories are not separate or distinct from one another; rather they are interrelated, much like building blocks that form a pattern in which it is hard to distinguish each separate part.

Although normal child development follows predictable patterns— and involves simultaneous physical, mental and social changes—there are only a few absolutes that, if not followed, will cause irreparable damage; parents have a wide margin for error.

Positive parenting involves accepting biological attributes of the child and then providing a nurturing environment that allows healthy development through good learning opportunities, appropriate role models, encouragement and discipline. It is to the parents' advantage if they understand the guidelines and methods that professionals use to evaluate children. The language used by physicians and psychologists may sound foreign to parents, perhaps even exotic, but the ideas behind the language are often based on common sense and can be understood by anyone.

For decades, there has been an ongoing debate about whether child development is more affected by genetics or environment—that is to say, whether we are the product of our genes or the product of our surroundings. It is the old *nature vs. nurture* debate. Presently, most professionals consider the debate a draw. They feel that the biological makeup of a child is just as important as environmental factors.

At birth, a child arrives with certain physical characteristics and inherited tendencies, which then interact with the environment. This complex integration of genetics and environment determines his overall development. The genetic influence is pretty much set in place at conception, so there is not a lot that can be done from that point on to alter that biological framework, other than corrective surgery to modify specific physical conditions.

The environmental influences begin at the point that the genetic influences end. Mothers submit their fetuses to a variety of life-changing environmental influences such as emotional stress, temperature changes, noise levels, changing voices, physical activity, and even dietary stimulation. That environmental influence begins in the womb, but it accelerates rapidly at birth, thus making environment equally important to genetics as a determining factor in a child's ultimate development.

Physical, mental and social development can be accelerated or diminished through this complex interaction. What that means is that a child can only benefit from environmental experiences that he is biologically capable of exploiting. Learning to play the piano is an example. Trying to teach an infant to play the piano would only lead to frustration for everyone involved. The infant is not mature enough to comprehend the task, nor is his body ready to use the eye-hand coordination necessary to produce socially acceptable music. The physical and mental changes necessary to produce music usually take some time. However, it is useful to keep in mind that child development is not absolute. One familiar exception is Mozart, who presented his first concert to the Imperial family in Vienna, Austria, at the age of six years. Mozart obviously possessed both the biological and environmental requirements necessary to express his musical genius at an early age. On paper, he was not supposed to be able to do that. Parents should remember that there are exceptions to every rule of child development, especially with children who possess special talents and abilities.

# Infant Development

Birth is not the beginning of physical development, but rather a continuation of what began in the womb. The child's heart has been beating, muscles contracting and many other organs have been functioning for some time. Even before birth, he can hear voices, respond to environmental conditions, and experience taste.

Only at birth does a child begin breathing and ingesting food. Behavioral development such as sucking and stretching, which also have already begun in the womb, continue at a rapid rate after birth. It is during this first two years after birth, what we traditionally call infancy, that the child evolves into a distinct person.

In early infancy, there are several standardized methods of assessing a child's level of functioning:

- **The Apgar Scale** is used to assess a newborn's heart rate, strength of breathing, muscle tone, color and reflex responsiveness within minutes of birth. It provides a preliminary evaluation of the child's overall health status. Often the pediatrician can determine problems that need further assessment as a result of the Apgar results.

- **The Brazleton Neonatal Behavior Assessment Scale** is given shortly after birth to determine the baby's general neurological health and behavior. To administer the Brazleton, an examiner purposely arouses the infant from a sound sleep and moves him through a series of activities in wakefulness and then allows him to calm himself again and go back to sleep. The examiner then notes the baby's ability to regulate his responses to over twenty stimuli, such as pictures, rattles, faces and voices. The examiner notes numerous reflexes and how the baby responds to being aroused from a deep sleep and then how quickly he can quieten himself again. A child's ability to respond and then quieten again shows good neurological development.

# Parent-Child Bonding

Parent-infant bonding has always been held in high esteem, as it should be, but contrary to earlier belief, there appears to be no absolute "critical period for bonding" that will result in catastrophic results if not adhered to. If it is not possible for parents and babies to be physically together within minutes after birth, the parents should not be overly concerned that a good relationship is in jeopardy, or that they will be less able to form close attachments.

The 1980s research of Dr. Michael Lamb and his colleagues showed that there is no significant difference in parent-infant relationships if bonding time is not available immediately after birth. Their findings have led to a shift in emphasis, making the quality of the bonding experience more important than any specific time frame. In other words, how you bond is more important than when you bond.

# Bonding Prefers the Slow Lane

"The bonding process is pretty gradual, but in the child's case it continues to develop throughout much of childhood. At least some of the slow pace has to do with the slow development of the brain, so when babies are really little they are just not capable of higher affinitive feelings.

They can certainly recognize the parent and they can elicit the kind of care giving they need, but I think it would be difficult to say the newborn feels 'love' toward the parent. However, the real size of the attachment starts emerging at about five or six months, when babies start showing a preference for or an aversion for strangers and they start fussing when mom leaves them alone.

This period, particularity the second six months of life when attachment is at its peak, coincides with a big spurt of development in the prefrontal cortex, which is where our awareness of our feelings starts to come up."—**Dr. Lise Eliot**

# Watching Baby Grow

The rapid changes in an infant's sensory development and reflexes are dramatic. Although the newborn can see, hear, taste, smell, and respond to touch, his acuity improves almost daily. He begins to follow his mother with his eyes, turn towards voices, and show an increased preference in taste and sensitivity to touch.

He will turn his head in the direction of touch and display a strong sucking motion with his throat, mouth, and tongue. Breathing is considered an early reflex, but it becomes partially voluntary with time. The Moro, grasping and stepping primitive reflexes, along with the survival reflexes, either disappear or gradually come under voluntary control within the first six months of life. These reflex responses are considered an important marker in his mental development.

Gender plays little role in development during the first couple of years. Although the brains of males and females are different even at birth, some of the differences are minor, but noteworthy. Dr. Lise Eliot, a neuroscientist and author of *What's Going On In There*, feels that, generally speaking, girls are about three weeks more neurologically mature at birth than boys. "That's probably the main reason girls are a lot less vulnerable in infancy," she said.[xxxv] "If you look at the different senses, there are subtle differences in acuity, with females generally having slightly better hearing, smell and touch. But males generally win out on measures of vision. They are better at predicting visual motion."

Boys show more activity, even before birth. Using big motor skills, they move about more, whereas girls spend more time using fine motor skills. That's a fancy way of saying that little boys like to use their large muscles, while little girls prefer to use their small muscles. Those differences appear to be genetically based, but most adults encourage those differences. By age two, boys and girls show different motor abilities. In nursery school, girls perform better in activities using rhythm and balance. They build block towers better and taller than boys. Boys run faster and are stronger than girls.

Other brain differences are apparent in how boys and girls behave. "In infancy, boys are definitely fussier and more emotionally labile than girls," said Eliot. "They are less able to handle their feelings and frustrations. That again, is presumably to do with their general lack of development."[xxxvi] Most adults reinforce the idea that little girls behave differently than little boys.

Eliot describes an innate bias towards different ways of interacting with the environment. "They are immersed in this environment, where men and women play very, very different roles—and by about eighteen months, they first become aware of whether they are a boy or a girl, and they very rapidly learn to identify with members of the same sex. So, once they hit that gender identification, or gender awareness, they sort of drive their own learning around how to be a boy and how to be a girl."[xxxvii]

Research suggests that children are greatly affected by how the significant people in their life respond to them. Dr. Marian Diamond, a brain researcher at the University of California, agrees with Eliot that society reinforces the inborn tendencies for "boys will be boys and girls will be girls". When a somewhat aggressive little boy smiles during very active, rough play, we play rough next time. And when baby girls respond more to touch and sounds, they, in fact, increase the likelihood of adults speaking and playing with them a bit more softly and gently in the future. Babies train us how to treat them at the same time we train them how to behave.

An infant's social development is evident immediately after birth. He will not only turn toward a human voice, he will actually seek its source and visually follow a human face. Eliot feels that newborns, only hours after birth, recognize and prefer their mother's face and voice.

As time goes on, infants develop emotional attachments to the important people in their life. Within the first two years, the infant learns whom he can count on and how to make independent decisions. During this time, his psychosocial development primarily revolves around developing a sense of trust and autonomy.

These major social themes are influenced by the child's interactions with his family. Parents who engage in frequent and sustained play with their babies help promote their social development. By imitating and trading smiles, gazes, vocalizations, and touches, a mother and child can create a very special relationship that, in turn, can create a foundation for the child to seek additional social contacts. Typically, the infant learns that the significant people around him will return at the end of the day, will rescue him when in distress, and care for his needs.

At the same time, the infant learns that he can make decisions about preferences in foods, what he wants to investigate, and who will get his attention. Usually this sense of autonomy is developed simultaneously with his sense of trust. Unless trauma is present in the environment, such as abuse or neglect, most physically normal infants seem to achieve these social milestones fairly easily. These early social experiences with family provide the basis for the personality and emotional development that follows.

Our ability to understand a child's early emotions is restricted by their limited ability to communicate their feelings. Assumptions are often made about what an infant may be feeling based on observable behavior. Specific emotions such as joy, sadness, fear, and anger can be easily identified by observation, but the more complex feelings cannot. Laughter comes by four months, fear at about seven months, and the more complex emotions, such as shame, are not identifiable until about two years. Infants clearly pick up on subtle cues from the significant people around them. They are sensitive to the positive feelings, anxieties, and fears of their caregivers.

This sensitivity has a reciprocal influence on an infant's caregivers. A baby that is considered easy is often responded to more positively by his caregiver than a more difficult child. An "easy child" is usually treated with more warmth, affection and acceptance, whereas a "difficult child" may often be labeled as such and treated with less warmth, acceptance or affection.

The most familiar views of personality, mental, and social development originated in Europe. Sigmund Freud, an Austrian physician, offered his theory of personality development in the 1890s after studying and treating patients who suffered from extreme conditions such as blindness or paralysis, which had no apparent physical cause. Jean Piaget, a Swiss psychologist and father of four, spent endless hours observing children as they developed their mental skills. From his work, we have gained an understanding of the cognitive developmental process.

Influenced by both Freud and Piaget, Erik Erikson, a German-born researcher who studied under Anna Freud (Sigmund Freud's daughter) before coming to the United States, focused on the influence of social environment in the developmental process. All three European theorists emphasize that the progressive stages of human development are closely related to the care that children receive early in life.

## The Caregivers

A child's early focus is on his need to be fed and cared for. A good and responsive relationship with his caregiver is vital if the infant is to learn trust. He is totally dependent on his parents and quickly determines whether they can be "trusted" to meet his needs or not. Typically, this relationship centers on the mother and child, but in some situations there may be a different primary caregiver.

For the early months, the child has no feeling of being separate from his mother. Most mothers enjoy sharing this feeling of total integration, as if the child is an extension of herself. If this closeness is achieved, it contributes to the child's development of a sense of security from which he will later venture to seek his individual identity, develop self-control, and assert his autonomy. The child who suffers inconsistent, neglectful or inappropriate care may exhibit personality problems later that are based on trust issues.

Traditionally, mothers have assumed the role of primary caregiver, with fathers feeling more comfortable with a secondary role. Is the time that moms and dads spend playing and talking to the infant different? Yes and no. Both parents use what psychologists call "build-up and withdrawal" cycles with the child. Their play is similar, but their styles are different. Fathers push a bit farther and reach a higher peak before withdrawal from the play. They are more physically active, using bouncing and jostling. They talk and smile less, and they are less inclined to play peek-a-boo or other familiar games. Fathers spend about half of their time with the child in actual play, whereas mothers, who spend most of their time physically caring for the child, spend only about twenty-five percent of their time with the child engaged in play.

Under different circumstances, where the father is considered the primary caregiver, he smiles more, imitates the baby's vocalizations and facial expressions, and plays ritual games similar to most mothers. When placed in the primary caregiver role fathers are found to be as successful and competent as mothers. Unfortunately, society has convinced many fathers that they are not as competent as mothers.

Between the ages of one-and-a-half and three years, children learn bowel and bladder control. During that time, the child needs encouragement, guidance and sensitivity from his parents as he struggles to gain full control of his body's functions. If successful, the child achieves a feeling of self-control and perceives himself as capable of making things happen. In general, he achieves self-esteem. Parents who are unable, or unwilling, to provide a safe and emotionally secure environment during this child-development crisis may contribute to future personality problems in their child, such as low self-esteem and a sense of powerlessness.

The most important determinant of personality seems to be in the quality of care rather than the quantity of care. With the growing number of single families and working moms, it is important to understand that it is not essential that this close attachment early in life be only with the mother. Little or no differences have been found in most children's preferred attachments during the first two years of life. Fathers or other caregivers can serve as well as a mother. Again, quality of care is the significant factor. Babies can be in a stable, responsive daycare situation all day and come home each evening to a loving, stimulating home with no ill effects.

Is feeding, bathing, dressing, and keeping a baby warm and safe, enough to insure health personality development? Most experts would say no. But a child needs the intimate and enduring emotional attachments that occur between himself and the caregiver early in life. Studies have shown that this physical closeness is even preferred over the desire for food. Children who are denied this mutual interaction seem to suffer residual effects throughout life.

The mental development of a child becomes evident soon after birth. He is expected to demonstrate his intelligence by manipulating objects with his hand, following and seeking voices, gazing at pictures and imitating sounds. Early expectations appear rather simple; however, as the child matures he is expected to respond to verbal directions, execute activities on command, and figure out simple problems.

According to Piaget, the infant's primary thinking takes place through the use of the senses and motor skills. He uses reflexes to deal with the environment and most of his behavior is focused on his own body. During this first stage of intellectual development, he begins to actually "know" things. He actively interacts with the environment, becomes aware of cause-effect relationships, crudely imitates others, and understands that objects exist even when they are out of sight.

A marker of the end of infancy occurs when the child can form images in his head called symbolic thinking. He no longer must touch an object in order to understand that it exists. He now responds to the suggestion of a favorite toy without actually handling it. He learns quickly, but seemingly by trial and error, learning that thoughts, actions and objects are separate. He understands to open his mouth wide for a cookie and close it tight for carrots. By age two years, he will search for a hidden toy, understanding that it still exists, even if it is not within his reach or sight. With normal intellectual development the young child imitates other's behavior, even hours or days later. Inappropriate words he overheard days earlier may be blurted out, usually at the most embarrassing moment.

Many communities offer new parents workshops, training, or home visits by educators to assist the caregiver in providing the appropriate attention and stimulation for the baby. These programs have been well received and seem to improve long-term outcomes for the children involved. Often new parents need the role models, training, encouragement and support they would not have otherwise.

Hopefully, during the first two years of life, the child has doubled in size and tripled in weight; his brain should have reached 75 percent of its adult weight. He has realized his own sense of self and can express a range of emotions. He is sensitive to the environment and has formed important relationships. He now understands that he is a separate individual who is capable of listening, thinking and speaking.

Now he no longer has to cry loud and long enough to annoy his parents into either changing is diaper or feeding him. Somehow, they always seemed to read the cry wrong and assume his diaper needed attention when he really was hungry. He has tried to be patient with his young parents as they learned to distinguish his different cries, but by the time they became fairly well trained at understanding his system of communication, he began saying words and going to the potty.

The first two years are the most critical in promoting healthy physical, mental, and personality development. Although he no longer needs feeding or changing hourly, he continues to demand attention throughout the day. The family may have experienced some stormy moments along the way, but he, like most youngsters, will have achieved the foundation necessary to build new skills.

Unless there are significant physical or mental handicaps, most children are ready by the age of two to venture into a new phase of learning and experience.

# Chapter 9

## What You Need to Know About Older Children

The years between the total dependency of infancy and the responsibility of elementary school are considered some of the most carefree years. It is a time of rapid growth and development, during which a child transitions into a true contributing member of the family. Physical changes during the preschool years are less dramatic than earlier, as the child begins to take on more adult-like body proportions. He seems to jump into a larger clothing size even before one season ends. He becomes less chunky and his appearance goes from gender neutral to masculine. He starts using motor skills more effectively to run, jump, walk and ride a tricycle.

The development of fine and gross motor skills become very important as he gets more involved in organized learning activities. The rate of his physical development can be affected by numerous factors, including his genetic makeup, his ethnic background, cultural influences, nutrition, and his overall physical health.

Boys have more muscle and bone and less fat than girls. For both, the growth process follows a predictable sequence. The toddler appears top-heavy because growth takes place from top to bottom. During this transition, his "pot-bellied" abdomen is considered normal for a while because it is holding almost full-grown internal organs. Shortly his lower body will grow to catch up, causing him to grow taller and better proportioned, losing the "pot-belly". By the time he actually enters school at age six, he will resemble the children in the upper grades more than his younger sibling.

Physical changes become more evident as motor skills develop:

- At about three years, he can run in a straight line, jump with both feet, copy a circle, use simple utensils to eat and stack a few blocks.
- By four years, he is skipping, hopping and catching a large ball. His fine motor skills now include buttoning large buttons, copying simple shapes and drawing a simple figure.
- At age five, when he is ready to enter kindergarten, he is usually using scissors, copying letters and numbers, balancing on one foot, running without falling, and building fairly complex structures with blocks.

Another achievement of most preschoolers is acquiring total bladder and bowel control. Typically, daytime bladder and bowel control occur concurrently, usually before the third birthday. Debate continues over whether reminders are helpful, hurtful, or make no difference in his success. However, too many reminders or harsh responses to accidents can create anxiety or defiant behavior. Nighttime bladder control takes much longer and is associated with several factors such as the size of his bladder and how deeply he sleeps. Usually, by kindergarten he seldom, if ever, has accidents.

Much of the brain's growth has already taken place by age two or three. It will reach about 75 percent of its total weight by age three and about 90 percent by age six. During the preschool years, the brain develops the structures necessary for higher mental functions and acquires the specific brain activity associated with separate regions of the brain. With the completion of these brain processes, the child is able to write and draw. During his kindergarten year, boys are more likely to be evaluated for Learning Deficits, Attention-Deficit Hyperactivity Disorder, and Autism. Professionals must be cautious in diagnosing such disorders too early since some children with learning problems seem to "blossom" after being placed in a structured learning environment.

Play is the primary activity of a preschooler. His play is usually designed to meet his own enjoyment needs. He is more interested in the process of play than the outcomes of play. Psychologists use play as a means of observing a child's attempt to resolve conflict and gain power over the environment. The child initially watches others, only engaging in play for a minute or two at a time. He then learns to play alone, avoiding interaction with others. Later, he tries to engage others in his play, only slightly at first, but then moving into cooperative play.

Erickson noted that children this age have a greater feeling of mobility, are more communicative, and have an increased imagination. In his efforts to bring secret fantasies under control, the child learns to experience feelings of guilt. He seems to have an inner voice offering judgments concerning his behavior of right and wrong, and he fears punishment for fantasies that he labels as "wrong."

Verbal and physical aggression are usually part of the preschooler's repertoire of behavior to express his needs and resolve conflicts, but as time goes by, most find other means of dealing with conflicts in a more socially acceptable manner. The preschooler that is unable to alter his aggressive behavior finds that life only gets more complicated as he progresses through the educational system.

# Thinking Like a 4-Year-Old

Socially, preschoolers engage in conversations, play with siblings and exhibit a sense of belonging. Emotionally, they exhibit complex feelings that sometimes vacillate from being witty and performing for anyone that will watch, to being very absorbed in their very private thoughts. Parents are sometimes embarrassed, at other times entertained, but continuously amazed at their precious creation.

As Piaget's research revealed, preschoolers exhibit egocentric thinking, which means that they are unable to think beyond self to consider another's point of view. They can only focus on one aspect of a given situation. They believe that nonliving objects are, in fact, alive and that all objects, whether living or nonliving, are made the same way. They tend to over-generalize on many levels. They learn to classify objects according to several categories. With practice they are able to sort according to color, size and shape.

Preschoolers sometimes have difficulty retracing behavior, such as "what did you do with the ball this afternoon?" Neither can they understand that mass and volume remain the same when circumstances change. They have a difficult time believing that eight ounces of juice in a large pitcher can remain the same when poured into a tall glass.

Matthew, who is four years old, loves to play with his dad's car keys. He will play with them anytime he has a chance. When his dad couldn't find the keys one night, he became frustrated and insisted that four-year-old Matthew must find the keys he had played with earlier in the day. Dad tried to motivate Matthew by promising to take him to buy ice cream if he found the lost keys.

Unfortunately, Matthew was not capable of recalling details of previous events and retracing his actions from earlier in the day. He simply couldn't remember where he was playing with the keys, no matter how motivating the ice cream offer sounded. Matthew's mom tried to intervene by offering him his favorite juice while he thought about where the keys might be. Matthew loves juice, so as usual he whined and fretted until his mom poured the juice into his favorite tall glass instead of the wide-rimmed, shorter glass. Matthew insisted there was more juice in the taller glass, even though mom poured the juice from glass to glass to help him understand that the amount does not change.

Matthew has two very well meaning parents who are simply uninformed about reasonable developmental expectations for a four-year-old. It would benefit both Matthew and his parents if they understood that Matthew should not play with anything of much value or any object his parents might need in the near future. If adults allow children to play with such items, they should take responsibility for retrieving the valuables after playtime. And for mom, only time will help Matthew understand that 6 ounces of juice is still 6 ounces of juice, no matter into which glass it is poured.

# Gender Differences

Sex differences in preschool play may appear only slight, but what begins in preschool, continues throughout life—boys prefer to play with other boys, girls with other girls. There seem to be visual cues as to who plays with whom: girls tend to walk in a straight line, arms at their side or folded across their mid-section; boys shuffle back and forth in more of a sideways motion, their arms swinging. Boys are often larger and stronger than most girls, and they may be able to hit, throw and catch a ball better.

One of the most significant gender differences in preschoolers is how they choose to use their time. Boys are active and rough. Girls prefer quieter play, such as drawing or playing with stuffed animals. Girls are more proficient at manual dexterity, hopping and skipping; but boys can go up and down steps and jump better than girls. Boys prefer playing outdoors and girls usually enjoy indoor play more. Boys enjoy playing in the sand, climbing, and playing with outdoor gadgets more than their female peers.

# Where Parents Fit In

The development of language skills is a major accomplishment during the preschool years. Parents are very instrumental in language acquisition as the child initially masters the grammar of his native language. During the preschool years, he learns to combine words into meaningful thoughts. Gender, culture and socioeconomic class all contribute to differences in syntax and language usage.

By the end of his second year, the child understands that he exists as a separate individual, apart from his parents, although he continues to be deeply attached to them. He identifies with his parents and feels that they are powerful and may even be viewed as somewhat dangerous.

As the preschooler is busy trying out new ideas and behavior, parents are busy trying to provide appropriate structure and discipline. Parents fear the unintended effects of being too lenient or harsh. Parents who provide a high level of control and demand maturity—but offer limited communication and nurturing—seem to produce children that are distrustful, less happy, and more likely to have lower school performance.

Permissive parents that are communicative and nurturing, but that make few demands for control or maturity, tend to produce children that have difficulty with self-control and self-reliance. Authoritative parents that show a high level of control, clear communication channels, and a nurturing attitude seem to provide the healthiest parenting style. Their children are more likely to be better adjusted and described as self-reliant, and they are more likely to have good self-control and achievement.

# What You Need To Know About the Middle Years

Many remember the middle years of life with greater fondness than any other time. Children that age have a good command of language, they can think clearly, and they contribute to conversations with their opinions. Usually, they have plenty of play time and start developing friendships that may continue the rest of their life. Often neighbors and family members comment on "how big he's getting" and "how smart he is." He's growing up, learning daily, and should feel that "life is good."

On the first day of school, most first graders are filled with excitement and anticipation. Some may be shy, others very outgoing and others even a bit aggressive. They arrive in a variety of sizes and shapes. The largest child may be six inches taller and sometimes twenty pounds heavier than the smallest in the class. These dramatic differences are only amplified within the next several years as children grow at different rates. Girls usually reach this growth spurt earlier than boys, so by late childhood, girls are sometimes standing head and shoulders above the boys.

The timing of this phenomenon is interesting since it often coincides with their initial interest in one another. Awkward as it may seem, boys and girls cope fairly well with their height differences. It's when height, weight or physical features fall outside the "accepted range" of tolerance that peers can be cruel and hurtful. Children that are obese, have large ears, wear glasses, or have other anomalies, are often the target of ridicule by their peers.

The middle-to-late childhood years are full of physical challenges. Baseball, soccer, basketball, swimming, tennis and football seem to be the sports of choice. Socially it's important to participate, whether it is in organized sports or with sandlot friends. Boys particularly feel the pressure to be part of a team activity. Physically their bodies are increasing in strength and endurance, and their motor skills are improving quickly with practice.

Dramatic differences in abilities are evident in boys between the ages of six to ten. A major difference is noticed in the older boy's coordination and timing. He can now anticipate the baseball better, swing the bat in time to connect, and run, jump and catch the ball in the outfield.

Although injury is always a possibility and fear of failure is ever-present, participation in team sports seems to be beneficial for most boys. It not only refines his motor and coordination skills, but it also offers social contact and teaches him to play by the rules. However, parents must be careful in their approach with sons that are involved in sports. Encouragement is important, but constant pressure to excel may cause extreme harm. Participation in organized sports can be an opportunity for families to have fun together while providing the child with valuable life lessons.

The school-age child learns at a remarkable rate. He learns to read, spell, compute math, comprehend concepts, get along with others, follow directions, and work independently, all in the first year of his formal education. During this time he begins to perform mental operations that demonstrate his ability to focus on various aspects of a problem. He can think beyond the present, incorporate more than one aspect, and begin to reason out issues. Soon he will be able to challenge the adults in his life.

# Navigating the Challenges

As the child makes his way through the middle years he is faced with many challenges. He must learn a self-discipline if he is to conquer math, reading, spelling and science. Facing homework nightly can create a family crisis if he has trouble with attention, motivation or ability. He begins to take on chores around the house, earn an allowance and explore a world beyond his own backyard. Friends become increasingly more important and many aspire to being a valued member of a sport's team.

Both Freud and Erikson described the years between six and twelve as the time the child begins to focus on building skills and developing a feeling of competency. By now most children have pushed aside some of the internal conflicts with each parent. He no longer waits for magical wishes to come true, including replacing his father. He is now ready to independently prove himself to be worthy of notice. He may concentrate his efforts on sports, academics, music or other activities. Few children dodge all the snags along this path; most do achieve a healthy sense of self-confidence, even if it is accompanied by the nagging voice of inferiority from time to time.

On the playground gender differences may be noticed. Boys tend to show more achievement motivation by racing against one another, while girls often spend their time developing social relationships by chatting in small groups. Peer relationships become increasingly important during this time regardless of gender. Although most children during the middle years do not share intimate thoughts and feelings with their peers, they do show more self-confidence in the presence of friends. Developing friendships offers feedback for the child and helps to slightly reduce his self-centered thinking.

Boys usually play in large groups with lots of tossing and tumbling around. They claim multiple "best friends," even when it is not a reciprocal relationship. Girls develop a much smaller circle of close friends and play games involving conversations and feelings. Peer relationships contribute to the child learning to cooperate and share.

Peers can offer a different perspective on many issues for the child. On the positive side, peers can offer feedback that fosters confidence in ways that parents cannot. They can even influence social behaviors. At times, the child at home appears totally different than the child known by his peers. Unfortunately, children with negative attitudes are the peer group's weakest link. They often bully and threaten smaller or weaker kids, ridicule underachievers, tease, or embarrass those who may be slightly different. They may ridicule children who live in homes without both parents. Parents should take quick action in those situations.

The concept of popularity becomes increasingly important during this time. Often popular children have a slight advantage over the others in school achievement, athletic abilities, confidence, physical attractiveness or advanced social skills. Girls seem to desire popularity slightly more than their male counterparts.

The middle years consolidate a "sense of self" for youngsters. Less adult supervision is necessary and, if things are going well, parents feel confident of their parenting skills. Their son engages in conversations with them. He expresses his unique feelings and desires, and he will quickly protest any hint of unfairness. Parents begin to see their own behavior in their son. The affectionate parent is usually pleased to see their son be affectionate to his younger sibling. The angry parent has little reason to be surprised to hear foul language in a son that has been exposed to it in the home.

It is sometimes helpful to remember poet William Wordsworth's observation that "the child is father of the man." The joy, frustration, laughter, and heartbreak that a child experiences on the road to adulthood will combine, eventually, to make him or her into the person that they become.

# PART II

# The Practice

## ADOPTIVE
## AND
## FOSTER PARENT
## SCREENING

# Chapter 10

## Home Study Interview Techniques

The phrase "home study" seems to mean different things to different people. To many of the self-help writers who have written adoption manuals, it is an entitlement that applicants have earned by virtue of having paid taxes. To many adoption applicants it is a mirror image of how they see themselves as prospective parents. To some social workers it is a report that provides a family genealogy of the applicant.

In truth, it is none of the above. A home study, when properly done, is an in-depth psychosocial analysis of a foster or adoptive applicant's potential as a parent, complete with a detailed look at a series of interrelated social and emotional variables that have shaped the individual from childhood to the present. The challenge is to look at the past with enough clarity and insight as to be able to make reliable predictions about the future.

For the screener the first goal of a home study is to evaluate the applicant's potential for sexual, emotional or physical abuse toward a child. Until that can be determined, everything else involved in the home study process is secondary. Once the screener is satisfied that the applicant is not a risk to a child, the second and third areas of concern are the individual's emotional stability and the nature of the individual's relationship with his or her spouse and family members. Other areas of concern include the individual's relationship with society as a whole (as documented by arrests or treatment for alcohol or drug abuse) and his or her experience with children and their attitudes about major parenting issues.

Doing a first-rate home study requires a lot of thought and effort.

113

Unfortunately, issues arise from time to time that make the work more difficult than it should be for screeners that are serious about their work. Since there is no regulation of adoption or foster homes at the national level, there are no uniform standards for home studies and the requirements vary widely from agency to agency, even within the same state. Screeners that do home studies for private agencies and international adoptions must constantly second-guess themselves about the information they include in the report for fear of violating privacy rights, or for fear of being sued for defamation by an applicant who disagrees with the assessment. It can have a chilling effect on the truthfulness of the report by intimidating a screener into withholding critical information.

The best way for a screener to approach a foster or adoptive applicant is as a complicated mystery that requires a level of sleuthing worthy of Sherlock Holmes. Is the applicant the person she seems to be? Or is she little more than a façade, a poser who has been coached about the "right" and "wrong" answers to give during the interviews?

The home study we advocate in this book is the optimum level of assessment we consider appropriate for screening foster and adoptive applicants. Admittedly, some agencies hold their screeners to a lower standard, especially when it comes to details of the applicant's emotional and sexual relationships.

We don't approve of shortcuts in the home study process since we think it puts children at risk, but we know that is the reality. Our hope is that increased scrutiny of the process will elevate professional standards to a level commensurate with the responsibility of the task.

# HOME STUDY FORMAT
(should be 15-25 pages in length)

**INTRODUCTION**

An explanation for the applicant's contact with the agency.

**INTERVIEWS**

Dates and structures of the interviews with the applicants. For example, "Individual interview with Mrs. R. on May 15. Joint interview with Mr. and Mrs. R. on June 1."

### FAMILY HISTORY

A detailed history of each applicant's family background and social history, beginning at birth.

### EDUCATION

Schools attended, graduation dates, majors or field of study.

### EMPLOYMENT HISTORY

Complete work history, with dates and summaries of responsibilities.

### MARITAL (OR SIGNIFICANT OTHER) RELATIONSHIPS

A detailed analysis of the applicant's relationships.

### EXPERIENCE WITH CHILDREN

If there are children in the family, names, ages, descriptions of each child. If not, an analysis of the applicant's experience with children.

### ATTITUDES ABOUT ADOPTION (OF FOSTER PARENTING)

Discussion of applicant's views on adoption and foster parenting.

### HEALTH

Discussion of any health problems that could affect ability to care for children.

### REFERENCES

Names, address, telephone numbers of the individual listed as references, along with quotes from each reference.

### RECOMMENDATIONS

Statement of acceptability as adoptive parents.

# The Introduction:
# Don't Overlook the Details

This section should provide the details of the agency's initial contact with the applicants. Did the applicants write a letter? If so, quote from the letter. Was it by telephone? If so, the intake worker should have recorded the date and the time and noted any comments the applicant made. Did the applicant walk into the office without an appointment to request information? If so, provide details of the visit. Did anything unusual happen during the visit?

In any case, indicate what information was given to the applicant. Most agencies provide the applicant with an application form and a booklet that explains the agency's policies about adoption and foster homes. If so, note the date they were given an application and then later note the date the completed application was returned to the agency. The dates are important because if there is a long interval between when they receive an application and when they submit it to the agency, you will want to investigate the possibility that the applicant or the applicant's spouse may have mixed feelings about adoption or foster parenting.

# The Interviews:
# How to Get What You Need

Once the applicant submits an application, it is important for the screener to respond with a telephone call to acknowledge receipt and to set up a time for the first office interview. When the applicants arrive, pay attention to how they are dressed. Are they trying to convey identical—or different—messages? Is one person dressed in a revealing or radical manner and the other dressed conservatively? Is one person casual and the other dressed in formal attire?

If you have a comfortable sitting area in your office, use it instead of staying behind a desk. It will make the applicants feel more relaxed and it will enable you to manage the conversation more easily. Use a tape recorder for the interview, after asking the applicants (on tape) for permission to record them, and keep a notepad on your lap so that you can make notes about follow-up questions.

---

**CASE STUDY**

Alice and Josh were a study in contrasts. Alice wore a pastel pants suit with frilly cuffs and a white blouse that was set off with an antique necklace, while Josh wore jeans and a black T-shirt that broadcast the message "Life Sucks!" The screener let the T-shirt message slide until the individual interviews, at which point he made inquiries about it.

Alice apologized and made it clear that she did not approve of Josh's attire. "I don't know why he does things like that," she said. "He knew better than that." Although he did not apologize, Josh readily admitted that he did know better. He explained that a friend had asked him to help move his mother into a nursing home that day and it took longer than he expected and it left him no time to go home and change clothes.

Josh grinned and said, "I guess you see all kinds, don't you?"

The screener acknowledged the truth of that and had decided to overlook the fashion error when the second shoe dropped with a thud. "To tell you the truth," Josh added, "I'm not sure I would have changed, even if I had time. Alice gets too uptight about how I dress sometimes." Josh winked at the screener. "I think the T-shirt taught her a valuable lesson, don't you?"

---

Body language and clothing choices are important vehicles for non-verbal behavior. Clothing is one way for people to use body language to express their feelings and you should never be dismissive about the clothing that applicants wear to an interview because it usually says something about the individual. Always ask yourself what image you think they are trying to get across to you.

If you are interviewing a couple, are both partners able to maintain strong eye contact with you? Do they communicate with each other in approving or disapproving ways while the other person is speaking? Do they sit with their arms folded, showing resistance to your questions? Do their eyelids flutter, indicating possible deceit when you ask them direct questions? Does either partner seem defensive or reluctant to be there? Does either partner interrupt you when you are speaking (an attempt at dominance) or do they interrupt each other when they think their partner is faltering?

If they seem anxious during the first interview, that would not be unusual. They know they are somehow being tested but they don't know exactly how. Their voices may be pitched slightly higher than normal. Their words may sound breathy at times. Put yourself in their position and try to be understanding. Be supportive and maintain a friendly, matter-of-fact demeanor; but at the same time be alert to anxious mannerisms that are paired with negative body language such as shrugs or eye avoidance, any signals that could indicate negative or deceptive thinking.

Look for signs of dominance—head inclined forward, with chin dropped, tightened eyelids, and raised outer brow—and signs of contempt directed toward the partner: rolled eyes, dimpled cheek with crooked smile, along with sarcasm and insults, even if delivered behind a mask of forced laughter.

Take note of the frequency with which applicants nod and shake their heads so that you will be aware of whether they are in agreement with you on important issues, especially as they relate to policy. Richard Petty, an Ohio State psychology professor, conducted research in which he found that head nodding and shaking not only influences other people, it self-validates the person displaying the head movements.[1] Sometimes interviewers nod their head out of habit when they are listening to something that doesn't particularly interest them and they don't want to spend time discussing it; in those instances, nods are seen as a way to move on to something more interesting. If you have that habit, break it—your nods are communicating unspoken approval to the applicant on subjects about which you may not wish to be offering agreement.

Be aware of the influence that emotions can have on physical characteristics. Anger experienced over a long period of time can sculpt the face with telltale signs about the eyes and lower forehead that give the individual a "hard" combative look even if the individual is smiling at the time. It is very difficult for a person to control his facial expressions because human anatomy has been wired in such a way that facial muscles react to a stimulus twice as fast as the brain can process it. In other words, humans react faster than they can think about reacting to a particular stimulus. As a screener, that gives you the advantage, but only if you are clever enough to understand the signals.

While doing research on how emotions affect the face, Paul Ekman and Wallace Friesen, both psychology professors at the University of California, determined that facial muscles are capable of producing forty-three movements that can create ten thousand different facial expressions. Some expressions, they concluded, can be seen as "microexpressions" that are displayed in less than a fifth of a second.

Ekman and Friesen discovered the existence of microexpressions while studying films of a depressed woman seeking a weekend pass from a mental hospital. The first time they viewed the film, the woman appeared stable. It was not until they switched to slow motion and studied her face that they caught flashes of the despair she attempted to conceal: The corners of her mouth were pulled down and the insides of her eyebrows arched up, fleeting expressions that were camouflaged by a broad smile. Fortunately, the doctors at the mental hospital turned down her request for a pass—a good thing since it later turned out that she planned to leave the hospital so that she could commit suicide. Ekman and Friesen characterize facial expressions that are revealed in quick bursts as emotional "leakage" that betray a person's true feelings.[1]

Along those lines, the co-author of this book, James L. Dickerson, became aware quite some time ago of emotional "leakage" of the type described by Ekman and Friesen that occurs with female children and adults who have been sexually abused. He first noticed it in women that had confided in him about their abuse as children. The leakage manifest itself in the form of a distinct smile, fragile in appearance and marked by minute tugs at each corner of the mouth, and intense, searching eye contact that falls just short of a stare. Once, while the author was working as a consultant for a group of psychologists, he passed through the waiting room while it was filled with about a dozen girls that ranged in age from five to eight. As he walked past, one girl in particular caught his attention with the telltale smile and stare. After he entered the inner office he asked the receptionist why the girls were there.

"They're being tested," the receptionist answered.

"For possible abuse?"

"No."

"One of those girls has been abused."

"Why do you say that?"

"I just know."

"What girl?"

"The one in the blue sweater."

The receptionist pulled the girl's file and quickly read through it. Suddenly, she gasped. "You're right," she said. "She was sexually abused."

The point of the story is that emotional leakage of various kinds is always at work on the human face, affecting the way individuals look, if only for a fraction of a second. There is no scientific basis for the author's observations about the relationship between sex abuse and facial expressions, but there is an intuitive basis that has been influenced by many years of observation.

A good screener will react to those types of intuitive insights with follow-up questions, even if he does not exactly understand why. Intuition may well turn out to be more scientifically substantial than simply a vague foreboding. Intuition may be a reaction to the micro-expressions discovered by Ekman and Friesen, intellectual calculations that occur too rapidly for our brains to register as anything other than a vague feeling.

# Chapter 11

## First Interview with Adoptive Applicants

One of the things you want to establish at the first interview is why the applicants do not have birth children. Is one of the partners infertile? If so, that certainly solves the mystery of why they want to adopt. If not, then it is important that you establish why they would want to adopt instead of having a birth child. Is it because one partner has a high probability of passing on a genetically based disease?

Is it because the applicants do not have a satisfying sexual relationship? If the reason is the latter, it is unlikely to reveal itself in the first joint interview. The screener should keep that unacceptable possibility in mind while eliminating other acceptable reasons such as fear of a genetically based disease. If he suspects a dysfunctional sexual relationship he should put the issue aside until he can re-visit it during the individual interviews.

The first interview is a good time to establish the perimeters of adoption insofar as the applicants' expectations are concerned. When you discuss the ages and types of children that become available for adoption, it is important that you not allow one partner to do all the talking. If the husband says he would be accepting of a child up to age 10, don't let the issue slide—ask the wife if she agrees. Make certain that each person makes his or her opinions known about every issue you present to them.

Many applicants are intimidated by the interview process and that makes them prone to provide positive answers to questions that they perhaps have never even thought about. Never accept a statement such as, "Well, I guess so," without pressing the issue. Make certain at all times that they understand what you are talking about. If they say, "Well, I guess so," to a specific issue it may be because they haven't really considered it, in which case you should explain to them that you would prefer that they think about the issue before committing to a half-hearted response such as, "I guess so."

It is critical for the screener to pay close attention to the applicants when they discuss the gender of the child they want to adopt. That is often a source of disagreement with a couple. More often than not, the woman will want to adopt a girl and the man will want to adopt a boy. How they resolve a conflict like that is important.

Research conducted at the University of Washington shows that fathers work about forty hours a year more after the birth of a son than a daughter, and their hourly earnings are higher if they have sons rather than daughters.[1] It also shows that women are 42 percent more likely to marry the father of their baby if the baby is a boy.

The results of this study are important to consider during the home study because it supports anecdotal evidence that suggests that women who support their partner's desire to adopt a male child are creating a greater margin for success in the relationship than are women who oppose the man's desire and insist on adopting a female child. Well-adjusted couples instinctively avoid this dilemma by striking a compromise, with the wife saying, "Let's adopt a boy first and then adopt a girl later," or with the husband saying, "I really want a son, but I'm fine with a daughter first if you will agree to adopt a boy the next time."

Screeners should be skeptical of couples that express, upfront, a desire to adopt girls, one after the other, especially if the husband has ever expressed a strong desire to have a son. Should that occur, the screener should spend as much time as necessary during the interviews to determine whether the husband harbors any resentment over his wife's reluctance to adopt a boy. Disagreement on this issue is as strong an indicator as any you will see at this stage of the interviews of the couple's potential for divorce.

---
**SAMPLE QUESTIONS
FOR FIRST INTERVIEW WITH ADOPTIVE APPLICANTS**

---

**1) How long have you been considering adoption?**

This question is important since you need to rule out impulsive decisions or decisions made as a result of a recent trauma.

**2) Why do you think the time is right for adoption?**

Why is the applicant in your office on this particular day and not on another day? The applicant will have an explanation for why the time is right for adoption, but you probably won't hear that explanation unless you ask.

**3) Have you had any experience with adoption?**

Has anyone in the applicant's family ever adopted a child? Does the applicant have friends who have adopted? Has the applicant's employment put him or her into contact with adopted children?

**4) Are you able to have birth children?**

If the answer is no, your agency may require you to obtain verification from a physician. If the answer is yes, you must determine why the applicant would apply for adoption. Do they have an aversion to sex? Are they fearful of childbirth? Do they have a family history of genetically influenced disease?

**5) Do you ever feel angry that you can't have children of your own?**

Anger is not a good emotion with which to begin adoption proceedings.

**6) Have you ever applied elsewhere to adopt children?**

If the answer is yes, you must determine the status of the previous application. Was the applicant rejected? Did the applicant withdraw the application? Why?

**7) What age child would you like to adopt?**

Good adoptive prospects typically have a specific age in mind. Beware of the applicant who says, "I don't care." Or "I don't know—I've never thought about that."

**8) Describe the child that you think would fit best into your home?**

Good adoptive prospects will know how to respond to this question and will give you important information.

**9) Would you be able to accept a child that has special needs?**

Few applicants will understand the phrase "special needs," so you will have to explain it to them before asking the question. Subsequent questions will allow you to discuss their reactions to specifics conditions or situations.

**10) How do you think that adoption will change your life?**

Good prospects will have an answer to this question. If the applicant responds, "I don't know," you may want to give the applicant a reading assignment that must be completed before the next interview.

**11) What do you think is the most difficult part about raising an adopted child?** This question will give you insight into their biases and false expectations.

**12) How does your extended family feel about adoption?**

It is very important for you to ascertain any negative attitudes that family members may have toward adoption. If the applicant is evasive in their response, then you must press for details.

**13) How would you feel about adopting a mentally challenged child?**

The response could be positive, negative or something in between. If the response is that the applicant could not be accepting of a mentally challenged child, don't try to persuade—just move on. If the response is "yes" or "maybe," pause long enough to describe the different levels of intellectual disabilities and discuss with them their ability to adopt a child with mild, moderate or severe retardation. If the response is still positive, you will still have a lot of educational work to do with the applicants at subsequent interviews. If the response is "no," reassure the applicants that they will not be penalized in any way for not agreeing to accept a child that is mentally challenged.

**14) How would you feel about adopting a physically challenged child?**

Follow the same procedure as above. You want to make certain that the applicants understand all the implications, both short and long range, of caring for a physically challenged child. Be specific in discussing the types of handicaps that are at issue.

**15) How would you feel about adopting a child with emotional problems?**

Follow the same procedure as above. Provide the applicants with examples of children with emotional problems and listen carefully for any reservations on their part. Also be alert to any unrealistic expectations from either partner.

**16) How would you feel about adopting a child that had been sexually, emotionally or physically abused by her parents or caregivers?**

Same as above. Provide the applicants with examples in each category.

**17) How would you feel about adopting a child of a different race?**

As in other areas, you should let the applicants know that there is no penalty for wanting to adopt a child of the same race. One thing you want to be alert to in their response is a negative attitude toward a particular race. If they explain their rejection of a different-race child in terms of comments such as, "We wouldn't want a black child because they have criminal tendencies," or "We wouldn't want an Asian child since they can't be trusted," then you will have to follow-up those comments during the individual interviews to determine whether the applicants' attitudes are pervasive enough to be grounds for rejection.

**18) How would you feel about adopting a child of a different religion?**

Same as above. You don't give negative points to an applicant that is reluctant to adopt a child of a different religion, but you do want to be alert to negative or hostile comments about other religions since it may be indicative of a life view that would be incompatible with good parenting.

Religion is a passionate issue for many individuals and could have a very strong impact on how children are raised in an adoptive home. Unfortunately, religion's relationship to adoption has not been the subject of any in-depth research and many screeners are uncomfortable with the issue. That should not be the case. Religion should be explored by the screener with the same thoroughness he devotes to other issues that have a bearing on an adopted or foster child's growth and development within a family.

**19) How would you feel about adopting for a child whose birth parents are under court order not to try to contact the child?**

Applicants that are apprehensive about committing to a child under those conditions should not be penalized since caution is a fairly normal reaction. As in other situations, you want to be alert to what else the applicants say while responding to your question. If the applicants say "yes" but then add, "We have enough guns to stop a small army, so we wouldn't be concerned about any trouble," you would want to pursue that line of thinking during the individual interviews.

**20) How would you feel about adopting a child whose parent is in prison?**

If the applicants say they would have no problem with that you will want to question them in detail about their attitudes toward people who go to prison. You need to be alert to attitudes that later would result in the child being told disparaging things about their birth parent. For example, a situation in which a parent would discipline a misbehaving child by saying, "You are going to end up in prison just like your mother."

**21) How would you feel about adopting siblings?**

This is an important question since many adoptable "special needs" children have siblings and should be placed as a family and it is important for prospective adoptive parents to understand that many children in this category do not necessarily have problems or disabilities of any kind. If the applicants say they could accept siblings that have no serious problems, ask them to define what they consider to be "serious" since their definition and yours may differ.

**22)    How would you feel if you received an infant who was believed to be healthy, but later showed indications of a serious condition?**

We know of a case in which a couple received an infant whoaw 9-month pregnant mother dies as the result of bullet wounds. After the infant was placed, it was discovered that the infant had bullet fragments in her brain. How would you cope with that?

# Acceptable reasons
# For wanting to adopt a child

**To experience a more complete family life.** It is probably safe to say that most couples enter into a relationship with expectations of starting a family. If it turns out that one of them is unable to conceive a child, it is natural for them to consider adoption, provided both individuals are capable of loving another person's child.

**To contribute to the development of another human being.** This is a rare motivation, admittedly, but one that is deserving of consideration. It is no secret that most children are born of a passion that is totally unrelated to a desire to contribute to the development of another human being. However, sometimes couples deliberately set out to have a child, doing everything possible to increase their odds of pregnancy, for the purpose of bringing a child into the world. If they cannot have children of their own, they may see adoption as an acceptable substitute.

Couples that cannot have children of their own are free to contemplate how they wish to spend their advancing years. Some focus on building a business or establishing a profession. Others devote their lives to the arts. Sometimes couples come to the conclusion that contributing to the development of another human being is something that is very important to them. Couples and singles that approach adoption from that perspective often make excellent parents.

**To accept parental responsibility.** Wanting to adopt to contribute to the development of another human being and wanting to adopt to accept parental responsibility represent two different motivations. Those who adopt for this reason have more of a need to contribute to the development of society as a whole. They feel that society needs them to accept parental responsibility to help raise children that have been abandoned by society. This is not the best reason in the world to adopt a child, but all other criteria having been met, it is an acceptable reason.

**Because they are capable of giving and receiving love.** During the first several months of his career, a screener will notice that the one thing that all foster and adoptive applicants have in common is a determination to impress him with their capacity to love children. "Love" is the one word that everyone uses to explain his or her motivation for wanting foster or adoptive children. However, by the time a screener has heard the "L-word" used a few hundred times, it loses meaning to him and he tunes it out of the conversation.

The ability and desire to provide genuine love to a child is indispensable to being a good adoptive or foster parent, but it is not the sort of thing that can be demonstrated in conversation. The best way for a screener to evaluate an applicant's capacity for love is to examine the individual's existing relationships.

Does the individual have a loving relationship with his or her partner? Children, if they already have them? Parents? Siblings? Friends? Neighbors?

The "L-word" has little meaning coming from the applicant, who after all has a self-interest in its application, but it has great meaning coming from a reference, especially one who cites specific examples of how the applicant has shown love to others.

# Unacceptable reasons
# for wanting to adopt a child

**To make a troubled marriage stronger.** This is the sort of thing that seems reasonable to some applicants during times of stress. They have drifted apart. The great passions they once shared—music, art, sports—no longer bond them as a couple. One of them has grown more than the other as an adult. They conclude that if they are able to focus on a new passion, namely a child, it will restore their relationship and they will live happily ever after.

**To compensate for abuses experienced as a child.** Sometimes applicants who were sexually, physically or emotionally abused as a child want to right that wrong by demonstrating the "correct" way to raise a child. They see it as a second chance for happiness and they feel it will provide them with an opportunity to prove themselves worthy of love. They also may feel that they can "save" a child from the pain they experienced as a child.

**To give love they never received.** If their parents were cold and unforgiving and presented them with a bleak, colorless childhood, the applicant may want to compensate for that upbringing by raising a child in the "proper" way and by demonstrating how deficient they were as parents.

**To promote a religious agenda.** They have been told by a priest, minister, rabbi or mullah that God expects them to raise a family. They aren't sure if they can love another person's child, but they are afraid they will displease God if they do not pursue every avenue possible to obtain a child.

**To please a partner.** One partner doesn't feel a strong need to have a child in his or her life, but it is very important to the spouse and she very much cares that he or she is fulfilled in life. They rationalize that they will learn to love the child. Having a child is a sacrifice they are willing to make.

**To give meaning to their life.** Everything in life has disappointed them. They thought they would be more successful at this point in life. They thought they would have more close friends than they do. They thought they would be earning more money. They feel like a failure, their good qualities overlooked or rejected by society. A child seems the perfect solution.

**To confirm beliefs about the debate over nature vs. nurture.** One partner is of the opinion that environment trumps genetic makeup, or the other partner is of the opinion that the opposite is true—that is, you are the person you are genetically programmed to become. The applicant is white and wants to adopt a black child to prove that he or she can be raised to have "white values." Or just the opposite: the applicant is a person of color and she wants to raise a white child to prove that skin color determines the kind of person you become.

**Because all the applicants' siblings have children and the applicant feels left out of family events.** The applicant has been competitive with her siblings her entire life. The only area in which they have been able to out-perform her is by having children. She has none and her brother and sisters have a total of seven children. The applicant feels left out at family gatherings when stories about children are exchanged. The applicant reports that she sometimes has to leave the holiday dinner table because of headaches.

**Because the applicant is sexually attracted to children.** Most pedophiles spend a lifetime denying the truth, even to themselves. It is a myth that they are all single, weird looking and effeminate in appearance. They are often married and have children. In appearance, they look no different than their neighbors.

We once were asked to do a home study on a grandfather who wanted to adopt his deceased son's pre-teenage daughters. The girls had become wards of the state after their mother had abandoned them. The grandfather had a lot to gain by putting himself across in a positive manner to the agency, but from the beginning he was belligerent, angry that the state would intrude into his so-called "private business."

Hostility is always a red flag during the home study process. Sometimes it indicates consciousness of guilt. Other times it indicates a level of intolerance that is incompatible with child-rearing. Other times it is used as a defensive weapon to discourage questions in sensitive areas.

In the grandfather's case, it was an indicator for all three of the above. We were able to determine, though interviews with him and his neighbors, that he fit the profile of an unrepentant pedophile. By that, we mean someone who had a history of inappropriate behavior toward pre-teenage girls that lived in his community.

When his application to adopt the girls was rejected, he angrily filed a lawsuit to press the issue, thus opening the courthouse door on his earlier transgressions. The girls who were molested by him had since become adults and they came forward with testimony that not only backed up our assessment of his potential as an adoptive parent, but resulted in criminal charges against him. For his efforts, he got ten years in prison.

Since pedophiles tend to be obsessive they are prone to overcompensating when confronted with criticism. Often they display anger management problems. They disagree with society's definition of inappropriate behavior and they often feel a high level of righteous indignation over being singled out for engaging in behavior that they consider acceptable. It is the main reason why rehabilitation is not successful in changing their behavior. They go to their graves convinced that they have done nothing wrong.

# Chapter 12

## First Interview
## With Foster Parent Applicants

One of the first things that a screener needs to establish is the applicant's stated motivation for wanting to be a foster parent. Their stated reason may have no relationship with the actual motivation, but it does offer a starting point for the discussion. Typically, foster home applicants will say they have applied because they "love" children. Sometimes applicants will use the "love" word to distract from what they perceive to be the real reason, as in, "We love children—and we could use the money."

Since you cannot measure the "love" they have for children, or gauge its intensity, it does not have much value to you as an evaluative tool. Finding out why the applicant has applied will require the full scope of your talents as a screener for the duration of the interviews. As a screener you cannot possibly arrive at an informed decision about the applicant's value as a foster parent until you understand their motivation—and you cannot do that until you can define, within the context of the Foster Parent Syndrome (see Part I), the specific needs they hope to satisfy by being a foster parent.

Whether financial motives for caring for foster children are acceptable will depend on the individual agency since it is essentially a policy decision. It is difficult to rationalize prohibiting foster parents from having a financial motivation for caring for children when everyone else involved with the child—the screener, the caseworker, the supervisor, the psychologist who administered tests to the child, the judge who ordered the child placed into the care of a child-welfare agency—receives a paycheck for their efforts. Some foster parents see themselves as part of a team, as co-workers who coordinate their efforts with those of the other agency personnel.

Our feeling about a financial motivation is that its acceptability should depend on its context. For example, if the applicants are in dire financial straits that would be a situation that is not conducive to good parenting. In that situation, you should look at the problems that contributed to their financial situation. The financial problems may be symptomatic of deeper problems in the applicants' relationship such as marital discord, the inability to hold a job, drug or gambling addiction, etc. If the applicants admit to a financial motive, but establish that they are not desperate for money, then it should not be discounted unless agency policy clearly states it is a reason for rejection.

One of the continuing debates about foster parents is whether they should be treated as co-workers, on an equal footing with the social workers with whom they work, or whether they should be treated as clients or patients in need of continuing casework. That debate has been complicated in recent years by lawsuits filed by foster parents in efforts to clarify their legal rights on a variety of issues, including adoption and the removal of foster children from the foster home by the state without due process. In 1976, a federal district court ruled unconstitutional a New York law that allowed the state to remove children from foster homes without affording a hearing to either the foster child or its foster parents. Appealed to the U.S. Supreme Court, *Smith v. Organization of Foster Families for Equality and Reform (OFFER)* was reversed the following year on the grounds that the procedures used by the state of New York were adequate. Noted the court in a ruling that did not address the constitutional rights of foster parents: "Whatever emotional ties may develop between foster parent and foster child have their origins in an arrangement in which the state has been a partner from the outset."[1]

One major area in which foster parents have been able to claim important shifts in agency policy is adoption. In 1974, *Child Welfare* published an article that of forty-four states surveyed, twenty-seven had agreements with foster parents that specifically prohibited them from adopting children in their care.[1] Seven years later, another survey asked state welfare officials if foster parents were given a preference to adopt a child that has been in their care and the response from forty-three of the forty-six states that replied was foster parents were given a preference.[1] Those new numbers represented a major shift in agency attitudes that continues to this day insofar as granting foster parents increased rights is concerned; but it only made the "co-worker/client" debate more difficult to resolve from a professional standpoint since it is contradictory to be both a co-worker with responsibilities to the agency and a client with constitutionally protected rights at the same time. And, of course, there is no getting around the fact that foster parents and adoptive parents are two separate groups from a profile standpoint.

To accept foster parents and adoptive parents as interchangeable requires an intellectual acceptance of the reverse—namely, that adoptive parents have the same legal right to move from adoption to foster care without negative effect, and that, of course, would be a potentially devastating shift of opinion as far as adoption is concerned.

Foster parent rights are an issue whose time has come, in many different ways; but it would not serve the profession of social work well for screeners to confuse the evolving political, legal and social rights of foster parents with the well-established rights of foster children to be placed in safe and loving homes. Whether you call foster parents co-workers or clients in need of casework, the work of the screener remains unchanged.

---

## SAMPLE QUESTIONS
## FOR FIRST INTERVIEW WITH FOSTER PARENT
## APPLICANTS

---

**1) How long have you considered becoming a foster parent?**
It would be rare for an applicant to have a long-term desire to be a

foster parent. The motivation usually builds over a relatively short period of time.

**2) Do you know any foster parents or foster children?**

If the answer is yes, it will provide you with an opportunity to find out those aspects of foster parenting that the applicant finds attractive or unattractive.

**3) Have you ever applied elsewhere for foster children?**

If the answer is yes, you should determine the status of that application.

**4) How did you find out about our foster home program?**

What you want to do here is determine whether their information is based on negative news coverage or agency advertising or conversations with foster parents.

**5) What age child would you like to have in your home?**

Uncertainty on this issue from a foster parent applicant does not have the same negative connotations that it would have with an adoptive applicant. That's because the foster parent's expectations are short term and that makes them more open to suggestions from the agency. If they specify an age, it will typically be within a broad range of, say, school age, or pre-school-age—and not specific to a particular year.

**6) Would you feel comfortable caring for a child that has emotional problems?**

Same procedure as in adoption.

**7) How would you feel about caring for a mentally challenged child?**

Same procedure as in adoption.

**8) How would you feel about caring for a physically challenged child?**

Same procedure as in adoption.

**9) How would you feel about caring for a child that had been sexually, emotionally or physically abused by her parents or caregivers?**

If the applicants say they can be accepting of this, you should review the various problems that can arise in this situation so that you can be certain that they understand what is involved. Sometimes foster parent applicants idealize what is required of them in abuse situations, with they express with phrases such as, "All that child needs is a big old hug around the neck." Just make certain their expectations are realistic.

**10) How would you feel about caring for a child of a different race?**

Hard-core racists sometimes mask their true feelings. Be alert to any hesitancy from the applicants on this issue. It is better for an applicant to be specific that they prefer a child of a certain race than to express ambivalence.

**11) How would you feel about caring for a child of a different religion?**

Same as above. Ambivalence can lead to problems later.

**12) How would you feel about caring for a child whose birth parents are under court order not to try to contact them?**

If the applicants say they have no problem with that, yet ask no questions about what the implications are, you will need to spend more time with this question to make certain that they understand. Of course, the best response to the question is, "We don't know—could you be more specific?" If after hearing the particulars, the applicants say that they do not feel it will be a problem, then you will be on firmer ground making a placement of that type with them.

**13) How would you feel about caring for a child whose parent is in prison?**

Some applicants are opposed to caring for the children of prison inmates. Now is when you need to find that out.

**14) How would you feel about caring for a child that has used violence against her parent or caregivers?**

As in Question 12, you want to determine if they have realistic expectations.

**15) How would you feel about caring for a girl that is sexually active?**

Once again, you are probing for realistic expectations.

**16) How would you feel about caring for a girl that is pregnant?**

Probe for realistic expectations.

**17) How would you feel about taking a child that has been arrested for substance abuse?**

Probe for realistic expectations.

**18) Have you ever considered adoption?**

Unless your agency encourages foster parents to adopt, you should explain that foster parenting is a poor introduction to adoption.

---

In selection, as in all other aspects of the foster care program, the social worker makes crucial decisions. They affect the life of the child, the welfare of the parents and the foster parents, the agency's status, and the worker's own professional integrity. His task is not an easy one. It is complicated by pressures upon the agency, by role confusion and, apparently, by inadequate communication of agency views to all participants. The problem is compounded by an apparent marked absence of specific knowledge about the meaning of theoretical positions presumably held by the profession.—**Martin Wolins**, *Selecting Foster Parents.*

# CASE HISTORY

The screener's telephone rang at 2 a.m. with an ominous urgency. It was the Provincial Police and they needed the screener right away at a farm on the outskirts of town. The screener dressed and rushed to the address he was given, the newly fallen snow barely impeding his progress.

When he arrived at the address, he saw four squad cars pulled up in a circle, with four sets of spotlights focused on the two-story farmhouse. The officer in charge explained that the house was owned by a man who had taken his two grandsons, aged three and four, from his daughter's house because of suspected abuse and had refused to allowed OPP officers to see the children.

"He's one of those old-time loggers," explained the officer. "A pretty rough fellow."

"So why am I here?" asked the screener.

"The old fellow called us after he took the children and reported his daughter's abuse and we did an investigation and took her into custody, but when we came to talk to him about the children he wouldn't allow us into the house and threatened to use force to keep us out."

"So what are we going to do now?"

"What do you mean 'we?' We have no authority to enter the man's house. You do. We'll be here if you need us."

A cold wind whipped around the farmhouse and sent shivers up the screener's legs. He looked down and saw that in the rush to leave his house he had not replaced his slippers with boots. Slowly he made his way through the snow into the glare of the intersecting spotlights and knocked on the door.

Moments later a grizzled, decidedly unhappy looking, man in overalls slowly cracked the door open and glared at him: "What do you want?"

"I'm with the Children's Aid Society and I need to see your daughter's children."

"They're asleep."

"Sir, I still need to see them."

"You can see them tomorrow."

"I'm afraid I have to see them tonight."

The old man peered around the door at the police officers standing outside their patrol cars. "I'll let you in but if you cause me any trouble I'm strong enough to break your back before those fellows can do anything to help you."

The old man stepped back and allowed the screener to enter the house. "Let me show you something," he said, and led the screener into the kitchen. He opened the refrigerator door and showed him that it was filled with food. "See, those boys got plenty to eat," he said.

"Where are they?"

"Upstairs. Asleep."

"I need to see them."

"You're the fellow that puts children in foster homes, aren't you?"

"Yes."

The old man shrugged and led the screener through the living room to a staircase and then slowly made his way up the creaky stairs into the loft, where the two boys were sound asleep on the same bed, their mouths streaked with chocolate.

"See, they're fine," said the old man.

The screener explained that he was going to have to remove the children, not because the old man wasn't a loving grandfather but because he wasn't set up so that he could care for the boys on a daily basis. The old man grumbled and mumbled and paced, waving his arms at imaginary enemies who had been "after him his whole life," until, finally, he simply wound down and collapsed into a chair. He made one last, half-hearted threat to break the screener's back, but when the screener replied that would only land him in jail and he probably would never see his grandsons again, he relented and told the screener to take the children " . . . and quick, before I change my mind."

The screener awakened the boys, named Todd and Eric, and loaded them into his car and drove them across the county to a foster home located on a farm near a scenic river. Mrs. Bland was a fifty-something woman with a jovial personality who had raised two sons of her own on the farm with her husband, an easygoing man who relished his role as a foster parent. Together they provided what the screener considered to be his best foster home. Over the past eight years they had given dozens of foster boys and girls a fresh start in life, all without incident.

No sooner did the screener pull up to the farmhouse than Mrs. and Mrs. Bland dashed from the house into the snow, their arms outstretched. "Let's get them inside before they freeze to death," she said excitedly, lifting both boys up into her arms. Once inside, she looked over the boys, wiping the chocolate from their faces with her apron. "I can see now that the first order of business will be a good nutritious breakfast."

Over the next few weeks, it became obvious that Todd and Eric had been severely abused by their mother. She was charged with child abuse and released on bond to await trial, but the court prohibited her from having any contact with her children. The way these cases usually precede is that it takes years of hearings and trials before they can be resolved. Sometimes the children are returned to the parent; sometimes they are not and end up in adoptive homes. Less than a week before the first hearing in this case, the boys' grandfather took it upon himself to settle the matter on his own terms. Upset that his daughter had abused his grandchildren and unconvinced by her remorse, he shot her to death and then turned the gun on himself, making the boys orphans.

The screener wasted no time finding them an adoptive home. Seth and Caroline were in their late twenties and operated a farm in an isolated part of the county. The thing that had struck the screener the most when he first met the couple was how similar they were to the Blands, except for being nearly half their age. They had the same child-friendly personalities and the same optimistic approach to life.

During their screening interviews, Seth had said he wanted a boy and Caroline said she wanted a girl, but they said they could be accepting of either. They also said they would be willing to adopt siblings, especially brothers. By the time Todd and Eric became available for adoption, more than a year had passed and they had become quite attached to the Blands. For that reason, the foster parents were invited to the visitation so that they could help Todd and Eric feel more at ease.

The screener was not surprised that Seth and Caroline reacted instantly to the boys—nor that the boys responded in a similar manner to them—but he was surprised at the way that the foster and adoptive parents embraced each other. As it turned out, this proved to be a very successful adoption, not just for Todd and Eric, but for everyone involved, with Seth and Caroline forming a lifelong relationship with the Blands that allowed Todd and Eric to accept them as an extended family.

# Chapter 13

## Follow-up Interviews
## With
## Foster and Adoptive Applicants

Second and third interviews should be individual interviews with the applicant and his or her spouse. Usually it is better to schedule the second interview at the home with the partner that handles most of the homemaking duties. In addition to the interview, the screener should use the visit as an occasion to tour the house. Notations should be made of the number of bedrooms and baths, cleanliness levels, whether the kitchen is organized and tidy or otherwise, and whether there is anything inappropriate in the home that might raise questions—for example, a prominently displayed calendar with nude photos of women, artwork that suggests violence or radical causes or demeaning language, or firearms on display in areas potentially accessible to children.

In addition to discussing the house, the screener should use the home interview to collect information about the applicant's childhood, family life, relationship history, and employment and health history.

The third interview should take place in the office with the spouse and it should follow the same outline used for the partner during the home visit. The screener should use this interview to answer questions raised during the first and second interviews, and to gather information from the spouse on a variety of subjects, including family history, relationship history, employment history, parenting attitudes, etc.

The fourth interview can take place in the office or at the home, depending on what is convenient for everyone involved. Its primary value is the opportunity it provides the screener to bring up issues raised during the individual interviews. It is during this interview that applicants sometimes withdraw their application when questioned about troublesome areas in their family and relationship histories. The fifth interview is usually scheduled if the supervisor or placement board has questions that need to be addressed prior to approval of the application.

## INTERVIEW TECHNIQUES

To be an effective interviewer, the screener must have a clear understanding of what he is expected to do and he must transfer that understanding to the applicants in such a way that they will understand his role in the proceeding. His responsibility is to the child and not to the applicants, at least not until they have been approved as foster or adoptive parents. His job is to obtain information, not to provide therapy.

As a result, his interview style will be noticeably different from the other social workers at the agency, almost all of whom will be doing interviews in therapeutic situations involving emotional dysfunction of one kind or another. Unlike the professionals engaged in therapeutic interviewing, the screener can afford to be less reserved in his interactions with the applicants. Friendliness is an asset, especially when it projects an image of warmth and understanding. It is important that the applicants feel comfortable throughout the interviews. A screener that fails to create such an environment will have a more difficult time obtaining the information that he needs.

Screeners should be cautious about appearing overly stern when asking questions. Most people confronted with sternness have a tendency to shut down emotionally out of a sense of self-preservation. The best interview environment is one in which the applicants have no reservations about answering each question without giving thought to the screener's motivation for asking it.

For the routine questions, it is best to establish a rhythm in which the screener asks them in quick succession, without emphasis on any one particular question. The screener should understand that if he asks a question and looks up at the applicants with full eye contact they will interpret that question to be more important than the others and that will usually work to the interviewer's disadvantage. Save the full eye contact until such time as you really need it.

It would probably prevent misunderstandings if the screener explained to each applicant that he or she has no constitutional right in either the United States or Canada to be a foster or adoptive parent. It is a privilege that is granted by the state when certain conditions are met. However, since screeners cannot explain that concept without seeming overly aggressive and putting the applicants on the defensive, it usually remains unspoken unless the applicants are rejected and the issue comes up before a review panel or a judge. If an agency wants to stress that point with applicants, the place to do it is in the agency's booklets or perhaps on the application itself, where the information could be presented in a less threatening manner.

There will be times during the interviews when it will be necessary for the screener to be aggressive in his questioning, especially if he feels the applicant is being dishonest or evasive. It is all right to challenge an applicant's response, particularly if it contradicts a previous statement made by the applicant.

When the screener gets to the point where he is keying in on the essence of the applicant's family or marital relationship, one technique that always works wonders is the **white space effect.** What that means is that a good interviewer will use long silent pauses to lure the applicant into filling in the white spaces of the conversation. Think of the interview as a blank canvas. You want the applicant to look at the blank canvas and feel greater pressure to fill in the spaces than you do. Most people are made so uncomfortable by a long pause that they will start talking and say things that they perhaps had decided not to say. The white space effect is a power tool. Use it sparingly but with great flare.

# The Family History Interview

The most effective way to gather family history information is to begin with the basic facts—names, birthdates and physical descriptions of both parents and all siblings, if any. Does either parent have a previous marriage? If so, ask for details and whether previous marriages ended in death or divorce. As far as siblings are concerned, you will need to ask their cities of residency, what they do for a living, the names and ages of their children, physical descriptions (is anyone obese?) whether they have been married and divorced, whether any of their children have ever been in foster care, and whether any of them have arrest records. When gathering this information, make the questions seem as routine as possible, maintain an even tone with your voice—and make notes to follow up later on items about which you have serious questions.

Arrest records are an important part of a foster and adoptive applicant's family history. If the applicant reports arrest records for parents or siblings your interest in viewing those records will depend on the nature of the charges. Allegations involving abuse, either sexual or physical, will be of interest, as will allegations of drug use or trafficking. In international adoptions it is customary for applicants to be fingerprinted and undergo a police check. That's not necessarily the case with domestic agencies, public or private, though it should be mandatory. Even if a police check is not stated policy at the agency, as the screener you have the option of doing a police check on any applicant about whom you have reservations. All you need to carry out the check with your local police department is the person's name, birth date and/or Social Security number. Arrest records are public information and the police are required to make it available to anyone who requests it.

How deeply you probe a history of arrests depends on the nature of the crimes. Obviously, if the applicant's father, mother or siblings were arrested for sexually or physically abusing children, using or selling drugs, public drunkenness, etc., it will be of greater concern than if the charges related to property theft or traffic offenses. The reason for that is because crimes of child and substance abuse radiate throughout the family and affect relationships in varied and substantial ways. Ex-pedophiles, ex-drug users, ex-alcoholics or ex-drug traffickers always remain a threat because those classes of behavior are subject to such high recidivism rates. It is the reason that Alcoholics Anonymous insists that members speak of alcoholism in the present tense, as in "I am an alcoholic."

American and Canadian jurisprudence maintains that a person is innocent until proved guilty. That is an admirable principle upon which to base a legal system, but as a screener whose main responsibility is to protect innocent children you will be just as concerned with charges and allegations as you will with convictions since they may be indicative of harmful patterns of behavior. A person's right to a fair trail does not translate to a right to have a foster or adopted child.

Once you have the names and dates out of the way, you should concentrate on the relationship issues that characterize the family history. Before you leave this line of questioning and move on to other topics you will want to understand the family's interactions with each other in great detail.

---

**SAMPLE QUESTIONS
FOR FAMILY HISTORY INTERVIEW**

---

**1) How would you describe your childhood? Was it different in any important ways from your friends' childhoods?**

The point in asking this question is to determine if the applicant experienced any social isolation as a child. If so, it will have a bearing on his or her motivation for wanting a child.

**2) How would you describe your relationship with your parents?**

Listen carefully to the responses given here. What you hope to hear is, "Fine (or great)," followed by examples of how the relationship was beneficial. An applicant who says simply, "Fine," without elaborating, may have issues with a parent. Of course, if an applicant admits to a dysfunctional relationship with a parent you will want to explore that relationship in detail since it will have a bearing on the applicant's relationship with any child you place in the home.

**3) In what ways are your mother and father different?**

Once you understand the parents' relationship you will be able to apply that knowledge to a better understanding of the applicant's significant-other relationship.

**4) Who was dominant—your father or your mother?**

You should use this knowledge to determine if the applicant has dominance issues in his or her significant-other relationship. For example, if a woman grew up in a family in which the father exerted dominance over the mother, she may either expect that of her life partner or she may resent it. If she expects that quality in her partner and he does not deliver, it could be a festering issue in the relationship. Or, if her life partner is dominant—and she resents it—it could result in relationship issues.

**5) Were you ever emotionally, sexually or physically abused as a child?**

Screeners usually dread hearing the answer to this question because a "yes" means that they will have several difficult decisions to make about the applicant. When applicants admit to abuse as a child they usually do so with the expectation that their admission will score points with you.

**6) Which of your parents was the most loving?**

Be alert to applicants who have bad relationships with opposite-sex parents since that correlates with bad relationships with the opposite sex and should be a consideration in making opposite-sex placements into the home.

**7) Did your parents ever have arguments about your behavior? If so, describe the behavior.**

Be prepared for anything with this question. Examples include: "My folks said I was cruel to animals, but I wasn't"—"My mom always accused me of deliberately having bicycle accidents with my father, but I don't know why she would say that"—or, "My parents always thought that I set fire to the house on purpose, but burning down the house was the last thing on my mind, really."

**8) Did you ever feel you had to "walk on eggshells" around your parents or siblings?**

If the answer is yes, you will want to question the applicant in more detail to determine if one of the parents could be classified as a borderline personality. If that is the case, then you will want to find out how the applicant adjusted to living in the home with that person. Did the applicant withdraw to avoid conflict? Or did he or she meet the conflict head-on?

**9) What are the highlights of your childhood?**

When the applicant reports positive experiences, does he or she attribute those experiences to hard work or to blind luck? Does the applicant take responsibility for the good and bad things that happens in his or her life?

**10) Do you undergo any traumatic events as a child?**

If the applicant draws a blank, be more specific by asking if he or she had any serious accidents or experienced the death of a loved one, etc.

**11) Were you ever hospitalized as a child?**

If so, was it a negative or positive experience? If it was a negative experience, has it affected his or her willingness to seek medical treatment?

**12) Did either of your parents have previous marriages? If so, please tell me about them and explain why and how (death, divorce, etc.) the marriages ended.**

**13) Have your parents ever had a marital separation?**

If the answer is yes, you will want to know how it affected the applicant.

**14) How were you disciplined as a child?**

Ask for specific examples. If the applicant was spanked, does he or she plan to spank children that are placed in the home?

**15) Were your parents fair when disciplining you?**

An applicant who was unfairly disciplined will most likely avoid a middle-of-the-road approach to discipline: They will either be too strict, repeating their experience, or they will be too lenient in an effort to repudiate their past experiences.

**16) Tell me about your relationships with your siblings?**

Good adoptive and foster parents report good relationships with their siblings. If the applicant reports a bad relationship, you will need to explore that relationship in more detail with a view of determining who was at fault.

There are no tests that you can administer to the applicants to determine if they have "love" to give to a child, but you can assess the love that they have given to their parents, siblings and extended family members. Good foster and adoptive parents invariably have good relationships with their siblings and parents.

Sometimes individuals apply for adoption in the hope that being a foster or adoptive parent will repair bad relationships within their family.

They think that an adopted or a foster child will give them a new start in life. One of the worst things that an applicant can tell a screener is that they have a bad relationship with their mother/father or brothers/sisters and hope that adopting or fostering a child will give them an opportunity to have someone with whom they can have a loving relationship. That type of reasoning should be a definite red flag to the screener.

The reason for a bad family relationship should be explored by the screener to determine if it is the fault of the applicant. Perhaps the cause of the bad relationship is sibling jealousy based on a perception that the parents favor the applicant over the sibling or based on a high level of professional success. Or perhaps it is financial in nature, the result of an unpaid loan. Whatever the cause of the bad relationship, the screener may want to suggest to the applicants that they make an effort to repair damaged relationships with siblings and parents before continuing with their application, since the addition of a foster or adoptive child into the extended family could make the situation worse and create unwanted problems for the child.

One of the most complicated and painful issues that a screener can face while compiling a family history is childhood sexual abuse since it provides grounds for rejection for both foster and adoptive applicants.

Kristine W. did not feel the slightest bit of discomfort when she and her husband applied for adoption at the same agency that had placed her into a foster home as a teenager. "It'll be like having a family reunion," she told her husband with great enthusiasm. "To me, they're home folks."

As luck would have it, when they arrived at the agency for their first joint interview, they encountered Kristine's former caseworker in the hallway. The two women embraced and the caseworker told her how happy she was that she was married. Afterward, the interview with the screener went well and they left optimistic about their chances of getting a child.

The following week, when Kristine returned for her individual interview with the screener, she told him a secret that she had never told her caseworker, or anyone else for that matter. "While I was in that foster home, my foster brothers made me have sex with them and their friends for a period of two or three years," she explained. "I never told a soul because I was afraid I would be kicked out of the home."

The screener was devastated to learn that her placement into one of the agency's foster families had proved so traumatic for Kristine. It represented failure of the worst sort.

"How does your husband feel about that?" he asked.

"Oh, he doesn't know," she said. "I could never tell him that. You are the only person that I trust with that information."

"What would happen if you told him?" asked the screener.

"He wouldn't love me any more, I'm sure of that."

"How would you describe your relationship with your husband?"

"Good."

"In what way is it good?"

"He doesn't get all upset when I get emotional. He says he understands what makes me tick and he wants to be there for me."

"But he doesn't understand, does he?" asked the screener.

Kristine suddenly looked profoundly sad. "No," she admitted. "But he thinks he understands—and that counts for something, doesn't it?"

After more discussion, the screener explained to Kristine that he would be unable to give additional consideration to her application because of the abuse she experienced in the foster home.

"I don't understand that at all!" she sobbed. "I'm one on your children and I've come here for help. You owe me that much. If you had put me in a better home I would not have been abused. You owe me!"

It hurt the screener to tell Kristine that she was not acceptable as an adoptive parent. He tried his best to explain: "I think you need to resolve your feelings about your abuse before you give any more thought to adopting a child."

Kristine tried to understand, but the betrayal she felt overshadowed all her other emotions. "I came to you for help," she sobbed. "I never expected this!"

"I know," said the screener. "I want to put you in touch with someone who can help you. Please trust me that adoption is not the solution that it appears to be."

Kristine's story points out the obvious: Parents who have not experienced childhood sexual abuse are considered better candidates for foster and adoptive parents than parents who have been abused. There are several reasons for that. In Kristine's case, she clearly had unresolved issues with her husband related to the abuse.

Males and females react differently to sexual abuse. Females are more likely to internalize their responses to childhood abuse with suicidal ideation, eating disorders, low self-esteem and psychological disorders—responses that are not conducive to good parenting.[1] Added to that is the fact that a statistically significant percentage of child abuse victims commit sexually abusive behavior as adults.[1]

Of course, statistics should never be used as grounds for rejection. In Kristine's case, the screener's concern about her suitability as an adoptive parent hinged on unresolved issues related to her abuse. If she had been able to successfully resolve those issues, the screener would have been more inclined to address the statistical probability of abuse by referring her to a psychologist for testing and evaluation to determine if she was a good candidate to beat the statistical odds of becoming an abuser.

It may seem unfair that child welfare agencies would reject would-be foster and adoptive parents because one of the parents was been a victim of sexual abuse, but it happens routinely. Rules like that may seem unfair to would-be parents, who otherwise have a great deal to offer to children, but the rules are in place to protect the children and not to protect the sensibilities of would-be parents. The screener's first responsibility of the adoption agency is to find the most stable home possible, even when that seems to run counter to the needs of the applicants.

# Chapter 14

## Health and Background Interviews

Few public and private agencies have minimum educational standards that are required of applicants, since there seems to be a consensus that the ability to be a loving and caring parent is not related to educational background, but some foreign countries do have such standards when it comes to international adoptions and screeners who do home studies in those situations need to be aware of the various requirements. As in most other areas of inquiry, the screener's questions will have a dual purpose. The first is to document the years of school attendance, along with the names and locations of the schools, graduation dates and diplomas and degrees received. The second purpose is to gain insight into the applicants' attitudes about education and to understand how the applicant was affected by their educational experiences.

Do the applicants have positive or negative views toward teachers? How do they rate education as an influence in a child's life? Where do they place education as a priority in a family's life? Another area that needs to be covered is whether either applicant was home schooled. If so, how does the applicant feel about being home schooled? Do they want to home school tier adopted child?

Since completing their own educations, have the applicants participated in any school activities or run for elective office such as school board member? If the home study is for adoption applicants, what financial plans have they made to provide for the child's education? Do they intend to set up a college fund? Do they have long-range plans of any kind related to education?

> # SAMPLE QUESTIONS
> # FOR EDUCATION INTERVIEW

**1) Were you educated in a private or public school, or were you home schooled? How would you describe your first years in school? Did you have any bad experiences? Were you able to make friends with the other students?**

You are looking for isolation issues here. If an applicant was unable to make friends in school, what makes him think he will be able to "make friends" with a child? Does the applicant have a need to reshape his or her childhood?

**2) Tell me about the best teacher you had. What made her special?**

Questions 2-5 will give you an indication of how the applicant reacted to authority at an early age—and how he or she adjusted in a competitive situation. If the applicant's grades were below average—and you feel the applicant has average or above-average intelligence—you will want to explore his home life in greater detail.

**3) Tell me about the worst teacher you had. What made her a bad teacher?**

**4) What were your strongest subjects?**

**5) What were your grades in grammar and middle school?**

**6) Did you participate in any extracurricular activities?**

Did the applicant feel like an insider or an outsider?

**7) How would you describe your high school experiences?**

Once again, you are looking for isolation issues, especially those that may have prompted anti-social behavior.

**8) How were your grades in high school?**

If their grades were bad, do they feel it is acceptable for children in their care to make bad grades? If their grades were good, will they put pressure on a child to excel beyond his or her capacity to do so?

**9) Did you participate in any extracurricular activities in high school?**

Did the applicant feel like an insider or an outsider?

**10) Do you feel you were popular in high school?**

If not, do they feel popular as an adult?

**11) Were you ever bullied by other students?**

If yes, how does the applicant feel it affected their life? How do they feel about bullies today? As an adult, has anyone ever accused them of being a bully?

**12) If you could revisit your school years, what would you do differently?**

Basically, you are looking for evidence that the applicant has the capacity to learn from his or her mistakes in life.


**If Applicable**

**13) Do you feel you benefited from going to college (trade school, etc.)?**

If the answer is no, will the applicant encourage children placed with him or her to pursue an advanced education?

**14) Were you able to make friends?**

Hopefully, if the applicant was unable to make friends in high school, he or she had better experiences in college.

**15) How did you adjust to being away from home for the first time?**

If the adjustment was difficult, what did the applicant do to compensate? Did the applicant withdraw socially—or did he or she rebel and display anti-social behavior?

**16) What was your grade point average?**

At some point, it may be important to know if the applicant is a high or low achiever.

**17) As an adult, have you ever considered returning to school?**

If both parents are working, you need to know if there are long-range plans for either parent to return to school, a decision that could deprive the child of additional time with the applicant.

*   *   *

In the narrative, the screener should reach conclusions about the applicants' educational experiences, especially as they have affected other areas of life such as interpersonal relations and employment. If the home study is for adoptive parents, the screener should reach conclusions about the applicants' abilities to parent children of low, average or high intelligence, and their commitment and financial ability to provide a child with a quality education.

If the home study is for foster parents, the screener should express an opinion about the applicants' ability to communicate with children of various intellectual abilities and point out any educational pluses in the applicants' background, such as degrees in teaching, social work, psychology, etc. Are the parents capable of dealing with children of above- or below-average intellectual abilities? Is there any reason to think they would not be good parents for a slow child or one who is very creative?

# Employment History

The screener will want to compile a complete employment record for the applicants, beginning with the first job (even if it was as a newspaper carrier at the age of ten) and continuing up to the present. Special attention should be given to the length of employment at each job, descriptions of the job requirements, salaries paid, and the reasons for leaving each job. Income verification will be necessary for the current employment for both foster parent and adoptive applicants.

Whether he thinks they need the money or not, the screener should advise adoption applicants that the U. S. government offers an adoption tax credit that can be applied on qualifying expenses paid for a child's adoption. In addition, various organizations offer financial assistance in the form of loans and outright grants. Typically, this assistance is to be used for private adoptions, domestic or international, or for public adoptions in which children with special needs are identified.

For example, the National Adoption Foundation has a $9 million fund from which it provides unsecured loans to adoptive families and grants that range from $500 to $2,500 per family. The program is open to all legal adoptions, whether public, private, special needs or international. There is no income requirement and the only requirement is that a home study be completed or underway at the time of application.

The Hebrew Free Loan Association, a California-based organization, offers interest-free loans qualifying Jewish families who have applied for adoption, but it requires that the money be repaid. Many employers help with employee adoption expenses by providing cash benefits. The U.S. military will reimburse active-duty personnel up to $2,000 on adoption expenses for one child or $5,000 for siblings.

All states offer financial assistance for "special needs" children as a result of the Adoption Assistance and Child Welfare Act of 1980 which was enacted to remove the financial disincentives to the adoption of special needs children. Children may receive a federally funded subsidy under Title IV-E or a state-funded subsidy as determined by each state's guidelines. The amount of money received is based on each state's foster home rate and varies from $325 to $1,283 per month, depending on the state.

To qualify as a special needs child under the federal legislation, the child must possess one of more of the following: 1) a physical disability; 2) a mental disability, defined as an IQ of 70 or less; 3) a developmental disability; 4) emotional problems; 5) membership in a sibling group of two or more who are placed together; 6) age 6 or older; 7) belong to a hard-to-place racial or ethnic group; 8) have a chronic medical condition; or 9) have a history of sexual, emotional or physical abuse.

---
### SAMPLE QUESTIONS
### FOR EMPLOYMENT HISTORY INTERVIEW
---

**1) Are you happy with your current job (or position)?**

Applicants who are contemplating job or career changes, relocation to another state, province or country, or other major changes in their lives while applying for adoption do not make good candidates for adoptive or foster parents for obvious reasons. They should be advised to wait until after they make those changes in their lives.

**2) Do you see yourself staying there until retirement?**

Don't give negative points to someone who says that they do not expect to stay in their current position until retirement, since that is a rarity in today's economy, but do give points to someone who responds in the affirmative since it shows an ability to at least think in terms of long-term commitment.

**3) How would you describe your relationship with your boss?**

In this instance, you will find the applicant's description of his or her relationship with the boss more revealing than the fact that it is either good or bad. Pay attention to why the applicant thinks the relationship is positive or negative.

**4) Do you ever feel that your job is a dead-end?**

If yes, you will want to probe the influence of a dead-end job on the applicant's relationship with his or her significant other.

**5) How often do you go to work early? How often do you work late?**

Individuals who consistently go to work early and return late may be having problems at work, or possibly at home. Question the applicant until you understand why it is necessary to maintain that type of work schedule.

**6) Does your boss appreciate all the hard work you put into your job?**

If the boss doesn't appreciate an applicant's effort at work, a form of rejection, the chances are that attitude will be taken home and transferred to the spouse. Remember that rejection is contagious.

**7) Have you ever resigned from a job without having a replacement job?**

If yes, ask for details.

**8) Have you ever been fired?**

If yes, explore in detail.

**9) If you could go into another line of work, what would it be?**

Another angle on life satisfaction. If the applicant has numerous dissatisfactions, it raises questions about his or her expectations for adoption.

**10) Have you ever been the target of a conspiracy by jealous co-workers?**

If yes, ask for details—and ask if anyone in his or her family has ever conspired against them.

**11) Have you ever been reprimanded at work for losing your temper with customers or co-workers?**

If yes, you should probe for other instances. If you see a pattern, you may want to talk to the applicant about a referral to a psychologist for testing.

**12) Do you ever socialize with your co-workers?**

If no, you need to understand why. A "no" answer here might be your first clue that the applicant is being ostracized by his or her co-workers because of radical beliefs or an alternative life style. If so, you need more information and you may need to interview the co-workers.

# Assessing Health and Reference Information

The foster parent and adoption applications should contain a questionnaire that asks for information about the applicants' health history. The purpose of the questionnaire is to ascertain whether the applicants have any diseases that could be transmitted to a child or which would affect their ability to care for a child.

What are the diseases that would be of interest to a social services agency? Anything that is potentially life threatening—heart disease, cancer, kidney disease, liver disease, AIDS, etc.—or anything that could place a burden on the child (advancing paralysis, for example). Typical questions would include: "Have you ever been hospitalized or treated as an out-patient for emotional problems? Have you ever taken medication for nervousness or anxiety or depression? Have you ever been treated for addiction? Has your driver's license ever been suspended for DUI? Have you ever been arrested for alcohol or drug-related offenses?"

Health insurance is also an important issue. If the applicants have health insurance, is everyone in the family included? Does the insurance company exclude adopted children for any reason? If the applicants don't have health insurance, do they plan to get insurance by the time they adopt a child? Insurance is a condition of placement with most agencies, so the screener should find out all he can about the applicants' coverage—or lack of coverage—at the first interview.

The agency will ask adoptive and foster parent applicants to provide the name of a physician to certify that they are in good health so that the screener can send the physician a questionnaire. The applicants will be asked to waive confidentiality so that the screener can discuss their health issues with the physician. Most of the time medical reports are straightforward and require no follow up by the screener.

Occasionally, it will become necessary for the screener to interview the physician about specific health issues. Those are sometimes difficult interviews because physicians are fearful of having the information they provide used by social service agencies as a reason for rejection. The physician interview will go better if the screener sticks to specific questions and does not come across as someone who is "fishing" for a reason to reject the applicants. Know your questions in advance and ask the physician to amplify any answers you do not understand.

# References Can Play an Important Role

References serve two purposes: First, they give the applicants validation as potential parents from their friends and relatives; secondly, they provide the screener with insight into the applicants' judgment.

The agency contact with the references will begin with a letter, but it may be followed up with telephone calls and a face-to-face meeting with the individuals listed. The screener should carefully evaluate the written responses from references, looking for hints of evasiveness or disapproval of the applicants as adoptive or foster parents. Follow-up interviews are often more revealing if conducted by telephone. Newspaper reporters have known for a long time that they can get more revealing information over the telephone than they can in person. The reason for that is that the telephone is a more personal contact than a face-to-face meeting because it does not allow the person interviewed to control the interview with body movements or gestures designed to gain the upper hand (lighting a cigarette or pouring a glass of water, or walking to the window, for example).

Most agencies will guarantee confidentiality to references so that they will feel free to respond honestly. In a way, the applicants' first test as an adoptive or foster parent applicant is the judgment they show in selecting their references. If one of their references responds to the agency with scathing comments about their potential as foster or adoptive parents, the screener will have to determine whether the comments are based in fact or merely an expression of the reference's hostility toward the applicants. If the screener concludes that the comments are not based on fact, he will still wonder about the applicants' judgment in choosing such a person as a reference.

Sometimes applicants choose references based on their standing in the community and not on the depth of their relationship with them. That is often a mistake since individuals with high profiles who don't have a close relationship with the applicants may be hesitant to go out on a limb to recommend them.

Screeners should never take negative references at face value, at least not until they are certain about the reference's motivation. Sometimes family members that are opposed to the applicants' decision to foster or adopt a child of a different race will make negative comments with the intention of blocking the child from becoming a member of the extended family. Sometimes friends who do not have children will fear the effect of children on the relationship and make comments they know will raise questions about the applicants' suitability as parents.

If the screener receives a negative reference, he must confirm or disprove the validity of the reference's claims. His options are to interview the reference to ask for clarification and supporting data, and to discuss his concerns with the applicants, without revealing the source of the information.

Confronting applicants with negative information is never pleasant, particularly if the interviews to date have been encouraging, but it must be done—and with as little fanfare as possible. A negative reference is a big deal, but it is important that the screener not come across to the applicants, either with words or body language, as suggesting that it is a big deal.

---

**SAMPLE REFERENCE LETTER**
**(for married applicants)**

Dear _____ :

Your friends, _____, have applied to us to adopt a child [to become foster parents] and they have listed you as a reference.

We would appreciate it if you would take a few minutes to complete the following questionnaire and return it to us at your earliest convenience:

How long have you known the applicants? _____

---

Would you describe the applicants as _____ acquaintances, _____ close friends, _____ relatives, _____other (please explain)

_____

How would you rate the applicants' parenting abilities: _____ poor, _____ average, _____ excellent, _____ unknown.

How would you describe the applicants' relationship with each other?

_____

_____

To the best of your knowledge, does either applicant have a problems with alcohol or drug use?

_____

_____

How would you rate the applicants' potential as adoptive [foster] parents? Please explain

_____

_____

_____

_____

_____

Thank you for your help in this very important matter. Your responses are confidential and will not be shared with the applicants. If we have any questions about your responses we will get in contact with you.

Sincerely yours,

Department of Social and Family Services

## SAMPLE REFERENCE LETTER
### (for single applicants)

Dear _____:

Your friend, _____, has applied to us to adopt a child [to become a foster parent] and he/she has listed you as a reference.

We would appreciate it if you would take a few minutes to complete the following questionnaire and return it to us at your earliest convenience:

How long have you known the applicant? _____

Would you describe the applicant as _____ acquaintance, _____ close friend, _____ relative, _____other (please explain)
_____

How would you rate the applicant's parenting abilities: _____ poor, _____ average, _____ excellent, _____ unknown.

How would you describe the applicant's relationship with members of the opposite sex?
_____
_____
_____
_____
_____

To the best of your knowledge, does the applicant have problems with alcohol or drug use?
_____
_____
_____
_____

How would you rate the applicant's potential as an adoptive [foster] parent? Please explain

_____
_____
_____
_____
_____
_____
_____

Thank you for your help in this very important matter. Your responses are confidential and will not be shared with the applicants. If we have any questions about your responses we will get in contact with you.

Sincerely yours,

Department of Social and Family Services

## SAMPLE REFERENCE LETTER (MEDICAL)

Dear Dr. _____ :

Your patient, _____ , has applied to us to adopt a child [to become a foster parent] and listed you as a medical reference.

We would appreciate it if you would take a few minutes to complete the following questionnaire and return it to us at your earliest convenience:

1) How long have you provided medical care to the applicant? _____

2)   Applicant's Height _____ Weight _____ B/P_____ Pulse _____

3)   Are you treating the applicant for a chronic condition? ___ If yes, please explain

_____

4) Has the applicant been tested or treated during the past 18 months for:

Hepatitis _____ Test Results _____ Tuberculosis _____ Test Results
_____

HIV _____ Test results _____ Other Sexually transmitted diseases _____
Please explain
_____
_____

Infertility _____ Please explain
_____

Heart disease _____ Please explain
_____

Liver disease _____ Please explain
_____

Kidney disease _____ Please explain
_____

5) Does the applicant have a medical condition that could interfere with their ability to effectively parent a child? _____ If yes, please explain
_____

6) To the best of your knowledge, does the applicant have a problem with alcohol or drug use?
_____
_____

7) How would you rate the applicant's potential as an adoptive [foster ] parent:
_____ poor, _____ average, _____ excellent, _____ unknown.

_____
_____

Physician                                                                    Date

Thank you for your help in this very important matter. Your responses to questions 6 and 7 are confidential and will not be shared with the applicants. If we have any questions about your responses we will get in contact with you.

Sincerely yours,
Department of Social and Family Services

# CHAPTER 15

## Marital or Relationship Interviews

Couples that are experiencing relationship problems sometimes apply to be foster or adoptive parents in the hopes that a child will bring them closer together and save their marriage. Or they may view the addition of a child to the family as a substitute for a waning or nonexistent sexual relationship.

Obviously, the relationship interviews are the most important ones that a screener will undertake while doing a home study. The areas of greatest concern are: **conflict resolution** (how the couple settle their differences); **emotional compatibility** (how suited their personalities are to one another); **sexual relationship** (to determine if it is mutually satisfying); and **ethical/spiritual compatibility** (do they share a common vision that enables them to pursue similar goals?).

Good foster and adoptive parents know how to argue within the rules, without resorting to flight, physical abuse or threats involving the withdrawal of love. That is important because couples tend to argue with their children in the same way that they argue with each other. Since foster and adopted children tend to experience more behavioral problems than other children, it is important that foster and adoptive parents have better than average skills in conflict resolution.

A good test of how adults will resolve conflict with children is how they resolve conflict with their relationship partners. The screener should ask for detailed descriptions of recent conflicts, with special attention given to cause and resolution. It is normal for couples to argue from time to time. What is not normal are situations in which one or both of the individuals in a relationship bury their feelings to the point of ignoring serious problems, or express their disagreements so vehemently that physical and verbal abuse become part of the pattern. If one of the partners withdraws when faced with conflict—and the other partner uses that withdrawal as a tool for dominance—it solves nothing and merely creates resentment that will build over time. If both partners express their angry emotions at every opportunity, arguing becomes the foundation of the relationship and that is ultimately a dead-end street.

What the screener hopes to find in the relationship is a mutual belief in moderation and a willingness to talk through the problem in an attempt to reach a resolution. Partners that lunge and then withdraw, or loose their temper and say deeply hurtful things they later regret, or resort to violent acts such as striking the wall or throwing furniture, are not likely to remain a couple for the long term.

One thing that a screener can count on is that a partner that is abusive toward his or her partner ultimately will be abusive toward any child placed in the home. A partner that withdraws emotionally from his or her partner is likely to withdraw from a child when faced with opposition or indifference from the child.

One of the options that a screener has when focusing on conflict resolution during the interviews is to deliberately create a hypothetical stressful situation in order to observe how the applicants react as a couple. One way to do that would be to take a hypothetical comment and magnify it out of proportion so as to suggest that it has negative connotations. The goal is to see how the applicants react to what would obviously be a stressful situation. Do they isolate from each other and attack? Or do they pull together and defend each other from the screener's incorrect assessment? Does one of the partners side with the screener and isolate the partner, even though they know that the comment was misconstrued?

An important part of the adoption home study is a discussion of the applicants' sexual relationship with their partners (note: sexual history is not an appropriate evaluation for foster home applicants since the long-term success of the relationship is not the primary issue). This makes many screeners uncomfortable, but it is essential that they overcome their personal feelings and be aggressive in pursuing an understanding of this critical relationship issue. In order to determine if the applicants have healthy sexual attitudes and practices, the screener will want to know how often the partners have sex, whether it is a fulfilling experience, whether they have ever undergone counseling for sexual dysfunction, how many sexual partners they had prior to marriage, etc. These are important issues because there is a strong correlation between the quality of sex in a relationship and the longevity of the relationship.

# Case History

Helen and Phillip T. were in their late-twenties, an athletic and attractive couple that radiated high energy levels. Both worked as professionals and both had good incomes. When they came into the office for their first joint interview, they told the screener that they had been married for four years and despite their best efforts Helen had been unable to get pregnant. Their family physician ran tests and determined that there was no physical reason why Helen could not get pregnant.

Helen and Philip showed a great deal of enthusiasm about adoption. Helen said that she had wanted to have children for as long as she could remember. She was disappointed that she had been unable to conceive but she felt that adoption was "the answer to a prayer." Helen was somewhat flirtatious during the interview, but it seemed to be consistent with her effusive personality. The screener concluded that she was probably the type of woman that flirts with everyone, men and women.

Helen and Philip related well to each other during the interview and each was respectful of the other's opinions. They looked at each other often and exchanged smiles whenever the subject of children was brought up. By the time the screener went to the home for his individual interview with Helen he was optimistic about their chances for approval. That feeling continued through his discussions with her about her family life, leading him to believe that she had enjoyed a remarkably normal upbringing.

However, once the discussion turned to her relationship with Philip, the situation became more complex. She expressed great satisfaction with the relationship—"In many respects, I think we are soulmates"—but when their sex life was brought up she confided that she had been unhappy with the frequency of intercourse over the past two years. "He's just so tired when he comes home," she explained. "He works so hard. I just wish he would make more time for me."

Asked why they had no children of their own, she said they had been tested by doctors who told them that neither of them was infertile. They could find no reason why she could not become pregnant. "The doctor told me that a lot of times women like me get pregnant after they apply for adoption," she said. "Have you ever heard of that happening?"

"Yes," answered the screener. "Not often—but often enough to keep doctors talking about it."

By the time the screener left the house, he had grown very pessimistic about their potential as adoptive parents. The individual interview with Philip was conducted one week later at the agency office. The screener was eager to get to the critical points of the interview, but he knew from experience that it was better to pace the questions, beginning with the most routine and slowly building to the most critical. When Philip was asked about his relationship with Helen, he expressed agreement with her that it was mutually satisfying . . . "Except for one thing," he added. "The sex."

"What do you mean?" asked the screener.

"No matter how much I make love to her, it is never enough," he said. "I just stay exhausted all the time. To me, sex is a great pleasure, but to her it's all tied in with her obsession with having a baby. Is that normal?"

The screener mumbled that normal probably didn't exist.

Philip thought about that for a moment and then dropped a bombshell. "You seem like a nice guy," he said. "Would you be interested in helping me out?"

"What do you mean?"

"You know, with the sex."

"Let me get this straight," said the screener, doodling on a notepad. "You are asking if I will have sex with your wife?"

"That's about it, yeah."

The screener told Philip that he was flattered to be asked, but would have to turn down his offer. As Philip left the office he turned and said, "I guess this conversation pretty much kills any chance we have of adopting, doesn't it?"

"Pretty much."

Helen and Philip were officially rejected as adoptive applicants two weeks later, but they did not contact the screener to ask why. The screener was never certain if Philip's "offer" was legitimate or merely an attempt to sabotage their application. Either way, the result was the same.

Philip's "offer" created a dilemma for the screener. He discussed the case with his supervisor, who agreed that the agency already had enough information and did not need to schedule additional interviews to reject the application, but he agonized over whether to write the incident up in the home study.

If he did, it would become part of the couple's permanent record and opened the door to possible privacy abuses that, while within the law, hardly seemed fair. If he did not write it up, he risked exposing himself to legal action if the couple later changed their story out of vindictiveness and accused the screener of being the one who made the "offer."

Although he did not feel good about doing it, the screener decided to protect himself and write the incident up as it happened. It was yet another reason why he was glad he taped all his interviews and another reason why he was glad his agency had a policy against allowing anyone other than agency staffers to read home studies.

When it comes to the dynamics of relationships, couples come in all shapes and sizes, any combination of which may prove acceptable. Since there is no perfect relationship configuration, screeners constantly have to weigh pluses and minuses to arrive at an acceptable weight of approval for a particular couple.

It is not possible to offer a standardized test to applicants to determine the strength of their relationship, or to equate their relationship with parenting potential, so that judgment must be made by the screener using variables that will provide information about the likelihood of the applicant's success as parents.

Often the time that screeners spend interviewing foster and adoptive applicants overlaps so that in any given week he has several applicants "up in the air" over approval. When that happens it is natural for the screener to compare the applicants to each other, with a view of deciding which of the couples offers the best potential and which offers the least potential. Sometimes borderline applicants will get approved because luck has brought them to the agency at a time when the other applicants are all unacceptable.

Read the following summaries and decide which couple makes you the most comfortable:

COUPLE NO. 1—Priscilla and Robert are proud of the fact that they have been married for five years and have never had an argument. If one does something the other doesn't like, they simply ignore the offending behavior. "My parents argued all the time—and it was horrible," explained Alice. "I swore to myself that when I got married that would not happen. I'd rather cut my wrist than get in an argument with Robert." Robert felt the same way: "When I hear couples argue, I want to leave the room—and sometimes I do. Nothing is worth arguing about. Life is too short."

COUPLE NO. 2—Lee and Caitlin are just the opposite. Whenever they argue, their friends scurry from the room with promises to return when "things calm down." Caitlin is proud that she has never let Lee off the hook when he's done something to offend her. "Just the other day, he left the milk out all night," she explained. "I had to throw it away the next morning." Lee laughed. "Yeah, she gave me hell for that. Of course, I deserved it."

COUPLE NO. 3—Simon and Wendy were always pleasant around their friends. It was when they were alone that sparks flew. Simon was an introvert who disliked confrontation. Wendy was just the opposite. She was an extrovert and she instigated confrontation over even the smallest issues. She pushed and pushed, often getting into Simon's face to scream at him. Simone took it until he reached a breaking point—and then he exploded, a reaction that always sent Wendy leaving the room in tears. Once the situation returned to normal, Wendy always rehashed the argument over and over, repeating from memory each comment that was made, until Simon apologized for losing his temper with her.

COUPLE NO. 4—Erica and Jock were alike in a lot of ways. They were both athletic and began each morning with a three-mile jog. They liked different books (he preferred nonfiction and she liked fiction), but they enjoyed the same movies and music. Since they were in the same profession their interests overlapped in many different ways. The one way that Erica was noticeably different was in her approach to competition. She was hypercompetitive in her dealings with Jock and had anger management problems during those occasions when he seemed to have the upper hand. As a result, she found it necessary to regulate his behavior in order to feel good about herself.

Out of the above-mentioned couples, you've probably figured out by now that it is couple number two that has the best chance of being approved as foster or adoptive parents. It is not good that they are so intimidating to their friends when they argue, but it is a good sign that they discuss problems as they arise instead of allowing them to fester and it is a good sign that Lee was able to verbalize his regret at leaving the milk out to spoil. They deal with problems as they arise and that is mandatory with children.

Couple No. 1 lives in a fantasy world that is certain to fall apart during a crisis. If that happens, they are less likely to survive as a couple for the simple reason that they have no experience working together to solve disagreements. Couples that say they never argue are either being disingenuous or they are so emotionally disconnected that they have no basis for a long-term relationship.

173

Couple No. 3 is a disaster waiting to happen. Simon and Wendy have opposite personalities and that guarantees that they will approach disagreements from different perspectives. Since their respective introverted/extroverted personalities prevent them from engaging at the first signs of a disagreement they both hold back until they are at the boiling point. For that reason, almost every disagreement they have escalates into a major argument in which doors are slammed and insults are hurled without regard to the damage they cause. Being an introvert, Simon always retreats and issues an insincere apology when he comes under Wendy's withering attacks. Eventually there will come a point when he will no longer be able to do that—and the relationship will probably end with the sound of a quietly closed door.

Couple No. 4 is burdened by Erica's hypercompetitive approach to their relationship. Richard M. Ryckman, a psychologist at the University of Maine, conducted some interesting research on hypercompetitive individuals that allowed him to conclude that such individuals do not offer much potential for successful, long-term relationships by virtue of the deep-seated emotional pain and unhappiness that often lies at the root of their competitiveness.[1] Hypercompetitive individuals tend to be possessive and require constant reassurance, needs that prevent them from showing understanding to a partner.

---

## SAMPLE QUESTIONS
## FOR MARITAL OR SIGNIFICANT OTHER INTERVIEW

---

**1) What quality of yours do you think your partner most appreciates?**

The answers to Questions 1-7 matter less than the fact that the applicant is able to answer them. If the applicant cannot answer those questions it is an indication that the relationship may be too insular to allow for the introduction of a child.

**2) What do you find most attractive about your partner?**

3) Who are your partner's best friends?

4) What are your partner's life dreams?

5) Explain your partner's basic philosophy of life.

6) What relatives does your partner like the least?

7) Does your partner listen to you when you talk?

8) Who is your best friend?

You are looking for two things here. First, you want to know the gender of the best friend. If the friend is of the opposite sex you will want to know if that creates problems with the significant other. Second, you will want to ask what qualities the friend has that the significant other does not have.

9) When you have disagreements with your partner, how do you solve them?

You will want to devote a significant portion of your time to Questions 9-11 since how the applicants deal with each other will reflect how they will deal with a child. Ask for numerous examples of disagreements and then ask the applicants to walk you through how they were resolved, if, in fact, they were resolved.

10) Who loses their temper the easiest—you or your partner?

11) Has your partner ever struck you during an argument?

12) How would you rate your partner as a problem solver?

You will need to decide for yourself which partner is the better problem-solver.

13) At what age did you become sexually active?

Sex is always an uncomfortable subject, but one that is important for a proper understanding of the relationship. The answers to Questions 13-19 will be critical to your recommendation for approval or rejection. You cannot place an adoptive or foster child in a home in which there is sexual dysfunction.

14) How old was your first sexual partner?

15) How often do you and your partner have sex?

16) How would you compare the sex you have with your partner now with the way it was in the beginning?

**17) Does your partner bear any grudges because of previous sexual relationships you had?**

**18) Does your partner know what pleases you sexually?**

**19) Do you schedule days for sex or is it mostly spontaneous?**

**20) Have you and your partner ever had a marital separation?**

If yes, you must explore in detail. You can approve applicants who have had marital problems that were addressed and corrected, but you cannot approve applicants who have unresolved marital problems.

**21) Have you ever filed charges against your partner for abuse?**

A "yes" here would be grounds for a referral to a psychologist for testing and evaluation. Frankly, not many applicants that answer yes to this question are able to be approved for adoptive or foster children.

**22) Would you describe your relationship as either romantic or comfortable?**

**23) Who makes the final decisions in your relationship, you or your partner?**

One of many questions you will ask that will help you decide who is dominant in the relationship.

**24) Do you ever feel you have to "walk on eggshells" around your partner?**

The "walk on eggshells" reference is a code phrase, of course, for individuals suspected of having borderline personalities. A "yes" response will be your cue to probe more deeply into the personalities of both applicants. If you suspect a borderline personality, you should ask the applicants if they would be willing to undergo testing and evaluation by a psychologist to resolve questions you have about their relationship.

**25) Do you and your partner ever have disagreements about the role of religion in your relationship?**

Do not underestimate the complications of a "yes" response. You do not want to place a child into a home in which there will be a constant tug-o-war over religion, with the child caught in the middle.

**26) Would you be friends with your partner's family if they were not family?**

A "yes" response is a positive indication about the long-term durability of the relationship.

*   *   *

If after dissecting the relationship—and then reassembling it—the screener is still uncertain about the couple's potential for maintaining the relationship, there is one question he can ask himself that is usually helpful: **Do the applicants see in each other mirror images of themselves?** One of the new understandings about the mechanics of relationships is the realization that married couples who perceive a kindred spirit or soul mate in their partners—someone whose values, personality traits, and day-to-day feelings mirror their own—report greater satisfaction in their relationships. It is another way of saying that we tend to fall in love with ourselves and we see what we want to see. For the sake of our own egocentric wellbeing, we will tolerate more negative behavior from our partner if we see them as mirror images of ourselves than if we see them as different.

Five psychology professors—Sandra Murray, Gina Bellavia, John Holmes, Dan Dolderman and Dale Griffin—published some interesting research in 2002 on the benefits of egocentrism in close relationships.[1] "People in satisfying and stable relationships assimilated their partners to themselves, perceiving similarities that were not evident in reality," concluded their research. "Such egocentrism predicted greater feelings of being understood, and feeling understood mediated the link between egocentrism and satisfaction in marriage."

Screeners searching for verification of their already-positive interview assessments of a couples' relationship would do well to give thought to whether the couple sees each other as kindred spirits at a high enough level, whether realistic or not, to overlook information to the contrary. If so, that is as good a marker as any in predicting the long-term survival of the relationship.

During the course of the interviews, it is also important for the screener to understand that couples sometimes apply for foster or adoptive children because they are experiencing problems in their relationship and think that a child will help them solve the problems. That is not an acceptable motivation to adopt or become a foster parent—and the screener must always be alert to the dynamics of a relationship in trouble. It is not the screener's job to repair a broken relationship or to tell applicants how to become more attractive as foster or adoptive parents. By the time that a couple decides to apply for foster or adoptive children as a means of getting help with their marriage, the odds are that several years will have gone by since their problems began and they will have experienced numerous failures in their effort to reconcile their differences. Foster parenting or adoption may be their last hope (in their minds). Screeners have to accept dysfunctional relationships for what they are— red flags.

Psychotherapy, whether administered by appropriately licensed social workers, psychologists or psychiatrists, can be very effective in many different areas, but marriage counseling is not one of them. In a 1995 Consumer Reports survey, marriage therapy ranked at the bottom of a poll of patient satisfaction with various psychotherapies. The magazine said that part of the problem was that "almost anyone can hang out a shingle as a marriage counselor." Recent research has shown that many popular treatments have shown few long-term benefits for couples who seek help.[1]

In other words, a broken relationship is one of the toughest things in the world to repair. Making an attempt to do so is beyond the scope of the screener's job description and training and he has no choice but to move on when he encounters applicants with marital problems, no matter how much he may want to help them. Situations like this sometimes take a toll on a screener. Most enter the profession because they want to help people. It is bad enough for a screener to want to help a couple in whom he has taken an interest, but then to have to reject them in addition to not being able to counsel them is stressful and one of the reasons that screeners tend to experience burnout and find other work long before they reach retirement age. Imagine how marriage therapists would feel if, in addition to failing in their efforts to save a marriage, they had to add insult to injury by formally rejecting the couple for one reason or another, in effect saying, "I'm sorry I couldn't fix your marriage . . . and by the way, I don't consider you parent material, either." Unfortunately, for screeners, that is part of the job description.

# Chapter 16

## Exploring Parenting Issues

There is a vast gulf between foster and adoptive applicants who have had experience with children—and those who have had none. Yet, the basic premise of foster and adoptive parenting is that everyone has the potential to be successful at it. As a screener, you should not discriminate against a couple because they have no birth children, or because they have had no experience with friends' or relatives' children, but that does not mean that you should not give added points to applicants who do report experience along those lines.

If the applicants have birth children in the home, you will want to focus on their parenting skills and you will want to interview the children about their relationships with their parents.

How do the children feel about foster or adoptive children coming into the home? Why do they feel their parents want more children? Do they interpret their parents' desire for more children as a rejection of their place in the family? Do they feel they would be able to accept foster or adoptive children in the home?

If the applicants have no birth children and report very little experience with children, the discussion becomes more of a philosophical exercise in which the applicants express their opinions about children. Whatever the applicants' experience level with children, the screener's job is to assess their parenting abilities. To accomplish that, he must look for both positive and negative attitudes—and hope that the positive outweighs the negative in those areas where it matters the most.

## SAMPLE QUESTIONS FOR INTERVIEW ABOUT EXPERIENCE WITH CHILDREN

**1) Have you ever been embarrassed by children and not known how to handle it?**

The answers to Questions 1-14 will tell you what you need to know about the applicants' experience with children. The "correct" answers are obvious, so what you will be looking for are answers that deviate from the obvious. The bottom line is do the applicants have realistic expectations about parenting?

**2) Have you ever been shown disrespect by a child and not understood why?**

**3) (If the applicants have siblings with children) If something happened to your siblings, would you want to raise their children?**

**4) From your experience, what is the best way to get a child to stop doing something you don't want them to do?**

**5) Did your parents spank you on a regular basis? If so, do you feel that it had the desired results?**

**6) (For applicants with children). How do you discipline your children?**

**7) (For applicants with children). Have your children ever had to undergo counseling at school for behavioral problems?**

**8) (For applicants with children). Have your children ever run away from home?**

**9) (For applicants with children) Have your children ever had run-ins with the police?**

**10) (For applicants with children). What would you want to do different with foster or adoptive children that you didn't do with your birth children?**

**11) Have you ever been the target of pranks carried out by neighborhood children?**

**12) When you watch movies in which there are children, what kind of scenes are most likely to bring tears to your eyes?**

**13) Have you ever kept other people's children in your home overnight or for an extended period of time? If yes, how did you feel when they returned to their parents?**

**14) Do you feel that children are sincere when they hug adults and tell them that they love them?**

# Adoption and Foster Care Parenting Issues

One of the first parenting issues that must be resolved from an adoptive couple is which partner will be the primary parent. Will either be a stay-at-home parent? If both parents plan to work outside the home, the screener must determine in specific terms their plans for physically caring for the child. Do they plan to hire a nanny? Do they have a relative who will help care for the child?

There is nothing wrong with both parents working, but if their schedules are such that their child-care plan is to let someone else raise the child, what motivation do you have as the screener to remove the child from a foster home, only to place the child in what amounts to another foster home?

If both parents plan to work outside the home, it is crucial that one parent take a leave of absence from work to stay at home with the child to be the primary caregiver. Different agencies have different policies on how long that should be and the time can vary from one month to six months, or possibly longer in some instances. The screener should make inquiries about what the applicants have worked out with their employers and then he should reconcile that with agency policy.

For foster parents, agency policy on whether mothers should have jobs outside the home varies according to the age of the children involved. It is unlikely that an agency would allow a foster mother to care for an infant or preschooler and hold a full-time job outside the home, since children that age need stable, consistent care-giving, but the policy may differ for individuals who want to care for school-age children. Agencies want foster care to reflect, as accurately as possible, the parenting norm in society as a whole and since most families find it necessary for both parents to work that reality is reflected in the foster parenting programs set up by most agencies.

Whether they are foster or adoptive parents, single or married, they should be questioned about their plans for alternative care in the event of illness or family emergencies. Who will care for the child if they have to stay overnight in a hospital or if they have to leave town for several days on business? If the applicant is single, they should be able to describe not only a plan for alternative care, but a back-up plan in the event the first plan does not work.

It is not necessary for foster parents to articulate a long-term plan for the child since their involvement is, by definition, for the short term, but it is essential that adoptive parents be able to discuss their plans for long-term care. Have they chosen a guardian for the child in the event of their deaths? Have they purchased life insurance polices that are sufficient to provide for the child's needs?

Once an interviewer has determined that an applicant possesses none of the negative characteristics that would make him or her a risk as an adoptive or foster parent, it is time to shift the focus onto those characteristics that make the applicant a good risk.

Children are egocentric in that they take love more easily than they give love. That characteristic is heightened in adoption for the simple reason that child-parent bonding fails in a higher percentage of cases involving adoptive children than with natural children. A good adoptive parent is one who will be able to accept the possibility that he or she may go through a lifetime in which they give more love than they receive. It takes a parent with a good self-image to be able to adjust to a one-way relationship with a child that frustrated friends and relatives might depict as "unappreciative."

183

Characteristics that adoptive and foster parents need in order to make them good parents to an adoptive or foster child include:

- **Optimism in the face of adversity**. Adoptive and foster parents typically experience more problems associated with bonding and attachment than do birth parents. One measure of a parent's ability to deal with bonding and attachment problems is his or her ability to function in a family without frequent confirmation of the parent's contribution to the family. Parents that are able to navigate through the minefield associated with bonding and attachment disorders typically are optimistic, able to accept personal criticism, and able to demonstrate patience while dealing with situations that are not quickly resolved.

- **Strong self image**. Good adoptive and foster parents will be able to deal with the likelihood that their child will one day want to locate his or her natural mother and father, and perhaps want to maintain a relationship with them as well. This is an area where the screener will want to engage in direct questioning and offer numerous "what if" scenarios to the applicants and be prepared to talk to them about their feelings.

- **Positive attitudes about adoption.** When and how to tell children that they are adopted is a gradual process that begins around or before age five and continues until the child is old enough to understand the more obvious implications of adoption. It is essential for the screener to determine an applicant's feelings about this very important issue. If the parent has negative attitudes about adoption, such as a belief that it represents a failure for the parent that she cannot have children of "her own," then those negative attitudes will influence the child's view of adoption.

- **Flexibility (if an open adoption is involved).** In open adoptions the child's contact with her birth parent may take the form of personal visits, or it may be limited to telephone calls and letters. This is becoming increasingly common with private agencies in situations in which birth mothers relinquish their children only on

184

the condition that they are allowed contact with the child as he/she is growing up. If the applicant says that they can accept an open adoption, it is important for the screener to provide them with numerous hypothetical situations and evaluate their response. If the applicant says that they cannot accept an open adoption, the screener should accept their answer and not pressure the applicant to change his or her mind.

- **Ability to accept things as they are.** Many adopted children enter adolescence with a deep sense of loss concerning their birth parents. It is not unusual to hear adopted teens describe that feeling as a "hole in my soul." It is important for the screener to look 10 or 15 years down the road into an adoption and discuss issues that are certain to arise. The only way that an interviewer can do that is with hypothetical questions: "How would you feel if a child you adopted as an infant and raised to adolescence spent her teens complaining that she had a "hole in her heart" over the loss of her birth mother? Would you feel you had failed?"

- **Problem solving ability.** Adopted children experience problems that other children do not have to face, such as pain-causing prejudice among other students and teachers, especially if it is a biracial adoption. Difficulties can arise out of routine assignments—writing an autobiography, for example. The screener needs to present hypothetical problems that the applicant can "solve." There are no pass-fail scores here, merely a greater understanding of the applicant's parenting potential.

- **Ability to accept delayed gratification.** Most adoptions and foster home placements provide parents with great joy, but those good feelings do not always arrive in a timely manner. It is not unusual for adoptive and foster parents to seek counseling over their perception that the love they receive from their children does not equal the love they give. Again, the screener wants to probe with hypothetical problems designed to measure an applicant's ability to be productive in delayed gratification situations.

185

# Case History

Medgar, who is eight, is an African-American who was placed into a foster home with a white family that had two birth children aged six and ten, both boys. Medgar's mother had abused him when he was much younger and subjected him to a drug-culture household that was always buzzing with activity. The house was usually very quiet until there were problems late at night, at which point it would explode and Medgar would be awakened by angry voices making threats—"I know you've got it here somewhere. Give it up or I'll cut that boy of yours into pieces!"

Not long after Medgar moved in with his foster parents, it was apparent that he had two problems that needed addressing. On the one hand, he was hyperactive—unable to sit still long enough to carry on a conversation with his foster parents or to play with his foster brothers, and subject to sudden temper tantrums that made him appear to be always on edge—and on the other hand, he was reluctant to engage emotionally with his foster family, which meant that he frequently withdrew to his room so that he could be alone. He found it very difficult to maintain eye contact with anyone in his foster family, a response that only set him apart even more so from their perspective.

Since Medgar's foster parents were convinced it was a racial issue, as was his caseworker, they made an effort to invite African-American couples with children into their home at every opportunity to make Medgar feel more "comfortable." Unfortunately, the more guests they invited into their home, the more withdrawn and hyperactive Medgar became, as if he were stuck in a groove from which he could not budge. His caseworker was perplexed.

When the time came to place Medgar into an adoptive home, the screener chose an African-American couple who had no birth children. Advised of Medgar's problems in the foster home, the couple voiced disagreement that it was a racial issue. "Just let us see what we can do," said the adoptive mother. "Black faces won't cure that boy's problems. What he needs doesn't have a color."

186

To everyone's surprise, Medgar showed definite signs of improvement before the probationary period ended. Instead of sending him to his room when he engaged in disruptive hyperactive behavior, as his foster parents had done, his adoptive mother told him that he could not leave the room until he had calmed down and could figure out what he wanted to do next. It was the latter challenge that had the greatest impact because it required him to interact with his environment.

Encouraged by his progress in that area, his caseworker and adoptive parents tackled his habit—yes, by then it was habitual behavior—of retreating to his room to be alone. Soon they realized that behavior was related to his inability to maintain eye contact with his parents and not to any discomfort he felt around whites. The caseworker realized that Medgar had never attached to his birth mother—an inability to maintain eye contact is common in those situations—so the caseworker made suggestions to the adoptive mother on how to encourage his eye contact. "Don't scold him or punish him for not making eye contact," the caseworker explained. "Just tell him you can hear better when people are looking at you."

The adoptive mother took the caseworker's advice and saw dramatic results. The more eye contact Medgar made with his adoptive parents, the less he retreated to his room—and the less time he spent in his room, the easier it became to maintain eye contact with his adoptive parents. In the end, it proved to be a very successful placement.

The lessons that Medgar's adoptive parents and caseworker learned can be applied to many other situations. When it comes to changing a child's behavior, it is important to give them choices, such as the adoptive mother did when she challenged Medgar to figure out what he wanted to do next before he left the room. The other important lesson has to do with eye contact. What may appear to be hostile behavior in children may actually be a defensive reaction caused by bonding and attachment issues. Work through that and you work through the problem.

## SAMPLE QUESTIONS
## FOR INTERVIEW ABOUT PARENTING ISSUES

1) **Does it concern you when you see children who do not appear to love their parents? Why do you think that happens?**

The answers to Questions 1-20 are important when it comes to providing you with information about the applicants' parenting skills, but of equal importance is whether the applicants agree with each other on critical parenting issues. In those instances when the applicants disagree with each other, is the nature of the disagreement such that they complement each other and provide balance to their parenting philosophy—or are the disagreements counter-productive and destructive in nature?

2) **What do you think is the biggest disappointment that a parent can have with a child?**

3) **Should children be punished for telling their parents that they hate them?**

4) **Do you think that you are responsible for whether your child loves you?**

5) **Do you think it is possible for a child to love two parents equally?**

6) **What is the biggest thing that a child could do to disappoint you?**

7) **As an adult, have you had a dog or a cat?**

8) **Where you able to housebreak your pet?**

9) **How did you correct your pet when it displayed bad behavior?**

10) **What did you do with your pet when you went out of town?**

11) **Did you ever have to leave work to take care of your pet? If so, did you get in trouble with your boss?**

12) **Have you ever given away a pet that you no longer had time for?**

13) What did you do if you told your dog to stop barking and it did not?

14) In what situations do you think spanking a child is acceptable? If yes, would they use a hand or a belt?

15) Do you and your spouse agree on how children should be disciplined? If not, how do you differ?

16) (For open adoptions) How would you handle the situation if you told your 14-year-old adopted daughter that she could not smoke, and the birth mother told her that she could smoke? Would they seek help from a professional?

17) (For open adoptions) If you had negative information about your child's birth parents, at what point would you share it with your child?

18) (For open adoptions) In your eyes, is there an "unforgivable sin" that a birth parent could commit against you or the child?

19) (For open adoptions) How is sharing the love of a child with a birth mother different from sharing the love of a husband with another woman?

20) If there anything that your mother or father did to you that you would never do to your child?

# Nurturing as an Indicator

Every day that the sun rises, an adoptive or foster parent somewhere in America tells their son or daughter that if they ever cross a particular line, "you are no longer a child of mine." Sadly, too many parents mean exactly what they say.

Of all the qualities that are essential to be good foster and adoptive parents it is probably the capacity to nurture or "mother" that is the most important, for it sets the tone for everything else that happens in a family.

# Case History

When Patrick O'Hara was a young adult attending college, friends told his father, Mike, that he was seen drinking in a saloon. That was especially grievous news because Patrick's brother Martin had died after getting drunk and falling under the wheels of a moving train. Mangled, he was brought home to die on the sofa in the family living room.

Patrick's father told him that he didn't want the same thing to happen to him and he administered the temperance oath to him, an act that made Patrick duty bound not to drink until he was twenty-one. After that age, Patrick refrained from drinking, simply because he thought it would interfere with his main goal in life—becoming a surgeon.

Later in life, when Patrick married and had a family of his own, he maintained that same attitude toward alcohol abuse. It wasn't so much a moral issue as it was a family issue. In his eyes, the individual was subordinate to the family and its tradition.

Then along came Patrick's son, novelist John O'Hara, who didn't see what all the fuss was about. When he was sent off to college, he rebelled against family tradition and became an alcoholic. To one friend, he confided that it was his intention to "get drunk just as much as I can." To another friend, according to biographer Finis Farr, he wrote that he and his father were at odds over his drinking: "This time he has good and sufficient reason to become perturbed; someone has told him of my boozing. He told me about what he had heard and made several dire threats which aren't even interesting; he hasn't the nerve to carry them out, but nevertheless, life henceforth will be a veritable hell for me. He has made it so before and he'll use every means he can to make it hell, because of all things he hates, liquor receives double its share."[1]

Despite John's perceived injustices by his no-nonsense father, the older man, who was a revered doctor in the community, did what he could to get his son started in a profession. He very much wanted his son to follow in his footsteps as a doctor. He took him on house calls with him and talked up the benefits of a life as a doctor. When John was twelve, he

190

told his son that if he would agree to pursue a career as a doctor he would deposit ten thousands dollars in a fund for his medical education. John refused the offer.

When it became apparent that medicine was not John's forte—he knew that writing was what interested him most—Patrick asked the publisher of a local newspaper to give his son a try as a reporter.

John excelled at his job, though it was not so much the news gathering that excited him, but rather the comradeship on the newspaper staff and the opportunity it gave him to hone his writing skills.

A few years later, when John was twenty-five, his father was diagnosed with Bright's Disease, a now obsolete term for serious kidney disease. During his final days, he was cared for by loved ones in a hospital bed that had been moved to his home.

At one point, during one of his rare lucid moments, he called out to his wife, "Katharine, I'm going to die," to which she answered: "Who will take care of the children?" Patrick's answer was perhaps not what she hoped to hear: "The world will take care of them."

When the attending doctors told the family that the end was near, according to Farr, John entered his father's room and drew close to his bedside when he realized that he was trying to tell him something. As it turned out, it was his father who had the last word in their relationship. "Poor John," he said in a faint whisper, "—poor John!"

After the funeral, John wrote to a friend that his father's death had had a "sobering" effect on him. He did not mean that literally, for he continued to drink heavily for another two decades, not quitting until a failed suicide attempt and a bleeding ulcer made it clear that if he wanted to continue writing he would have to stay sober. Later in life, he realized that his father had been right all along, but at what price to father and son had the lesson been learned?

Sadly, many families operate on the same principle that guided the O'Haras. There are many lessons that parents must teach their children, but all too often parents focus on one issue that—if it is ever breached, whether intentionally or by accident—results in what amounts to lifelong estrangement. For the O'Haras, the issue was alcohol. For other families, it is politics or race or religion or choice of employment.

Patrick O'Hara was right to warn his son about the dangers associated with alcohol use, but he was wrong to threaten him with dire consequences that, whether implemented or not, would affect his son's perception of him for the remainder of his life. Patrick went to his grave convinced that his son was doomed to a life of being "Poor John"—and John eventually went to his grave alone, without family present, leaving behind, for all eternity, a needlessly fractured relationship with his father.

Of all the mistakes that parents make in life, none are more poignant than the ones that could have been repaired by a few well-chosen words of apology. Was John O'Hara's dad a nurturing individual? By today's standards, the answer would probably be no. However, by the standards of that time, he would have been considered a nurturing dad. The Random House Dictionary of the English Language defines nurturing as providing "nourishment, support, encouragement, etc.," during childhood. Patrick O'Hara did all that—and more—for his son. He gave him his most heartfelt advice. He supported him. He helped him enter a career of his choosing. At the end, with his final breath, when he uttered "poor John" to his son, it could be interpreted as either dismissive or caring.

What Patrick O'Hara did not do was make his son feel that he could talk to him about the things that concerned him. It is that type of nurturing that psychologists and social workers would like to see adoptive and foster parents dispense in larger doses. For that reason, screeners should make an effort early in the interview process to evaluate the nurturing levels present in a marriage with questions such as:

1) **If your pets are ill, who takes care of them?**

2) **If you are ill, who takes care of you?**

3) **When was the last time you made an effort to nurse your partner when he or she was ill?**

4) **When was the last time you made dinner for your partner?**

**5) When your partner is not feeling well do you inquire about them during the day?**

**6) When you hurt your partner's feelings do you tell them you are sorry or do you just ignore the transgression and hope the moment passes?**

**7) When was the last time you went out of town and brought a gift back for your partner?**

**8) When you are ill or "in the dumps" is your partner a good person to have around?**

**9) When you have made a mistake are you reluctant to say you are sorry?**

**10) Do you think that children have a good understanding of a parent's need for love?**

The final question is important because of research that has linked the parents of battered children with the common belief (for both males and females) that children have an adult's awareness of what it takes to satisfy adult needs. In other words, parents who batter their children attribute adult qualities to them and believe that they can think and respond like adults. In a four-year study of the parents of abused children, Brandt Steele identified a common denominator characterized by a demand for high performance and the satisfaction of parental needs. "In all our patients who have attacked children, we have seen a breakdown in the ability to mother," Steele concluded. "There is no great difference between men or women in this breakdown. By 'mothering' we don't mean the superficial technique of care, but the deep, sensitive, intuitive awareness of, and response to, the infant's condition and needs, as well as consideration of the infant's capacity to perform according to his age."[1]

Any interviewee who responded "yes" to the above question No. 9 should be questioned in great detail about his or her beliefs about what children are capable of understanding and accomplishing. There is anecdotal evidence that adults that abuse pets do so for the same reasons: They punish the pets because they think the pets should "know better."

Batterers feel that children understand their needs in the same way that other adults understand their needs and they lash out because they feel rejected and betrayed by the children who "knew better."

Screeners take note: It is rare to see a batterer who displays strong "mothering" behavior, so be alert to any and all mothering behavior that arises during the interviews. The absence of any mothering behavior in an applicant should be a cause for concern. We know of a screener who, baffled by an applicant's seeming total lack of mothering behavior, took his affectionate, well-behaved dog with him to one of the home visits to see how the applicant would react. When the dog made a friendly overture to the woman, she shrieked and reacted by squirting him with a water bottle.

When people speak of making fathers more nurturing, they usually mean increasing verbal communication between father and son. John O'Hara grew up with the feeling that something was missing in his life. He later explored that void to great benefit in his novels. Highly charged words such as feminized and androgynous, when used by mothers or psychologists or social workers to describe a heightened nurturing ability in males, do not persuade fathers to be more nurturing with their children. A better way of addressing the issue is for women to be more specific in the requests that are made of fathers. Consider the following husband-wife exchange:

"Ed, I wish you were more nurturing with little Eddie."

"What do you mean?"

"You know, more nurturing."

If at that point, Ed does what so many husbands do and merely says, "OK, dear," without having a clue about what she is talking about, then nothing will be resolved. If, on the other hand, he presses her for a more accurate definition, he is more likely to take her advice. "But what do you mean by nurturing?"

"Talk to Eddie more. Spend more time playing with him—you know, take him places with you."

"I can't take him many places with me because I'm at work all day, but I can talk to him more—and play with him more. I like doing that anyway."

"Thank you, honey."

# Chapter 17

## Screener Recommendations for Adoptive and Foster Parents

Once the interviews are completed, the screener will write up a home study and present it to a supervisor and an adoption placement board. The screener will recommend that the applicants be approved or rejected—and the supervisor or board will either agree or disagree. If there is agreement that the applicants should be approved, they will be notified by telephone and/or letter. If they are rejected, they will be notified by letter and invited to discuss the matter with the screener or supervisor if they have any questions.

Most public agencies do not provide the applicants with copies of the home study, nor do they provide copies of the home study to the judges who approve the final adoption order. The reason for that is simple: while applicants have the right to know why they were rejected or approved, they do not have the right to read what their spouse or family members or physician provided to the agency on conditions of confidentiality.

That guarantee of confidentiality also extends to information presented to the judge, who is not trained to evaluate the psychological nuances inherent in a home study. The judge may direct questions of his own to the agency or to the adoption applicants, based on the report provided to him by the agency, but he cannot base those questions on information provided in confidence to the agency. In both the United States and Canada rights of privacy come into play, which is why adoption laws have recognized the separate confidentiality needs of the agency and the court.

Some private agencies do provide applicants with copies of the home study. If so, applicants should approach such a home study with caution. If the screener included the confidential information received from the applicants, family members or physician, it could have a very negative effect on the relationships of the people involved if shared. If the screener did not include that information in the home study, then all the applicants have is a watered-down version of a home study that almost certainly does not contain the real reasons why they were approved or rejected. Our experience has been that agencies that do not provide applicants with copies of their home studies generally are more professional in their evaluations and more successful in their placements.

# When Approval is in Order

The absence of negative factors is not a good enough reason for a screener to approve an applicant as an adoptive or foster parent. There must be positive reasons for acceptance and it is important that the screener articulate those reasons in the home study. Typically, the screener will reference parenting skills, relationship strengths, strong family ties, stable employment history, good health and whatever unique characteristics he feels the applicant has that qualifies him or her as an adoptive or foster parent.

An important part of approval is the screener's recommendations about the type of child that should be placed in the home. If the screener is unable to articulate those reasons, then they probably do not exist and may be little more than guesswork, a clear red flag to the screener's supervisor.

In his recommendations, the screener should voice opinions on the gender, sex, age, race, religion, and temperament of the child that would be the best fit for a particular family, even if that conflicts with the description of the child that the applicant has requested. Child placement is sometimes an amalgamation of what the screener and the applicants perceive to be the ideal placement (sometimes couples have different perceptions of what type of child is best for them).

One aspect of approval that social service agencies do not like to discuss is the effect that supply and demand has on the process. When the number of children who require care far exceeds the number of available foster parents, there is a tendency for screeners and their supervisors to lower their standards in response to pressure to approve more homes. Screeners sometimes broaden the range of acceptance in the belief that a foster home which presents some minor problems is better than no foster home at all. Martin Wolins calls it the "skimming" effect. He writes: "When the ratio of applicants to children is low (as in foster care), the agency is forced closer to the threshold and must often invade the risk area of the continuum, where poor homes may be numerous. The emphasis then changes from completely eliminating risk to reducing it as much as possible."[1] That is seldom the case in adoption, since the supply of applicants always exceeds the number of children available for adoption.

When applicants are approved for adoption, they typically feel an immediate sense of joy. Then as the days go by, they realize that they are on a waiting list with many other applicants and may not hear from the agency again for months or even years. How quickly they hear from the agency will be directly proportional to the flexibility they showed when they were asked what kind of child they could accept.

If they specified a white infant boy with a good health history, then they will likely wait for years. However, if they stated that they could accept a child of either gender or any race, or one with possible "special needs" related to physical, emotional or mental challenges, then they could hear from the agency fairly quickly.

Sometimes applicants who presented a narrow window of acceptability during the interviews will approach the agency, after approval, and ask to expand their acceptability requirements when the reality of a long waiting period sets in. That is permissible, of course, but it does put a burden on the screener to be certain that the applicants that change their mind about special needs children, or a child of a different race, or a child with health or emotional problems, are capable of dealing with the problems that could arise in those situations. It is at times like that that the screener will be glad that he went over every placement possibility in great detail during the interviews.

# Grounds for Rejection

The screener is more than merely a taker of information; he is a psychosocial profiler who must **evaluate** the information that he gathers. He must examine the applicants as individuals and as a couple (if they have a significant other). He must balance their strengths with their weaknesses and come to a conclusion about their suitability as foster and adoptive parents.

In small agencies, the decision to approve or reject will rest with the screener and his supervisor. In larger agencies, the decision may rest with a board composed of social workers, psychologists, and health professionals who vote as a group whether to approve each application. Decisions about adoptive and foster child approval are unique in social work in that they are basically irreversible and subject to verification.

Many times the supervisor may read something in the home study that raises questions that she wants answered. In those situations, she will address the questions to the screener, who may or may not have information on hand to provide the answers. If he doesn't have the information, he will call and set up another interview with the applicants. Most of the time additional questions do not indicate that an application is in trouble. It may simply mean that the screener forgot to ask something that his supervisor considers important. After the new information is gathered, it should be written up and attached to the home study and re-presented for approval. If the amended application is approved, the screener should telephone the applicants and give them the good news, and then follow up the call with a letter.

It is the job of the agency to find the best homes possible for children, and to protect them from emotional or physical abuse. The agency's first responsibility is always to the children. On those occasions when it is necessary to reject an applicant's application for adoptive or foster children, it should be done with clarity.

If an agency finds it necessary to reject an application, the best way of notifying the applicants is by letter. A rejection letter delivered by the postal service should not be viewed as being cold and distant, but rather a means to eliminate any confusion about the agency's decision. It also gives the applicants space in which to come to terms with the rejection without feeling the pressure of offering an immediate response (which would be the case in a telephone or in-person rejection).

The letter should state the reasons for the rejection in the most general terms possible and withhold the particulars until such time as the applicants request a face-to-face meeting. It has been our experience that most applicants who are rejected understand the reasons without asking for details. However, if an applicant vociferously protests the rejection—and no history of combative behavior is reported in the home study—the screener should take the time to do a self-review of the decision on the off-chance that a mistake has been made.

If that proves to be the case, the screener should schedule an interview with the applicant as soon as possible and address any doubts that he has about the applicant's potential as an adoptive or foster parent. If, after that follow-up interview, he still feels that rejection is in order, he should be prepared to defend that decision. If, on the other hand, he collects new information that prompts him to change his mind, he should not consider that a weakness. He should admit his mistake and move on.

## CHECKLIST FOR REJECTION

- Lack of financial resources
- Sexual abuse in the applicant's past
- Caseworker concerns about pedophilia
- Alcoholism or drug addiction

- History of spousal abuse
- Inadequate socialization
- Alienation from family members
- Membership in a radical organization that advocates violence
- History of unresolved marital difficulties
- Hostile statements or attitudes toward the country of origin of a prospective adopted child
- Arrests or convictions for assault, substance abuse or drug trafficking.
- Poor health prognosis.
- Emotional problems such as depression, borderline personality, obsessive-compulsive disorder, etc.

# Sample Policy Statement
# From a Private Agency

We reserve the right to reject the following applicants:

1) Individuals with felony convictions.

2) Individuals who engage in substance abuse.

3) Individuals with serious medical problems that could greatly reduce their life span.

4) Individuals who cannot demonstrate a history of healthy relationships with members of both sexes. A cause for rejection would be an attitude of hostility toward members of the opposite sex.

5) Individuals who cannot demonstrate an ability and commitment to provide for the continued care of adopted children in the event of the applicant's death.

6) Individuals who have a history of child abuse or adult sexual abuse.

7) Individuals who have been the victims of severe child abuse.

8) Individuals who have been convicted of assault.

9) Individuals who cannot demonstrate an ability to financially provide for a child until the age of majority.

10) Individuals who belong to organizations that advocate violence and/or disobedience of U.S. law.

11) Individuals who have made hostile statements or have hostile attitudes toward the country of origin of a prospective adopted child.

12) Individuals whose physical appearance or manner of dress could result in social ostracism for an adopted child.

13) Couples with a history of unresolved marital difficulties.

# What Should You Expect From Rejected Applicants?

An important aspect of the rejection letter is an invitation for the applicants to meet with the screener and/or his supervisor in a face-to-face meeting to discuss the matter in greater detail. Explanatory interviews are always emotionally draining. If screeners did not already possess high levels of empathy, they would never have chosen social work as a profession, so it is a given that he or she will find it difficult to dash the dreams of individuals who entered the process with high expectations. Even so, conducting rejection interviews is an integral part of the process.

Rejection interviews are difficult for many reasons. They are not query interviews—they are essentially defensive conversations in which the interviewer justifies his or her assessment of the individual's potential as an adoptive or foster parent. Such interviews require a great deal of preparation. It is one of the few areas of social work in which the rejection of a client is an option.

Just imagine if you went to a physician or a lawyer or a bookkeeper and you were told that you are not worthy of their services! Imagine the hurt and anger that you would feel! Rest assured that when you inform adoptive or foster applicants that they do not meet the agency's standards they will feel similar emotions.

Sometimes the reason for the rejection may originate in a reference letter from a friend or family member. The interviewer cannot disclose the source of that information without violating confidentiality agreements (and inviting a lawsuit), so it is essential that the precipitating information be confirmed from other sources, including follow-up interviews with the applicant. If the information that led to the rejection came from an applicant who asks that the information not be shared with the significant other, it is important that confidentiality protections be observed. Legal considerations aside, the screener does not want to be responsible for breaking up a relationship.

The bottom line is that it requires great skill to conduct a rejection interview in such a way that everyone's rights are observed and everyone's tender feelings are taken into consideration. It is not a job for beginners.

Every agency should have in-house appeal procedures in place so that if the applicants are unhappy with the agency's reasons for rejecting their application, as explained to them by the screener and/or his supervisor, they can ask for a more formal review of that decision by the agency's governing board.

Applicants who undergo that process and emerge with a belief that they have been unfairly treated by the agency have the right to file a lawsuit as a means of addressing their grievances. Since there is no constitutional right to foster or adopt a child, there is no basis for a court to hear a case based on claims that the rejection was unconstitutional. There would be a basis for a court to hear a case based on some form of agency negligence or wrongdoing, although that type of charge is extremely difficult to prove.

Lawsuits sometimes are initiated by private agency applicants when they receive a copy of their home study and can find no real explanation for rejection. There may be a good reason for that. If a screener knows that the applicants will read the home study, he may withhold all information that would be a violation of the confidentiality agreements he made while gathering information about them. As a result, the reasons for the rejection will have been stated and discussed off the record.

Of course, one of the most common sources for rejection is the spouse or an immediate member of the family. Examples of that would be the spouse who confides that he is simply not interested in raising another man's child and knows that if he tells his wife his true feelings it would end their relationship. Or the mother who confides that her daughter's marriage is a shambles and she doesn't think that adoption or foster children is the solution. Or the aunt who confides that she suspects that her nephew molested her nieces.

# Chapter 18

## Finalizing the Adoption

Once the applicants have been notified of their approval, the screener and his supervisor will review the list of children that the agency has available. If they have requested an infant, the screener and supervisor will probably decide on the placement without consulting with other caseworkers. They will review the various files that have been compiled on the infants—medical reports, physical descriptions, family histories, reports of the infant's progress in the foster home—and they will select a child that is a good match based on family background, hair and eye color, race, personality, possibly religion or ethnic background, and development in the foster home.

Once a candidate has been identified, the screener will talk to the caseworker who supervises the foster home and he will visit the child in the foster home so that he can see the child and talk to the foster parents. Many times the caseworker for an infant will be a nurse and not a social worker since the problems that foster parents face during the first year are almost always health related.

If the applicants have requested an older child or a child with special needs, the process will be much different. Instead of the screener and the supervisor reviewing the files, they will meet with the caseworkers that supervise the children in foster care. The screener will describe the adoption applicants and the caseworkers will describe their children, much like traders in the marketplace. The case workers will usually have a good idea what kind of parents their children need based on the type of problems encountered in foster care. The screener and the caseworker should visit the foster home of each child considered so that the screener can meet the child and the caseworker can deal with the child's fears or apprehensions about the meeting and discuss the child's development with the foster parents.

Once the screener, the supervisor and the caseworker are in agreement on a placement, plans should be made for a **viewing** (if the child is an infant) or a **visit** (if the child is older). If none of the agency's children seem right for the applicants, they will be added to the waiting list. It is impossible to predict how long an applicant will remain on the waiting list. It could be weeks, months or years.

When the time comes for a viewing or visit, the screener should make it clear to the applicants that they should not feel pressured to accept the child that is presented to them if they have doubts or misgivings about that particular child. It will not be a "take it or nothing" situation. The last word in adoption always belongs to them and the screener should make that clear so that there are no misunderstandings.

The viewing or visitation room should be warm and friendly and uncluttered. It should contain comfortable chairs, a changing table, a bassinette, diapers, cleansing towels, small toys, etc. If the child to be shown is an infant, the screener should leave the child in the room with the caseworker (the foster parents will not be present) while he goes to the waiting room to get the applicants. If the child to be shown is older, the foster parents may be present, depending on agency policy.

Some screeners, upon returning to the room with the applicants, prefer to take the infant from the caseworker and physically hand the child to the applicants. Other screeners prefer to allow the applicants to approach the child and ask to hold him or her. The first way is more rewarding to the screener, but the second way offers more insight into the applicants' initial reaction to the child.

The screener will want to pay close attention to the applicants' body language when they react to the child. Are they hesitant to touch the child? Do they reach out to the child or so they fold their arms? Do they exchange glances with each other? Do they display any signs of stress, such as pursed lips? Are they smiling, frowning or displaying blank slates? Does one partner seem more enthusiastic than the other? Do they speak to the child or only to each other?

Then there's the child's reaction: If an infant, does she recoil or cry when she leaves the arms of the caseworker? If an older child, does she seem at ease when introduced to the applicants? Older children have been known to run and hide behind furniture when introduced to their prospective parents. If that happens it is important for the screener to immediately take charge and, with the caseworker's help, mediate the introduction.

Once everyone is at ease the applicants should be left alone with the child. The length of the visit will depend on the age of the child: The older the child, the longer the visit. For infants, fifteen or twenty minutes are usually enough. For older children, thirty or forty minutes would be more appropriate, depending on the comfort level of the child.

After the visitation, the screener should meet with the applicants to discuss their reaction to the child. At that time, the screener should present as much information about the child as possible to the applicants, including development history, feeding or eating habits, medical data, family background, known heredity factors, personality and temperament, the results of any psychological examinations, and any other conditions that might appear later or adversely affect future development.

Once the discussion centers on the applicants' reaction to the child the screener should be sensitive to any doubts expressed or reflected, whether direct or indirect, and deal with those feelings before proceeding further. The applicants should never be pressured for a yes or no decision, but rather they should be encouraged to share all of their thoughts about the visitation, positive and negative.

If the discussion is positive, the screener should set up a time for a visitation in the home. If the applicants have some reservations and ask for more time to think about it, they should be granted additional time. Occasionally, applicants experience the opposite of "love at first sight" and they simply don't relate to a particular child. It's something they feel but not necessarily something they can explain. If that happens, they should not be ruled out arbitrarily for another child. If the child they failed to respond to was an older child, the caseworker should explain to the child that the decision not to place was the agency's decision and not the applicants' decision.

It is important for the screener to understand the reasons for the rejection to make certain that the applicants are in full agreement about adoption in general. Once the screener determines that they are still in agreement, he will want to carefully analyze their reasons for the rejection of the child.

# The Home Visit

The home visit should be scheduled within two weeks of the office showing or visitation. We have never seen adoptive parents who were not anxious about the first home visit, so it is not an ominous sign if the prospective parents are on pins and needles about the child's arrival.

By the time the home visits begin, the screener's role in the adoption is winding down, depending on whether agency policy is for the screener to supervise until finalization or whether the case is turned over to a caseworker. If it is agency policy for the adoption to be supervised by a caseworker, it is important for the screener to remain involved at least through the home-visit phase because he is the person who knows the applicants best and he is more likely to pick up on problems in the placement.

When the screener goes to visit a foster or adoptive parent with whom he has placed an infant, he should stay long enough to witness a diaper changing. In his book, *The Anatomy of Disgust,* William Miller notes that we lower the threshold for what we consider disgusting at certain times. "Parents are who will care no matter what; will cart away the excrement, risk getting it on their hands and clothing; suffer being shat upon," he writes. "Overcoming the disgust inherent in contaminating substances is emblematic of the unconditional quality of nurturing parental love."

Miller's observation offers a test as good as any in determining the presence of nurturing love. An adoptive or foster parent who can change the diapers of a newborn without displaying any of the facial characteristics of disgust is a parent who has crossed the threshold into nurturing parental love. By the same measure, if the screener witnesses a new foster or adoptive parent displaying disgust while changing a diaper, or perhaps even making disparaging comments, the screener should interpret those actions as an invitation to probe more deeply into the parent's true feelings about the child.

Subsequent pre-placement visits—and the agency may require three or four, depending on the age of the child—should be monitored carefully for any signs of trouble. At the end of each visit the screener should talk to the applicants—and the child, if she is old enough for such a conversation—about what happened that day.

The screener should be sensitive to the child's and adoptive parents' ability and readiness to accept each other and he should be prepared to move quickly to terminate the visits once it is clear the placement is not working out. Things can go wrong during visitation that could result in the screener terminating the visits, but unless something extraordinary happens the applicants will be the persons who decide the child's future.

If the child is older than two, she may well be anxious at the visit, even if she doesn't understand all the implications. She may sense that it is a test of some kind, but not know what to do to pass the test. She may look to the screener or the caseworker for guidance. For that reason, the screener should go out of his way not to place the child in situations in which she has to respond to questions she doesn't understand.

Here are some suggestions that might prove helpful:

- The screener should advise the applicants to give the child a walk-through tour of their home, but not to refer to her room as "this will be your room," since it would put pressure on the child. She will be able to figure out which room he prefers without anyone's help.

- The child should be asked what she wants for lunch, but if she is too shy to voice a preference, the applicants should be encouraged to offer her a choice: "Would you like to go get a pizza, or would you like for me to make you a peanut butter and jelly sandwich?"

- The screener should caution the applicants not to make the pre-placements public events to which friends and relatives are invited. Few things are more intimidating to a child than a room filled with excited adults reaching out to hug and kiss them.

If the pre-placements go well, the child will be placed in the home for a period of supervised probation that usually will last from six to twelve months (different agencies have different probationary periods). The purpose of the probationary period is to protect the child by giving the adoption time to gel, and to provide the applicants and the child with casework support to address any problems that arise.

The person that supervises during the probationary period may be the screener, or it may be the child's caseworker, depending on agency policy. Visits should be made to the home at regularly scheduled times, with unscheduled visits made at unpredictable intervals. During the visits, the screener should observe the child, talk to the child in private, provided the child is old enough, and discuss any problems with the applicants. During this time, the applicants should be encouraged to take the child to their physician for a checkup, especially if the child is an infant.

# Finalization: A Job Well Done

Most states require about twelve months from the time a child is placed into an adoptive home until finalization is possible. If the screener has any concerns about the placement, he can ask for an extension past the

# PLACEMENT CHECKLIST

Applicant _____ Birth Date _____

Applicant _____ Birth Date _____

Marriage _____No ____Yes _____ (Date) _____

Address _____

Telephone _____Cell _____

Email _____

CHILDREN IN THE HOME

Name _____ Age _____

Name _____ Age _____

Name _____ Age _____

INTERVIEW LOG

First Interview _____ Date _____ Home or Office
Second Interview _____ Date _____ Home or Office
Third Interview _____Date _____ Home or Office
Fourth Interview _____ ate _____ Home or Office

Fifth Interview _____Date _____Home or Office

Application Approved _____ (Date)

CHILD DESIRED

Gender _____ Race _____ Age _____ Religion _____

Restrictions _____

Special Needs _____

twelve-month period so that any uncertainties can be resolved.

Sometimes adoptive parents request an extension when older children are involved and there are reports of misbehavior. That is hardly ever a good idea since it puts the child in charge of the adoption and subjects her to greater emotional risk than she otherwise would experience. Finalization should be timely and presented as affirmation of the parent-child relationship and not as a reward for good conduct by the child or the parents.

At the end of the probationary period, the screener should have frank discussions with everyone involved with the placement—the applicants, the child, the child's caseworker, and the foster parents. It is rare for adoption applicants to pull the plug on an adoption at the end of the probationary period, but it happens on occasion and the screener should remain alert to that possibility. In that case, the screener should devise an exit strategy with as little emotional damage as possible to the child.

If, on the other hand, everyone involved is pleased with the placement at the end of the probationary period, the next step is for the agency to file a petition with the court in the jurisdiction of the applicants' residence to finalize the adoption. If the screener works for a private agency, the paperwork will be handled by the agency or by the applicants' lawyer, depending on the agency's policy. If the adoption placement was initiated by a facilitator or by the child's birth parents or guardian, the applicants will hire a lawyer to handle the adoption petition.

State laws differ, but most states require a post-placement investigation and report before an adoption can be finalized by the court. Typically, public and private agencies provide the report, but in the case of adoptions initiated by facilitators or the child's birth parents or guardian, the courts may hire an independent social worker or a psychologist to prepare the report.

Once all the paperwork has been done—and the necessary reports filed—the judge will conduct a hearing in her office or in a courtroom. If there are no problems and no opposition to the adoption, the judge will sign a decree or order that names the applicants as the legal parents of the child. This part of the adoption process is usually anticlimactic, with the applicants' presence not required.

# After Finalization: What Next?

The screener's final involvement in the adoption will be to offer advice to the new adoptive parents about how to proceed with some of the more mundane aspects of adding a child to the family. The new parents should be advised to:

- Apply for a social security number from the Social Security Administration for the child. To do that they will need proof of the adoption and proof of residency.
- Have an attorney draw up a will or trust that will ensure that the child will be provided for in the event of their deaths. Since state laws differ—and some states have special provisions for adopted children—the applicants must make certain that their will takes note of the child's adopted status.
- Make certain that the child is included in their health insurance coverage. Sometimes adoptive parents forget to change their policies from individual to family coverage and only learn that their child is not coverage during a health care emergency.
- If the applicants don't have life insurance, they should take out a policy as soon as possible. If they already have a life insurance policy, they should make certain that the child is listed as a beneficiary and pay particular attention to the language of the policy since some use limiting terms such as "descendants" or "heirs of the body" that could exclude an adopted child. Insurance companies should be asked for written confirmation that the child is included in the policy.
- If the applicants did not take the child to a dentist or physician during the probationary period, they should do so as soon as

possible so that they will have established health-care contacts in the event of illness. The physician or dentist should be told that the child is adopted since some physicians will not treat children when a full health history is not available. Parents should find out in advance if the physician they have chosen has any negative attitudes about treating adopted children. It is a good idea for a child to receive a complete physical, including blood tests, *especially if she has been adopted from abroad.*

# PART III

# Psychological Assessment

## A Means to Resolve Complicated Evaluation Issues

# CHAPTER 19

# The Referral Question: An Overview of Testing Possibilities

Most of the time a screener will be able to make decisions about a foster or adoptive parent application without asking the applicants to undergo any type of formal testing. However, there will be special situations in which the screener and his supervisor will want to engage a consulting psychologist for assistance.

Depending on the circumstances of the consultation, the role of the consulting psychologist may be to offer more insight into the data already collected, to add new data, or to answer specific questions relevant to the decision of approving applicants for placement of foster and adoptive children. The best way to reach that consultative goal is for the referring agency to be clear about what is needed prior to the psychologist seeing the individual or couple. Ideally, the home study, minus a final recommendation, will already have been written by the screener and made available to the consulting psychologist. The goal of consultation may include reporting specific test scores, interpreting results, and making specific recommendations.

Early in the consultative process, the psychologist must make sure that the referring agency understands the limits of the evaluation. Clearly, in a situation where emotions run high and the couple's goal is to impress the screener about their ability to be good parents, multiple data points are needed to make the most informed decisions about placement. Having another professional with different expertise and a slightly different theoretical perspective may help differentiate between simple idiosyncratic behavior and actual behavior that would dictate rejecting the applicant.

If a psychologist is asked to administer a specific test and simply report the test scores back to the agency, he will likely feel uncomfortable with the referral. Most clinicians prefer to be presented a referral question so that they can decide which, if any, standardized tests should be utilized to provide an answer. Some agencies are reluctant to use consulting psychologists to conduct assessments. Others may feel that they are capable of interpreting scores from certain standardized tests, although they may have no one on staff that is qualified to actually administer the tests. In that situation, if the applicant is referred to a psychologist for the administration of a specific test, the psychologist would be simply performing a psychometric task with no qualitative referral question and would have no real impact on the decision process.

When outside consultation is limited to test administration, the agency has to take full responsibility for integrating the test scores into the other data, rather than utilizing a consulting psychologist to respond to a referral question. Ultimately, the agency has the decision-making responsibility. Gathering the needed data, whether from a full psychological assessment, or from isolated tests scores, will assist the agency in making an informed placement decision.

# Defining Psychological Assessment

Psychological assessment is more than simply reporting test scores. It usually involves administering a variety of tests using multiple modalities interpreted within the context of the referred individual's background information, the referral question and any previous data available for review. Given certain circumstances, test scores alone can be very misleading. An individual who has had a head injury may have lost very specific cognitive skills. Individuals who are under tremendous stress at the time of testing may score much differently than they otherwise would score.

Clinicians know to use scores as part of the snapshot of the person's performance; however those scores must be viewed in the context of their whole life story. The engineer who can not tie his shoes on the day of testing due to a hand injury may make a fine adoptive parent, although he can't pass a task on a developmental test from early childhood. An average score on an IQ test may be fine for most of us, but the Mensa member who was recently suffered a head injury in an auto accident would not be pleased if the assessor simple reported scores without explanation. The process of assessment is often convoluted and demands a high level of competence to sort through all the factors involved in addressing the referral question.

It is expected that the couple will minimize any negative aspects of their relationship, family histories or other areas being evaluated and present themselves in the most positive light. Initially, applicants may deny real problems and try to convince the screener that "everything is just fine." Applicants may feel unfairly scrutinized in order to pass the "tests" to become adoptive or foster parents. They often feel that their altruistic gesture of offering a child a loving home suddenly turns into having to prove themselves far beyond any other parents.

We could not find any tests designed to specifically evaluate prospective parents in order to predict outcomes of foster or adoptive placements. The literature is rather scarce in terms of the relationship of a parent's emotional health, personality or cognitive skills as it specifically relates to foster care or adoption success. Professionals in the field of adoption typically generalize findings from parent-child research, although it is not clear if most of the subjects have a biological relationship rather than adoptive relationship. As with any interpretation, we would caution to not go beyond the data.

Even psychologists sometimes underestimate the value of psychological assessment. Of course, professionals should never go beyond their data, but integrating multiple points of data to reach well reasoned conclusions is not only acceptable, but expected. Tests are instruments from which we draw conclusions and make predictions about individuals. Psychologists use the data from test instruments in a similar manner as the medical field uses its instruments of prediction.

In 2001 *The American Psychologist* reported evidence that psychological tests predict outcomes comparably to the predictive value of medical tests.[1] The report concluded that the validity of psychological tests is strong and is comparable to medical test validity. Further, it suggests that psychologists should use more than one method in an individual's assessment to maximize the predictive validity of their findings.

# Making a Referral

A consulting psychologist can be an invaluable resource in sorting out complex issues and answering difficult questions that will guide the agency in making decisions about placement. To accomplish this, the agency must provide critical data to the consultant. The consultant must review the available data and determine the proper assessment methods and modalities necessary to address the issues of concern.

The success of the consultation is dependant on the agency's willingness to impart critical data and the skill of the psychologist to adapt the information. For the consultation to be effective, the consulting psychologist must fully understand the nature of the referral question. For that reason, the agency has a responsibility to be precise in what it expects from the referral. Consultations can be expensive and referrals based on vague requests such as, "please evaluate this applicant," are not helpful.

The first step in formulating a clear question is to describe the issues or problems in behavioral terms. Describing a couple who are applying for adoption as "poorly motivated" provides the psychologist with little useful information. A woman that is described as having "emotional problems" tells the psychologist very little. Clearly stating what the couple or individual does or does not do is much better. In the first example, it would have been better if the agency had reported that the couple missed two appointments without notice or excuse—or that they took four weeks to return a release form and wrote only one-sentence responses on the personal history forms.

With a clear description of their actual behavior the psychologist gets a better picture of what "poorly motivated" really means. In the second example if the screener had described the woman's actual behavios for the psychologist it would help clarify exactly what was meant by "emotional problems". The screener should report that the woman began crying during a seemingly non-threatening portion of the interview when asked where she graduated from high school. Later she exhibited agitation and hyper-vigilant when a male supervisor came into the room to explain agency policies. She did not maintain eye contact with him and kept jerking her head with her eyes darting from side to side to visually scan the room. Being vivid in your descriptions of specific behavior of concern will increase the likelihood that the consulting psychologist will be working from the agency's perspective.

The agency is not necessarily looking for a psychological diagnosis. It is concerned about the underlying causes of the described behavior and its impact on a child placed in the applicant's home. The agency hypothesizes that the identified concerns may adversely affect the family's ability to properly provide for a child and it calls upon the consultant to conduct a to help prove or disprove the hypothesis.

Any time and effort spent properly formulating the referral question will be in the best interest of the applicant, which is why a completed home study is helpful. A client's background information concerning medical, family, developmental, education, mental and social history may be relevant. Allowing the psychologist to have access to the basic background information that has already been gathered will be time-and-cost effective.

Psychologists usually conduct testing as part of a therapeutic protocol for individuals who have either requested the evaluation as part of diagnosis and treatment, or individuals who have been directed or requested to participate in an evaluation by the courts or in this case, requested by the screener. It is important from an ethical standpoint that everyone involved understand that evaluation requests made by agencies are made with the full consent of the foster and adoptive applicants who have chosen to participate in the evaluation. The applicants and screener must understand that the assessment is not a measurement of the applicants' ability to be good parents. No one will be given a pass or fail grade as a parent. Clinical interviews, testing, and record reviews are typical techniques used to complete a formal evaluation. The findings of a formal evaluation usually add valuable information to help confirm or refute apprehensions the screener may have about the applicants. Again, the referral question and subsequent hypotheses are paramount in the collaboration.

Examples of reasons for a referral to a consulting psychologist may include:

- approach to parenting differs significantly
- history or signs of depression
- emotionally labile applicant
- suspected mental illness
- suspected intellectual deficits
- symptoms of memory problems
- unusually disturbing behaviors
- questionable personality development
- exhibits extreme anxiety beyond expectancy
- concerns about couple's family dynamics
- suspected anger control problems
- concerns about couple's sexual compatibility
- history of sexual abuse
- couple exhibit conflicts during screening process
- couple present extremely different desires for children
- collateral source information offers disturbing data
- suspicion of sexual identity issues
- suspicion that "something" is being hidden
- suspected alcohol or drug abuse
- or other well reasoned referral questions

# Explaining the Referral to the Applicant

By the time an applicant has been referred to a consulting psychologist he or she will have been informed that the screener has run into difficulty making a decision about their application. It will be explained to the applicant that the goal of the referral is to gather additional information and not to make a specific diagnosis or to engage in treatment for any suspected emotional disorders or psychological issues. Depending on the nature of the problem encountered by the screener, the applicant may be informed that the application is likely to be rejected without the type of information that can be obtained from the referral.

The applicants must fully understand the intent of the evaluation and agree before any tests are given. Financial arrangements must be discussed and settled prior to testing to minimize any misunderstanding. After being informed of the intent of the referral, applicants should be encouraged to ask questions, clarify any issues and fully understand how the data will be used prior to making a decision whether or not they agree to testing.

Once the applicants agree to the requested testing, proper documentation is essential. Time-limited releases must be signed by the applicants to allow the professionals to share specific data and evaluation findings. We would advise that all Health Insurance Portability Accountability Act (HIPPA) guidelines for gathering, storing, sharing and releasing client/patient information be followed.

Before an agency ever utilizes the services of a consulting psychologist, they need to understand the milieu within which a psychologist practices. Because each profession has a different relationship with those they serve, each profession develops its own code of conduct. The American Psychological Association's (APA's) Ethical Principles of Psychologists and Code of Conduct (2002) set the standards by which all psychologists should practice. There are other formal ethnical guidelines, standards and codes of conduct, but we will review the APA's Ethics Code because it is the most widely recognized by psychologists.

225

The Preamble to the Ethics Code articulates the profession's intentions and commitment and offers a pledge for psychologists to perform professional services in a manner that will protect the welfare of those who seek the services. The document challenges psychologists to strive towards the highest ethical ideals. Psychologists must be aware of the affect that they have on those they serve and the magnitude of their professional responsibilities. They are reminded to take personal responsibility for their own physical and mental health and be cognizant of how that may affect their ability to help others. The general principles of the Ethical Code expect psychologists to maintain integrity, fairness and justice to all. There is a warning against potential biases and practicing outside the boundaries of competence, while promoting limitations based on expertise. Psychologists are reminded to have total respect for others and to uphold the rights of privacy and confidentiality. Psychologists should examine their ability to practice with respect to diverse cultures and make appropriate decisions based on that examination. Agencies should always consult with psychologists that are noted for their high standards and professionalism.

The Ethical Standards are the enforceable rules for the conduct of psychologists and they must be adhered to or else they will put the psychologist at risk for sanctions. They cover a broad spectrum of practice, but certain standards are of particular importance as related to this book. Standard 9 (Assessment) is dedicated to all aspects of assessment. Any psychologist who performs assessments on a regular basis should be familiar with this Standard. Both the consulting psychologist and the referring agency would be advised to review Standard 9 (9.01 – 9.11) for valuable guidance before engaging in conducting assessments to help determine the status of applicants for foster home or adoptive home placements. These guidelines apply if conducting full evaluations as a consultant or if only administering a single checklist or test.

The Assessment Standard (9) informs psychologists that their opinions must be based on sound information and appropriate techniques to support their findings. Further, it highly recommends that when an evaluator makes statements about the psychological characteristics of an individual, those statements are based on having conducted an examination of that individual. For our purposes, there should never be a situation occur that a psychologist would be expected to make statements about an applicant without having conducted a proper evaluation. In the event a psychologist supervised or briefly consulted with the screener, such as conducting a review of the records, an individual assessment may not be necessary. Whatever the circumstances, all parties must be aware of the nature of the involvement and the psychologist must make clear the sources of the information upon which any statements or clinical judgments are made. It is recommended that the psychologist limit his input to only the data that is documented and sufficient to draw any conclusions. In general, they should never go beyond the data.

A psychologist should only administer a test for the purpose for which it was designed to be used. The administration of any tests should follow the standardized procedures with any scores, test data, interpretations and recommendations consistent with the purpose of the test. We would caution examiners about using assessments that do not have a test manual that offers psychometric information.

The individual being evaluated should fall within the population for which the instrument's validity and reliability was established. In the event that validity or reliability has not been established for the test taker's population, yet for some compelling reason the psychologist feels it is necessary to use such an instrument, the psychologist has a responsibility to explain the situation and how this may impact the test results. An examiner must also appropriately address any language issues and its effect on the results.

A psychologist must fully understand Standard 9.04 "Release of Test Data" and comply with the agreement that exist between the client/patient, screener and psychologist. Evaluators feel a strong responsibility to maintain the security and integrity of test materials by trying to limit the distribution of test questions, protocols, manuals and test stimuli. Psychologists must guard against the use of obsolete or outdated tests, the use of untrained examiners, and using a test for which it was not designed.

Psychologists have a responsibility to interpret assessment findings in a manner that is consistent with the intended purpose. They must take all factors into consideration such as language and cultural differences, and they should let the interpretation reflect the influences of any such factors. The psychologist should make sure that assessment results are reported to the appropriate parties as determined by the consultant relationship. In general, a psychologist conducting assessments must be vigilant to practice within the boundaries of his competency, take responsibility for all aspects of the testing, even if he delegates some of the work to others, and guard against unfair discrimination during the testing, scoring and reporting results.[1] Psychological assessment can provide helpful insight into screening questions as long as the measures used adhere to basic scientific principles, peer review and sound methodology.

Psychologists should know who will be reading the report. If the report will be entered into a court record, given to the applicants or just read within the referring agency the psychologist should tailor it to best meet the needs. Even though other professionals in the mental health field may be familiar with psychological jargon, it is not necessary to fill the pages with such verbiage. When there is complexity in the subject matter it is even more important to write in understandable Standard English. Easy to read, well written reports can easily be incorporated into an overall assessment package.

We recommend that any consulting psychologist review the "Standards for Educational and Psychological Testing" (1999) for extensive information on testing individuals from diverse backgrounds and new uses for existing tests.[1]

The tester (psychologist) and the test-taker (applicant) should work together to produce the best assessment results. The psychologist should treat the applicant with respect, courtesy and without discrimination. Reasonable accommodations must be provided, if requested. The psychologist should inform the applicant of the type of feedback that can be expected and how it is expected to be used.[1] Again, we emphasize that the referring agency is the decision-maker, not the psychologist.

# CASE HISTORY

When Ellen and Pierre first came into the agency they made a terrific impression on the screener. In their late twenties, they seemed energetic and intelligent, and their social skills were well developed. They asked lots of questions and showed no evidence of evasiveness. As they were leaving the office after the first interview, Pierre cracked a joke and the screener was left with a parting gift of resounding laughter. Pierre was a salesman by profession and he did an excellent job of selling himself to the screener.

It was not until they were deep into the individual interviews that the screener encountered a problem. In response to a direct question, Ellen confided that Pierre had been abusive to her in years past. "But we went to a marriage counselor and we were able to work all that out," she said. "He hasn't struck me in over three years—and I don't think he ever will again."

The screener brought up the abuse during his individual interview with Pierre. "We knew we would have to talk about this," Pierre said. "What can I say? It happened and I'm sorry and it will never happen again."

"Why did it happen in the first place."

"I was under a lot of pressure at work at the time and I misunderstand a friendship that Ellen had with a male co-worker."

"What do you mean by misunderstood?"

"I thought she was seeing him and I slapped her around a bit. It turned out I was wrong and she wasn't seeing him at all. I felt like a fool. We went to a marriage counselor and worked all that out."

Subsequently, Pierre was asked if he had ever felt that a co-worker had conspired against him. He answered "yes," but explained it by saying that the co-worker was very ambitious and had made a habit of conspiring against the other salesmen.

The screener finished out the interviews and wrote up the home study, but when he got to the part where he had to make a recommendation he knew he had no option but to recommend that their application be rejected. The history of physical abuse was bad in itself, but when it was coupled with doubts about whether Pierre, through marriage counseling, had truly resolved the problem the potential for trouble was multiplied. Then there was Pierre's explanation for the workplace "conspiracy." It was a reasonable explanation, but it raised questions in areas that overlapped with the abuse issue.

The screener called Ellen and Pierre in for another interview. He told them the truth: Namely, that while he felt they had many wonderful qualities, he was troubled by the history of abuse in their marriage.

"Isn't there anything we can do?" asked Ellen.

"I could ask the agency to refer you to a psychologist for assessment. If we get a good report, I could approve you. If the report goes the other way, we would have to turn down your application."

Ellen and Pierre looked at each other for a moment and then Pierre said, "Sounds like we have nothing to lose!"

"That's one way to look at it."

"Sure, let's do it."

After the interview with Ellen and Pierre, the screener met with his supervisor and the agency director and it was decided to refer the couple to a consulting psychologist that had worked with the agency in the past on similar matters.

The procedure for the assessment will go something like this:

After being contacted by the agency, the consulting psychologist will ask for a clear indication of what the agency expects from the assessment. Does the agency want to know if Pierre is likely to abuse his wife again? Does it want to know if a child would be safe in the home? Does it want to know if Pierre have anger or impulse control problems that are responsible for his reaction to his suspicions that his wife was unfaithful? Does it want to know if Pierre has personality problems or even more serious pathology?

The consulting psychologist should have no difficulty answering any or all of those referral questions. After Pierre and his wife gave permission for the consult and signed all needed release forms, either the screener or psychologist meet with Ellen and Pierre to describe the nature of the evaluation, answer their questions, discuss limits of confidentiality and any applicable reporting issues and have a clear understanding of the financial responsibilities.

Once the preliminaries are attended to, the psychologist will request a copy of the home study and ask for specific behavior or statements that lead the screener to be concerned about the applicant. He also will be interested in the therapist's process notes, goals of therapy, termination criteria and prognosis.

After the psychologist gathered and reviewed all of the available data he would formulate an assessment protocol. There is no specific protocol to follow and psychologists will be lead by their own theoretical bases and utilize their individual approach.

The psychologist will likely interview both Pierre and Ellen and ask them to take various inventories to examine aspects of their marriage, current emotional state and personalities. Clearly, he will be looking specifically at Pierre's anger, impulse control, and satisfaction in his marriage, suspiciousness, jealousy, possible paranoid thoughts, past relationships with significant others, work relationships, and control needs. He may use both objective tests and projective tests to gather data. Pierre has been described as intelligent and using a multi-model method of assessment may be advisable in his case.

Driven by the data, the psychologist will pursue all avenues necessary to develop a comprehensive picture of Pierre's emotional development from childhood to present. He will gather data about his relationship with his father, with his mother, his father's relationship with his mother, other family dynamics, and any other possible contributing factors, including attachment issues.

The psychologist may have to juggle competing hypotheses about the "whys" of past behavior and the "ifs" of future behavior. A good evaluator will follow the leads and delve where necessary, using clinical judgment and administering the appropriate assessment instrument to unravel Pierre's past in order to make valid predictive statements.

Could Pierre be given a "good" report? Yes. Although his behavior was unacceptable, the circumstances under which he reacted inappropriately may be understood. Pierre may fully understand the magnitude of his anger outburst and may have taken the proper steps to recognize early signs of stress, and he may have learned coping strategies and feel remorse for his actions. Ellen may have contributed to his outburst and she also may have learned new skills. The couple may actually be more stable than ever before. And as for his work situation, additional information could prove that Pierre was accurate in his assessment of the "conspiracy ".

Could a psychologist recommend that the agency continue to consider Pierre a placement risk? Yes. Based on a formal assessment, the psychologist may determine that Pierre may be exhibiting a number of problems that could be exacerbated by the stress of a child being placed in the home.

There could be a wide range of possibilities for Pierre to be considered a risk. He may have had poor role models for dealing with anger. He may have had poor early attachments. He may have been abused himself. He may have a paranoid personality, impulse control problems, or he may be depressed. He may suffer from a substance abuse problem. He may be slightly narcissistic and he may have terminated therapy prematurely, against the advice of the therapist.

Depending on the outcome of the formal assessment, Pierre and Ellen may or may ultimately be approved to adopt a child. If, in fact, a child is placed with them, the psychologist will probably recommend some ongoing therapeutic contact for at least a while during the adjustment period and longer as indicted.

# Chapter 20

## Evaluating Mood and Anxiety Problems

A large number of adults suffer from anxiety and depressive symptoms from time to time. Many of these individuals are able to successfully hold jobs, interact with friends and be an effective parent; however, extreme anxiety and symptoms of depression are typically very problematic. Emotional problems that escalate to the possibility of drug use and suicide are devastating to families, friends and associates.

Agencies may find formal psychological assessments helpful in clarifying subtle hints of problems detected during the screening process. A consulting psychologist will help determine if simple statements made during the screening, labeled as fleeting feelings, may actually be hints of significant problems that need to be considered in the placement process.

Most of the research on how parental distress affects the ability to perform parenting skills primarily focuses on mothers. It is probably an accurate assumption that these mothers live with their biological offspring rather than adoptive or foster children. Therefore, the possible genetic influence must be considered when applying findings to the adoptive and foster home. Research findings indicate that depressed mothers tend to evidence constricted affect, are more negative, and describe their children as having more problems than would be the case with non-depressed mothers. Their children are more often referred by both parents and teachers for treatment due to behavioral and emotional problems. Depressed mothers reportedly have more difficulty applying consistent discipline, pay less positive attention to their children, and are at a higher risk for verbal aggression towards their children.

Parents with significant anxiety disorders are found to have children who have fewer friends, spend more time in solitary activities, and have

234

more difficulty in school. These children express more worry about their family as compared to children from parents with no known psychological disorder. The home environment for children of an overanxious parent is often much more tense, negative and fearful than in the homes of peers.

Depression and anxiety are among the risk factors that compromise parental effectiveness. They seem to impact vulnerable infants and adolescents more than middle age children. At their respective ages, infants and adolescents evidence a particularly high need for their parents to be "emotionally available" to help buffer the developmentally related stressors they experience. The responsibility of caring for other's stress can be overwhelming for a parent who is already emotionally compromised.[1]

Most people underreport their consumption of alcohol, use of tobacco and any other harmful substances. This tendency is even more noticeable when couples are being considered for foster and adoptive child placements because they fear some arbitrary point that dictates rejection. The screener may find that the couple frequents bars and often attends receptions and parties where alcohol flows freely. Reference data from collateral sources may report significantly different levels of consumption by the couple.

Within family dynamics, substance use or abuse is far more complicated than the actual level of consumption. The devastating effects of substances within a home are well known. Emotional and behavioral characteristics of the children of alcoholics are well documented, as well as the many other associated problems in the home. When there is even the slightest doubt about the influence of substances in the home, the couple should be referred for a formal assessment.

Stressors, physical and emotional problems, family issues, disappointments, substance use and the performance pressure have been identified as some of the major factors contributing to the escalation of emotional instability that may result in suicidal ideations. When an individual's emotional state includes feelings of hopelessness, the fear of suicide increases exponentially.

Some of the popular assessment instruments designed to evaluate depression, anxiety, hopelessness, substance use and suicide risk are summarized in order to assist the screener in understanding the range of data that may result.

**Title:** Beck Anxiety Inventory [1993 Edition]
**Author:** Beck, Aaron T.; Steer, Robert A.
**Purpose:** to measure anxiety in adults and adolescents
**Acronym:** BAI
**Publisher:** PsychCorp, A brand of Harcourt Assessment, Inc.
**Publisher address:** PsychCorp, A brand of Harcourt Assessment, Inc., 19500 Bulverde Road, San Antonio, TX 78259; Telephone: 800-211-8378; FAX: 800-232-1223; E-mail: customer_care@harcourt.com; Web: www.PsychCorp.com

The Beck Anxiety Inventory (BAI) is one of several tests by Aaron Beck and his associates. The series of tests by Beck are typically easy to administer and easy to score. The BAI is a 21-item evaluation of anxiety. It is considered a short and easy to understand test, highly reliable and valid, the scale can be administered in about 5 to 10 minutes. Each of the test items represent an anxiety symptom that is rated for severity on a 4-point Likert scale, ranging from "Not at all" to "Severely; I could barely stand it." Points for each item are simply added to equal a Total Score. The BAI can also be computer scored as well. The administration instructions are easy to follow.

The short manual is written for a clinician rather than researcher. Clinicians should find the BAI to be a very useful test, especially when combined with the other Beck instruments and integrated into a comprehensive computer-scored interpretive profile. This "profile" can be a combination of several of Beck's tests including the Beck Depression Inventory, Beck Hopelessness Scale, the Beck Anxiety Inventory and the Beck Suicide Ideation or can be developed for each of the separate tests.

The manual's discussion of the scale development primarily refers the reader to earlier work of Beck and his colleagues. It points out that the test is designed to measure symptoms of anxiety that only minimally shared with depression. The reliability and validity data reported is based on only three studies, although through and informative. The manual authors quite appropriately caution the reader the instrument was developed Caution should be taken when interpreting data with a non-clinical individual because the test was developed on a psychiatric population. Given the success of all of Beck's tests, the BAI will probably be considered a useful addition to the growing number of clinical anxiety measures.[1]

\* \* \*

**Title:** Beck Depression Inventory-II

**Author:** Beck, Aaron T.; Steer, Robert A.; Brown, Gregory K.

**Purpose:** to assess symptoms of depressive disorders

**Acronym:** BDI-II
**Publisher:** PsychCorp, A brand of Harcourt Assessment, Inc.
**Publisher address:** PsychCorp, A brand of Harcourt Assessment, Inc., 19500 Bulverde Road, San Antonio, TX 78259; Telephone: 800-211-8378; FAX: 800-232-1223; E-mail: customer_care@harcourt.com; Web: www.PsychCorp.com

The original Beck Depression Inventory (BDI) was developed by Beck and his associates in 1961. The BDI-II is based on that original test. It is a well-known self-report inventory that evaluates the severity of depression in adolescents and adults. The current edition assesses 21 symptoms and attitudes that are rated on a 4-point scale of severity. Those taking the BDI-II are asked to rate the items according to how they have felt the past two weeks including the day on which the test is taken. The items cover cognitive, affective, somatic, and vegetative dimensions of depression. The BDI-II usually takes no more than 15 minutes for total administration. The interpretation is based on total score, which may range from 0 to 63 and derived from simply summing the ratings given by the individual on all items.

Although the BDI-II is not considered a diagnostic instrument but simple a screening instrument for depression, the test identifies symptoms of depression according to DSM IV criteria. It is considered a good screening instrument for normal populations. It is well accepted and commonly used by clinicians. Although practitioners have found the BDI useful in other context, the test authors are careful to not endorse the use of the BDI-II for purposes other than for which it was developed.

Special attention is often given to Item 2 of the BDI-II (Pessimism/Hopelessness) and item 9 (Suicide Ideation) are often viewed as clinically relevant indicators. With this new edition, improved reliability is reported. The authors have tried to replace some of the older items such as weight loss, change in body image, and somatic preoccupation with more relevant symptom items.

The BDI-II is considered one of the most widely used instruments for detecting depression. It is now more sensitive to the DSM IV criteria including assessing symptoms for over a two-week period. The BDI-II is used in both inpatient and outpatient settings.[1]

*   *   *

**Title:** Beck Hopelessness Scale [Revised]
**Author:** Beck, Aaron T.; Steer, Robert A.
**Purpose:** to measure negative attitudes about the future (pessimism)
**Acronym:** BHS
**Publisher:** PsychCorp, A brand of Harcourt Assessment, Inc.
**Publisher address:** PsychCorp, A brand of Harcourt Assessment, Inc., 19500 Bulverde Road, San Antonio, TX 78259; Telephone: 800-211-8378; FAX: 800-232-1223; E-mail: customer_care@harcourt.com; Web: www.PsychCorp.com

The Beck Hopelessness Scale (BHS) is a test that evolved out of the Beck Depression Inventory of 1961. It is a 20-item self-report test for evaluating hopelessness, particularly as it relates to the risk of suicide. Hopelessness is considered a significant predictor of suicidology. Depression alone with symptoms of vegetativeness are not well correlated with suicidology, however, hopelessness is usually part of depression and when partialled out, it does help predict the risk of suicide. For these reasons, the BHS is unique and considered a valuable compliment to any measures of depression.

The BHS is by far a better predictor of suicide risk than the general evaluation of depression in the Beck Depression Inventory, however, more research needs to be conducted concerning the construct of hopelessness and its direct relationship to suicidality.

Within the context of adoption and foster parenting issues, hopelessness and pessimism may need to be considered differently than in the general population. The BHS may offer helpful information but should not be considered a strong diagnostic tool for this purpose.[1]

* * *

**Title:** Beck Scale for Suicide Ideation
**Author:** Beck, Aaron T.; Steer, Robert A.
**Purpose:** To detect suicidal ideation in adults and adolescents
**Acronym:** BSS
**Publisher:** PsychCorp, A brand of Harcourt Assessment, Inc.
**Publisher address:** PsychCorp, A brand of Harcourt Assessment, Inc., 19500 Bulverde Road, San Antonio, TX 78259; Telephone: 800-211-8378; FAX: 800-232-1223; E-mail: customer_care@harcourt.com; Web: www.PsychCorp.com

The Beck Scale for Suicide Ideation (BSS) is a 21-item test that was developed as a self-administered variation of the earlier Scale for Suicidal Ideation. The BSS is considered to be well constructed, easy to administer, and acceptable levels of internal consistency. The test is appropriate for use with English-speaking populations of average intelligence with a normative sample of primarily adults.

The test's clinical applicability is probably appropriate for psychiatric, psychological, and allied health settings. The BSS is a well-designed test that is time-efficient and popular.

Each item contains three statements, graded in intensity from 0 to 2. Part One evaluates the patient's attitudes toward wish to "Live or Die, Reasons for Living or Dying, and Suicide Attempt. Part Two screens the suicidal ideation and reactions to those thoughts.

It measures frequency, duration, and acceptance of suicide ideation; control over suicide ideation; and the deterrents and reasons for suicide are evaluated. Part Three asks about previous suicide attempts and the seriousness of intent to die during the last suicide attempt.

The BSS is considered a valuable tool in assessing suicide risk. Easy to administer and good validity and reliability help explain why the instrument is frequently used. Again, this test may be used as a part of a larger assessment utilizing several of Beck's test to combine information into a comprehensive profile.[1]

**Title**: Hamilton Depression Inventory
**Authors**: Reynolds, William M.; Kobak, Kenneth A.
**Purpose**: evaluate the severity of depressive symptomatology
**Publisher**: Psychological Assessment Resources, Inc.
**Publisher Address**: Psychological Assessment Resources, Inc., 16204 N. Florida Ave., Lutz, FL 33549-8119.

The Hamilton Depression Inventory is the successor to the Hamilton Depression Rating Scale of the sixties. The original 17 items of the HDRS are still embedded within the HDI; however, new items have also been added. The additional items seem to include more symptoms relevant to depression than some of the other tests available. However, reviewers feel that some of the various assessed by the HDI may be symptomatic of many disorders and hardly specific to depression. Sometimes multiple questions are used to assess a specific symptom. Intensity, frequency, duration, and latency are often explored concerning a significant symptom of depression.

The HDI offers sound psychometric properties with validity and reliability considered good. Administration usually takes from 10 to 15 minutes and the test is easy to hand score. Raw scores are used to determine T-scores and percentile. The manual offers interpretation of the scales with case examples. The manual also provides demographic information concerning the norms test sample. The HDI correlates well with other similar measures. Data gathered from the HDI should not be used in isolation for making adoptive placement decisions. [1]

**Title**:  Revised Hamilton Rating Scale for Depression
**Author**:  W. L. Warren
**Purpose**:  Designed as a clinician-rated scale for evaluating individuals already diagnosed with depressive illness.
**Publisher**: Western Psychological Services
**Publisher Address**: Western Psychological Services, 12031 Wilshire Blvd., Los Angeles, CA  90025-1251.

\* \* \*

**Title:** Reynolds Depression Screening Inventory
**Author:** Reynolds, William M.; Kobak, Kenneth A.
**Purpose:** to measure the severity of depressive symptoms
**Acronym:** RDSI
**Publisher:** Psychological Assessment Resources, Inc.

**Publisher address:** Psychological Assessment Resources, Inc., 16204 N. Florida Avenue, Lutz, FL 33549-8119; Telephone: 800-331-8378; FAX: 800-727-9329; E-mail: custsupp@parinc.com; Web: www.parinc.com

The Reynolds Depression Screening Inventory (RDSI) is a revision of the classic Hamilton Depression Rating Scale. It is used to provide a brief screening for the severity of current depressive symptoms. It is not intended to provide predictive information or to determine if the respondent meets DSM criteria for a diagnosis. The RDSI contains 19 items and administration usually takes from 5 to 10 minutes. The test evaluates moods, cognitive, somatic, neuro-vegetative, psychomotor, and interpersonal areas of depressive symptomatology.

Any mental health professional using the RDSI will find clear instructions for administration and scoring in the accompanying manual. There are built-in validity checks based on unusual or inconsistent response patterns. There are several critical items that would suggest follow-up with scores in a certain direction. The administration yields raw scores which the manual provides tables for conversion to T-scores and percentile ranks. Clinical relevance for depressive symptoms and recommendations for evaluations and considerations for treatment is discussed in the manual.[1]

\* \* \*

**Title:** Drug Use Questionnaire
**Author:** Skinner, Harvey A.
**Purpose:** to assess potential involvement with drugs
**Acronym:** DAST-20
**Publisher:** Centre for Addiction and Mental Health [Canada]
**Publisher address:** Centre for Addiction and Mental Health, Marketing Services, 33 Russell Street, Toronto, Ontario M5S 2S1, Canada; Telephone: 416-595-6059; FAX: 416-593-4694; E-mail: marketing@camh.net; Web: www.camh.net

The Drug Use Questionnaire (DAST-20) is a very quick screening test that assesses possible drug usage. This 20-item yes-no response, single score inventory derived from an earlier 28-item version, the Drug Abuse Screening Test developed by Skinner in 1982. It primarily focuses on features of drug dependence such as inability to stop using drugs, withdrawal symptoms, and several other relating behaviors associated with the use or abuse of prescribed, over-the-counter and illicit drugs. The DAST-20 may serve a useful purpose; however, psychometric information is not easily available. More details should be sought before using this instrument with confidence.[1]

**Title:** State Trait-Depression Adjective Check Lists
**Author:** Lubin, Bernard
**Purpose:** measures state and trait depression mood and feelings
**Acronym:** ST-DACL
**Publisher:** EdITS/Educational and Industrial Testing Service
**Publisher address:** EdITS/Educational and Industrial Testing Service, P.O. Box 7234, San Diego, CA 92167

The State Trait Depression Adjective Checklists (ST-DACL) is easy to administer and score. Administration is straightforward and the ST-DACL can be a self-administered or group-administered in less than 5 minutes. The examiner can usually score and develop the profile in another 5 minutes. To administer both the State-Mood and Trait-Mood lists can be accomplished in less than 10 to 15 minutes. The manual offers easy to follow instructions for either self or group administrations.

The ST-DACL was developed by item analysis conducting on a pool of 171 adjectives from the initial responses of 95 neuropsychiatric patients previously diagnosed as markedly or severely depressed. The instructions for the ST-DACL Trait-Mood lists instruct the individual to check the words that describe how you "generally" feel, instead of evaluating the individual's feeling simply on the day of the test.

The ST-DACL is applicable to a broad age range and diversity of clientele including college students, normal and depressed adults, and elderly. The test is appropriate for use with ages 18 to 89 years. The State-Mood lists have been thoroughly researched and the lists are relatively new, however, the levels of validity offered by the author is believed to support the use of this instrument as a simple screening instrument. Any clinical applications should be made only in conjunction with other measures.

Reviewer's Reference:
Petzel, T.P. (1985). Depression Adjective Checklists. In D. J. Keyser & R.C. Sweetland (eds.), *Test Critiques* (vol. III. Pp. 215-220). Kansas City, MO: Westport.[1]

\* \* \*

**Title:** Substance Abuse Subtle Screening Inventory-3 (The)
**Author:** Miller, Glenn A.
**Purpose:** to identify probability of having a substance dependence disorder
**Acronym:** SASSI-3
**Publisher:** SASSI Institute (The)
**Publisher address:** The SASSI Institute, 201 Camelot Lane, Springville, IN 47462; Telephone: 800-726-0526; FAX: 800-546-7995; E-mail: sassi@sassi.com; Web: WWW.SASSI.COM

The Substance Abuse Subtle Screening Inventory-3 (SASSI-3) is a very simple, quick to administer inventory designed to make inferences about substance dependence disorder. Respondents may make reference to different time frames including their entire life, the past 6 months, the 6 months before, or the 6 months since. The test is usually completed in less than 2 minutes.

The nine subtests evaluated in the instrument are: Face Valid Alcohol, Face Valid Other Drugs, Symptoms, Obvious Attributes, Subtle

Attributes, Defensiveness, Supplemental Addiction Measure, Family vs. Controls, and Correctional.

The scores yield a validity scale, five clinical scales, and two ancillary scales. There are three clinical scales that assess the presence of substance abuse. The last uses 12 - 14 questions to identify the extent of alcohol and/ or drug use.[1]

# Chapter 21

## Ruling Out Major Pathology

The research is clear that mental problems, including personality disorders, can greatly affect children and the family dynamics. It may seem unfair, but those who have been diagnosed with a psychotic or a severe personality disorder would be disqualified for a foster or adoptive placement because parents who suffer from these disorders are more likely to put their children at risk. These children may be forced to "take care" of the parent, to suffer neglect and be left without the parental guidance and emotional support they need.

Parents who suffer from certain personality disorders are often blamed for contributing to their children's difficulties in developing strong relationships, trust, self assurance and other crucial characteristics. The most common personality disorder, affecting about six million Americans, is borderline personality disorder. Children of mothers who have borderline personality disorder face a confusing world of contradictions. Until about age three, a child is unable to separate what they believe from what their mother believes.

An emotionally unstable mother who exhibits volatile, self-destructive behaviors in the presence of a young daughter creates a false, but powerful reality for her. The child is trapped in the emotional labyrinth of their relationship. Children who remain in the painfully fragmented, intense, and unpredictable environment often suffer devastating consequences. Infants of borderline mothers are typically unable to develop a secure attachment. They are at a higher risk of becoming aggressive, impulsive, oppositional, depressed and violent. Research has suggested that these children are eventually diagnosed with borderline personality disorder more often than their peers.[1]

246

The influence of parents who have any of a large array of personality disorders can severely alter the emotional development of their children. A histrionic mother whose dramatically exaggerated display of emotions, provocative sexual behaviors and high level of suggestibility, is unable to provide an appropriate role model for her impressionable children. A narcissistic father rarely shows his child empathy. He is often impatient with the child's shortcomings, is arrogant and denigrates the child. Often his child feels insecure, inferior and has low self-esteem.

Life long struggles are created by the traumatic effects of living with a parent with an emotionally damaging personality. Often these effects are subtle and hard to detect. Having a better understanding of applicants' personalities will equip the screener with valuable insight into the emotional environment to which a child could be exposed. An agency will find that a psychological assessment will provide the insights and prognostic data needed.

Some of the popular tests used to describe personalities, detect possible disorders and identify more severe pathology are described below.

**Title:** Clark-Beck Obsessive-Compulsive Inventory
**Author:** Clark, David A.; Beck, Aaron T.
**Purpose**: to provide a self-report screening for obsessive and compulsive symptoms
**Acronym:** CBOCI
**Publisher:** PsychCorp, A brand of Harcourt Assessment, Inc.
**Publisher address:** PsychCorp, A brand of Harcourt Assessment, Inc., 19500 Bulverde Road, San Antonio, TX 78259; Telephone: 800-211-8378; FAX: 800-232-1223; E-mail: customer_care@harcourt.com; Web: www.PsychCorp.com

The Clark-Beck Obsessive Compulsive Inventory (CPOCI) is a screening instrument used to measure obsessive and compulsive symptoms. The screening inventory is meant to be a compliment to the existing Beck measures. This screening instrument evaluates 25 symptoms of which 14 reflect obsessive symptoms and 11 compulsive symptoms. It usually takes approximately 10 to 15 minutes for most individuals to complete the screening; however, some individuals may take up to 30 minutes or more. The screening in instrument is close associated with the DSM IV Diagnostic criteria. The two subscale scores and a total score are calculated and interpreted with regard to non-clinical, mild, moderate, or severe clinical symptomatology.

An individual suspected of obsessive compulsive disorder should find the traditional Likert scales to be relatively non-threatening. An individual is expected to be able to read at least the eight-grade level to respond appropriately. The person being examined is instructed to complete the questionnaire in reference to their primary obsession or compulsion.

The standardization sample was overwhelmingly representative of young, single, white individuals. Reliability and validity are considered good. The authors of the CBOCI Screening Inventory warn that patient scores within the mild to moderate range may be difficult to interpret. In the event that the Clark-Beck Obsessive-Compulsive Inventory is used in assessing applicants for adoptive or foster care placement, care must be given to not use these test results in dependent of other assessment information.

1

*   *   *

**Title:** Hare Psychopathy Checklist: Screening Version
**Author:** Hart, S. D.; Cox, D. N.; Hare, R. D.
**Purpose:** To screen for psychopathy in forensic and non-forensic settings.
**Acronym:** PCL:SV
**Publisher:** Multi-Health Systems, Inc.
**Publisher address:** Multi-Health Systems, Inc., P.O. Box 950, North Tonawanda, NY 14120-0950; Telephone: 416-492-2627 or

800-456-3003; FAX: 416-492-3343 or 888-540-4484; E-mail: CUSTOMERSERVICE@MHS.COM; Web: www.mhs.com

The Hare Psychopathy Checklist: Screening Version (PCL:SD) is an instrument used to evaluate the presence of psychopathology in adults. The test was developed to shorten the format of the earlier PCL-Revised which often took over three hours to administer. This shortened version is primarily used to screen individuals in order to rule out psychopathology or to determine a need for more evaluation. The PCL: SD focuses on egocentric approaches to interpersonal relationships, manipulative behaviors, callousness, impulsivity, irresponsibility, and antisocial behaviors. The administration of the screening version usually takes less than one hour but does not include taking a case history of scoring the test.

The test manual describes good validity and reliability data. The manual discusses the semi-structured clinical interview format of the test. The rater inquires about the individual's academic achievement, behavior in school, employment history, patterns of interpersonal relationships, and involvement with the legal system. With collateral information and the interview data, the psychologist then decides how closely the individual matches a proto type for a specific category on the PCL. Although much of the decisions are considered subjective, the inner rater reliability data is considered good.

As with other tests, caution must be given to reaching a firm diagnosis or making speculative statements solely based on this test. Further, the test had limited numbers of minorities represented in the sample. Warning is also given in over-interrupting any scores falling in the "ambiguous" range. In general, the PCL may be a beneficial component of an overall assessment. [1]

\*　　\*　　\*

**Title:** Measures of Affiliative Tendency and Sensitivity to Rejection
**Author:** Mehrabian, Albert
**Purpose:** to measure social skills conducive to social exchanges and

submissiveness

**Publisher:** Mehrabian, Albert (the author)

**Publisher address:** Albert Mehrabian, Ph.D., 1130 Alta Mesa Road, Monterey, CA 93940; Telephone: 831-649-5710; E-mail: am@kaaj.com; Web: www.kaaj.com/psych/scales

The Measures of Affiliative Tendency and Sensitivity to Rejection Scales (MAFF and MSR) are brief self report measures that can be administered to groups or individuals. The MAFF has 26 items and the MSR has 24; that the individual responds using a 9-point Likert scale, indicating level of agreement or disagreement with each of the statements presented.

The norms for both measures were based on data from the mid 70's. No information about the gender and ethnic composition or socioeconomic status is reported in the test information. The MAFF and the MSR measures have adequate reliability and validity, making them helpful in the study of personality traits.

The Measures of Affiliative Tendency and Sensitivity to Rejection scales are self-report questionnaires designed by Mehrabian to measure traits related to social skills. The 26-item Affiliative Tendency Scale (MAFF) contains 13 positively worded and 13 negatively worded items; a similar division occurs with the 24-item Sensitivity to Rejection Scale (MSR). The author defines affiliative persons as being friendly, skillful in dealing with people and considered social. The author defines a sensitive person as a person who lacks controls or leadership in social interactions.

Although it is advised to use these measures with caution a clinician may feel comfortable with the scores obtained.[1]

$$* \quad * \quad *$$

**Title:** Millon Clinical Multiaxial Inventory-III [Manual Second Edition]

**Author:** Millon, Theodore; Davis, Roger; Millon, Carrie

**Purpose: measure ar**eas of personality disorders and clinical

syndromes.
**Acronym:** MCMI-III
**Publisher:** Pearson Assessments
**Publisher address:** Pearson Assessments, 5601 Green Valley Drive, Bloomington, MN 55437.

The Million Clinical Multiaxial Inventory- III was (MCMI-III) designed to measure personality disorders as defined by the categories of clinical syndromes in the DSM-IV. The Millon Clinical Multiaxial Inventory-III (MCMI-III) is a 175-item true-false self-report inventory for the assessment of psychopathology. This test is used in more research than any other personality test except MMPI and the Rorscharch.

The MMPI-2 is considered the MCMI-III's main competitor. A reviewer stated that the MCMI is considered to have some advantages over the MMPI-2 in that it clearer and more comprehensive in its assessment of the personality dimensions. Compared with other instruments designed to measure personality traits, the MCMI-III is considered a clinical measure. It is routinely used by itself as a screening instrument or as part of a test battery.

The MCMI-III is among the most popular self-report instruments for the assessment of personality disorders. It is shorter than the MMPI-2 but is considered as reliable and valid as the MMPI-2. The MCMI-III is often used alone, but at times it is used in conjunction with other tests. Scale elevations are considered evidence to be considered foe possible diagnosis only after a systematic interview and other data is gather.[1]

✳ ✳ ✳

**Title:** Minnesota Multiphasic Personality Inventory-2
**Author:** Butcher, James N.; Dahlstrom, W. Grant; Graham, John R.; Tellegen, Auke; Kaemmer, Beverly
**Purpose:**to assess personality and emotional disorders
**Acronym:** MMPI-2
**Publisher:** University of Minnesota Press; distributed by NCS

Assessments [Minnetonka]

**Publisher address:** University of Minnesota Press, Test Division, Mill Place, Suite 290, 111 Third Avenue South, Minneapolis, MN 55401-2520; NCS Assessments, Sales Department, 5605 Green Circle Drive, Minnetonka, MN 55343

The Minnesota Multiphasic Personality Inventory-2 (MMPI-2) is straightforward and easy test who may be administered by an appropriately trained psychometrist or psychological assistant. The MMPI-2 is a revision of an older version. The individual must read descriptions and determine which of two possibilities best fit his feelings. Test completion time is typically about 90 minutes, though less intelligent patients and those with other complicating factors may take two hours or more. Evaluators are warned to consider test results obtained in less than 60 minutes should be evaluated with possible suspicion. The test is usually completed in one session; however, more than one session may be necessary. Marginal reading ability and/or with certain psychiatric conditions, such as attention deficit disorder, mania, or severe depression tend to slow the testing. The MMPI-2 is recommended for individuals who are at least 18 years of age or older. The test's reading level is at about eighth grade level, with most items ranging from sixth to eight grade level.

Although Hispanics and Asian Americans may be slightly under represented, standardization is consistent with census data with regard to general ethnic composition. The standardization sample for the MMPI-2 consisted of individuals between the ages of 18 and 90 from seven states.

Important changes have occurred with the revision, there are no repeat items on the revision and many items have be re-written for clarity and to get rid if outdated terms.

Some of the non-scored, objectionable issues were taken out and replaced with items dealing with social situations such as alcohol and drug usage. With the changes, the cutoff score has been changed from a T of 70 to 65.

Elevations in scales offer valuable data about the individual. Prognostic statements may be made based on elevations in clinical scales, combinations in code types and elevations of specialized scales.

The controversial issue of racial bias in the MMPI remains unresolved. Numerous methodological difficulties are apparent in some of the investigations using the MMPI-2. Although black-white differences on the MMPI may be statistically significantly, they have limited clinical applications because of the small mean differences.

Several issues need to .be emphasized before attempting to interpret an MMPI-2 profile. It is recommended by the authors that the MMPI-2 never be interpreted in a complete vacuum. The clinician must seek additional data about the person before making strong statements solely based on the test results. It is important to seek information on a wide range of demographic data due to the potential influence on the test profile. These data include age, education, occupation, race, socioeconomic status, religion, marital status, and cultural background. A comprehensive knowledge of psycho pathology is necessary to interpret the MMPI-2. Scoring and interpreting the MMPI-2 is a time consuming process. Computer scoring and interpretive reports are available and often recommend for clinical who do not use the test very often

The MMPI-2 continues to be a valuable tool for the skilled clinician who has mastered its intricacies and is familiar with the criticisms.[1]

**Title:** Personality Assessment Inventory

**Author:** Morey, Leslie C.

**Purpose:** to screen for psychopathology

**Acronym:** PAI

**Publisher:** Psychological Assessment Resources, Inc.

**Publisher address:** Psychological Assessment Resources, Inc., 16204 N. Florida Avenue, Lutz, FL 33549-8119; Telephone: 800-331-8378; FAX: 800-727-9329; E-mail: custsupp@parinc.com; Web: www.parinc.com

The Personality Assessment Inventory (PAI) has been developed as a multidimensional alternative to the Minnesota Multiphasic Personality Inventory (MMPI) for assessing abnormal personality traits. The PAI is a self-report questionnaire consisting of 344 items. It is intended to be used as a screening instrument to help diagnosis and design treatment plans for psychopathology. A short form of 160 items is available, but the 22 scales have insufficient items to achieve adequate reliability.

Only small to moderate coefficients are found when the PAI is correlated with several other personality instruments. A positive for the PAI is that it includes current items, and avoids colloquial and slang expressions. There is criticism considered potentially bias on gender, ethnic, economic, and religious.

The PAI is designed for adults with a fourth grade reading level. The PAI uses a 4-point Likert type response format (i.e., false, not at all true, slightly true, mainly true, or very true). The inventory is available in English, Spanish, and audiotape versions.

Most reviewers feel that the PAI is a helpful inventory. The manual contains a good discussion on the scale development, reliability, and validity data. It is considered to be a worthy competitor to the MMPI-2, which remains the dominant objective personality inventory.[1]

$$* \quad * \quad *$$

**Title:** Rorschach
**Author:** Rorschach, Hermann
**Purpose:** A projective technique for clinical assessment and diagnosis
**Publisher:** Hogrefe & Huber Publishers
**Publisher address:** Hogrefe & Huber Publishers, 875 Massachusetts Avenue, 7th Floor, Cambridge, MA 02139; Telephone: 866-823-4726; FAX: 617-354-6875; Email: info@hhpub.com; Web: www.hhpub.com

The Rorschach, sometimes considered synonymous with psychological testing, is one of the most widely known psychological instruments and continues to peak the interest of the public. It is an old and widely used personality test that psychologists use with individuals as young as 5 years old and with adults of any age. It uses 10 cards with inkblots on them, 5 of which are black and gray and the other 5 have colors as well. All the cards have a white background.

The Rorschach is designed to present ambiguous visual presentations that are thought to evoke responses that suggest how a person experiences and handles real-life situations. Scoring and interpretations are determined based on elements such as location, the part of the blot used, movement, the use of color and texture. Debates over scoring and proper scoring and interpretations have been controversial from the beginning. The Exner Scoring System has been considered the most accurate and comprehensive; however, it too has been sorely criticized.

The mysterious nature of the Rorschach continues to fascinate the public. Only well trained clinicians should administer, score or interpret the test. Although subjective, it is considered an excellent test to use when problem-solving capabilities, emotional operations, interpersonal functioning and self-concept are of concern.[1]

\*   \*   \*

**Title:** Rotter Incomplete Sentences Blank, Second Edition
**Author:** Rotter, Julian B.; Lah, Michael I.; Rafferty, Janet E.
**Purpose:** to evaluate overall adjustment
**Acronym:** RISB
**Publisher:** PsychCorp, A brand of Harcourt Assessment, Inc.
**Publisher address:** PsychCorp, A brand of Harcourt Assessment, Inc., 19500 Bulverde Road, San Antonio, TX 78259; Telephone: 800-211-8378; FAX: 800-232-1223; E-mail: customer_care@harcourt.com; Web: www.PsychCorp.com

The Rotter Incomplete Sentences Blank (RISB) is a projective measure of maladjustment utilizing a semi-objective scoring system. The RISB, like its predecessor presents short sentences stems to the individual for him to complete the thought. Responses are rated on a 7-point ordinal scale with the higher scores suggesting greater maladjustment. Scoring considers omissions and incomplete responses, conflict responses, positive responses, and neutral responses. Generally scores range from about 80 to 205, with a possibility of 0 – 240.

Scoring should only be attempted by a skilled clinician who is cognizant of personality dynamics. Often clinicians score qualitatively for projected motivational needs; however, such interpretations are considered unreliable.

The RISM claims good face validity, therefore, caution is offered because responses are amenable to distortion, depending on the lack of self-insight, or conscious and unconscious motives of the respondent.[1]

\* \* \*

**Title:** Six Factor Personality Questionnaire
**Author:** Jackson, Douglas N.; Paunonen, Sampo V.; Tremblay, Paul F.
**Purpose:** to measure personality on six dimensions
**Acronym:** SFPQ
**Publisher:** Sigma Assessment Systems, Inc.
**Publisher address:** Sigma Assessment Systems, Inc., 511 Fort Street, Suite 435, P.O. Box 610984, Port Huron, MI 48061-0984; Telephone: 800-265-1285; FAX: 800-361-9411; E-mail: SIGMA@sigmaassessmentsystems.com; Web: www.sigmaassessmentsystems.com

The Six Factor Personality Questionnaire (SFPQ) is a test that measure personality according to a six dimension theoretical format. The six areas being examined are: Extraversion, Agreeableness, Independence, Openness to Experience, Methodicalness, and Industriousness. It consists of 108 items to which the individual respond using a 5-point Likert scale from *strongly agree* to *strongly disagree*. The individual marks on a carbonless answer sheet. The test typically takes only 20 minutes to complete.

It is considered short and concise and easy to understand. Reviewers agree that it does offer information on a broad range of personality constructs. Reading level of at about fifth grade, and the SFPQ can be administered on the computer by paper-and-pencil.It is considered fairly simple to take and the individual being tested seldom report feeling overly taxed.

The SFPQ offers the field of personality assessment that is practical in a variety of settings. It is considered appropriate for the use with individuals across a wide range of ages and backgrounds. In general, it is easy to understand and interpret.[1]

**Title:** Sixteen Personality Factor Questionnaire, Fifth Edition
**Author:** Cattell, Raymond B.; Cattell, A. Karen S.; Cattell, Heather E. P.
**Purpose:** to measure personality traits
**Acronym:** 16PF
**Publisher:** Institute for Personality and Ability Testing, Inc. (IPAT)
**Publisher address:** Institute for Personality and Ability Testing, Inc. (IPAT), P.O. Box 1188, Champaign, IL 61824-1188; Telephone: 217-352-4739; FAX: 217-352-9674; E-mail: custserv@ipat.com; Web: www.ipat.com

The Sixteenth Personality Factor Questionnaire, Fifth Edition (16PF) is an evaluation of personality that is primarily designed to b e used with normal adults with no psychiatric diagnoses. The 16PF is often administered to individuals, but it may be given to groups. It is either hand scored or computer scored.

The sixteen factors assessed are: Warmth vs Reserved; Abstract Reasoning vs Concrete Reasoning; Emotional Stable vs Reactive; Dominant vs Deferential; Lively vs Serious; Rule Conscience vs Expedient; Socially Bold vs Shy; Sensitive vs Utilitarian; Vigilant vs Trusting; Abstracted vs Grounded; Passive vs Self Assured; Open to

Change vs Traditional; Self-Reliant vs Group-Oriented; Perfectionist vs Tolerates Disorder; and Tense vs Relaxed. There are 5 global scores: Extraverted vs Introverted; High Anxiety vs Low Anxiety; Tough Minded vs Receptive; Independent vs Accommodating; and Self-Controlled vs Unrestrained. The 16PF yields 3 response style indices: Impression Management; Infrequency and Acquiescence. The test is easy to read at a fifth grade reading level.

The 16 PF interpretations of the results is considered complex. There are two computer-generated reports, the Basic Interpretive Report and Basic Score Report available and recommended for the less sophisticated user. The 16PF has stood the test of time and offers respectable psychometric data. The test is considered a valuable tool for clinicians who want more insight into their client's personality. [1]

\* \* \*

**Title:** Structured Interview for the Five-Factor Model of Personality
**Author:** Trull, Timothy; Widiger, Thomas A.
**Purpose:** to assess personality in a five factor format
**Acronym:** SIFFM
**Publisher:** Psychological Assessment Resources, Inc.
**Publisher address:** Psychological Assessment Resources, Inc., 16204 N. Florida Avenue, Lutz, FL 33549-8119; Telephone: 800-331-8378; FAX: 800-727-9329; E-mail: custsupp@parinc.com; Web: www.parinc.com

The Structured Interview for the Five-Model of Personality (SIFFM) is a structured interview between clinician and a respondent. The 120 items are designed to measure a person's personality according to a five factor model including: Neuroticism (vs. Emotional Stability), Extroversion (vs. Introversion), Openness to Experience (vs. Closedness

258

to Experience), Agreeableness (vs. Antagonism), and Conscientiousness (vs. Negligence).

The SIFFM closely follows the criteria for Axis II (personality) DSM disorders. The instrument may be useful for assessing normal and maladaptive personality patterns in both clinical and research settings. The interview format has found popularity among clinicians as an alternative to typical paper-and-pencil administrations. Graduate training on the administration of the SIFFM is not necessary; however, an understanding of psychopathology, personality, and structure interviewing is needed.

Although lacking in psychometric data, the potential is still considered good. The SIFFM is based in part, on the Revised NEO Personality Inventory. The major difference is in the interview format of the SIFFA and the opportunity to follow-up with questions for clarification. [1]

\* \* \*

**Title:** Tennessee Self-Concept Scale, Second Edition
**Author:** Fitts, William H.; Warren, W. L.
**Purpose:** Designed as a multidimensional self-concept assessment instrument.
**Acronym:** TSCS: 2
**Publisher:** Western Psychological Services
**Publisher address:** Western Psychological Services, 12031 Wilshire Blvd., Los Angeles, CA 90025-1251; Telephone: 310-478-2061; FAX: 310-478-7838; Web: www.wpspublish.com


The Tennessee Self-Concept Scale (TSCS-2) is an instrument that has both an adult and child form. The adult form is an 82-item assessment takes from 10 to 20 minutes to complete and about 10 minutes to score. There is a 20-item short form with only a total score calculated.

The TSCS-2 is based on six scales including: Physical, Moral, Personal, Family, Social, and a new Academic/Work. The six scales result in Total and Conflict scores. The overall goal of the evaluation is to assess self-view.

The manual offers a complete description on the development, administration, scoring, interpretation, restandardization, and psychometric properties. The TSCS-2 has maintained its popularity, especially since the revision has simplified the scoring and expanded the interpretation.[1]

* * *

**Title:** Thematic Apperception Test
**Author:** Murray, Henry A.
**Purpose**: is to assess various aspects of personality
**Acronym:** TAT
**Note:** This test was last reviewed in the Eighth Mental Measurements Yearbook (1978). Electronic access to this review is not available.
**Publisher:** Harvard University Press
**Publisher address:** Harvard University Press, 79 Garden Street, Cambridge, MA 02138

The Thematic Apperception Test (TAT) is a test made up of 31 pictures, some specific to adult females and males, others may be used by either. The TAT also includes cards for boys and girls from 7-14 years. The Thematic Apperception Test (TAT) was developed by Henry Murray in 1938 to assess personality by eliciting fantasy as a result of projecting past experience and present needs in response to ambiguous picture stimuli. The TAT uses a story telling format to elicit fantasy as a result of projecting past experiences and present needs in response to ambiguous picture stimuli. The first 10 cards evoked everyday situations while the second 10 could provide more unusual, dramatic, and bizarre fantasy.

Directions including asking the respondent to tell a story that includes describing the cards, explaining what the characters are doing, what they have done in the past or what led up to the situation, and what they may do in the future. The examiner may request information on feelings and thoughts of the characters along with a request for an outcome. Recording responses verbatim is used as much as possible.

The TAT is considered very hard to interpret and reports insufficient validity. There is an absence of consensual scoring. The TAT is not recommended to be used alone. Even formal training for use of the TAT is generally inadequate. TAT now obsolete by many.[1]

# Chapter 22

## Measuring Levels of Cognitive Function

In the screening process there may be some concern about the intellectual abilities of the applicant. Memory, specific academic skills or other cognitive concerns may warrant a formal evaluation. A parent's intellectual and academic abilities are very important. Parents are expected to be the support system for their children. They are expected to be the homework tutor and to remember all the facts and figures they learned in grade school. As a chauffer, they must juggle their own schedules to be available to transport their children from one venue to the next. Although millions of parents with low-average-to-borderline intelligence function very well as parents, they usually encounter more social challenges than parents that score higher.

Advocates for individuals with developmental disabilities, including mental retardation, have made great progress in the last few years convincing the public that these parents can provide adequate care for children. Often their family and social services agencies help by providing shadow assistance. Respecting the great strides in promoting the concept of keeping the biological children of cognitively challenged families together, adoption and foster care agencies typically would not place children in these homes.

Sometimes intelligent adults suffer diseases, injuries or early onset of neurological disorders that presents as memory or other cognitive deficits. Screeners should be alert to any memory problems displayed by an applicant. Early signs of dementia and other disabling disorders are associated with memory deficits. Depending on the specific diagnosis and prognosis, placement decisions will be affected.

Agencies must address cognitive issues as a part of the overall evaluation process. A referral for a psychological assessment is the best way to approach any doubts about cognitive deficits. The following tests are considered the leading instruments:

**Title:** Wechsler Adult Intelligence Scale-Third Edition
**Author:** Wechsler, David
**Purpose:** to assess the intellectual ability of adults
**Acronym:** WAIS-III
**Publisher:** PsychCorp, A brand of Harcourt Assessment, Inc.
**Publisher address:** PsychCorp, A brand of Harcourt Assessment, Inc., 19500 Bulverde Road, San Antonio, TX 78259; Telephone: 800-211-8378; FAX: 800-232-1223; E-mail: customer_care@harcourt.com; Web: www.PsychCorp.com

The Wechsler Adult Intelligence Scale (WAIS-III) is an individually administered test that evaluates intelligence. It consists of a series of various subtests that are scored individually and then collectively determines a Verbal and Performance Score, along with a Full Scale IQ score. This third edition of the Wechsler Adult Intelligence Scale retains the best features of the classic WAIS and WAIS-R. It also incorporates new scores that link to other Wechsler tests (memory).

The third edition has updated artwork. Although tests are still timed and it is important to evaluate how the examinee deal with the pressure of time; the timing of some of the subtests is now de-emphasized and processing speed will not confound other attributes measured by the subtests. The WAIS-III extends the intelligence quotient band from 45 to 155 points. Evidence suggests that the subtests are reliable.

The Wechsler Scales are typically taught in graduate school and due to the test's complexities, examiners should have received professional training and experience in its use. The full administration takes at least 90 minutes.

The test continues to maintain the high respect it has for many years due to its value in assessing a multitude of verbal and nonverbal skills. Another purpose of the test is the diagnosis of the extent to which neurological and psychiatric disorders may affect mental functioning.[1]

\*   \*   \*

**Title:** Wechsler Abbreviated Scale of Intelligence
**Author:** Psychological Corporation (The)
**Purpose:** to provide a short and reliable measure of intelligence
**Acronym:** WASI
**Publisher:** PsychCorp, A brand of Harcourt Assessment, Inc.
**Publisher address:** PsychCorp, A brand of Harcourt Assessment, Inc., 19500 Bulverde Road, San Antonio, TX 78259; Telephone: 800-211-8378; FAX: 800-232-1223; E-mail: customer_care@harcourt.com; Web: www.PsychCorp.com


The Wechsler Abbreviated Scale of Intelligence (WASI) is an abbreviated test to evaluated intelligence for ages 6 – 89 years. This abbreviated test was derived from the more extensive evaluations that are specific for different age groups. The WASI is a test utilizing only two to four subtests instead of the much more involved assessment. The WAIS is considered a brief, adequate screening instrument. In addition to assessing general, or Full Scale, intelligence, the WASI is also designed to provide estimates of Verbal and Performance intelligence consistent with other Wechsler tests.

An examiner may administer the recommended four subtests in about 30 minutes. The shorter version of the "short version" (WASI) uses only two-subtests (Vocabulary and Matrix Reasoning) and may be administered in about 15 minutes.

The raw scores are converted to T-scores that are converted into IQ scores. The test reports good standardization and adequate reliability and validity for the intended uses. In general, the WASI is considered a valid and reliable estimate of intellectual functioning that is quick to administer.[1]

\*   \*   \*

**Title:** Wechsler Memory Scale III
**Author:** Wechsler, David
**Purpose:** to assess memory functioning
**Acronym:** WMS-III
**Publisher:** PsychCorp, A brand of Harcourt Assessment, Inc.
**Publisher address:** PsychCorp, A brand of Harcourt Assessment, Inc., 19500 Bulverde Road, San Antonio, TX 78259; Telephone: 800-211-8378; FAX: 800-232-1223; E-mail: customer_care@harcourt.com; Web: www.PsychCorp.com

The Wechsler Memory Scales – Third Edition (WMS-III) is a test that evaluates both visual and auditory memory skills. This latest revision of the WMS-III is considered a significant improvement over the earlier versions. The new scale is very different than the older version. Clinicians will need specific training in the WMS-III because of the limited carry over from the former version. The test administration usually takes about 45 to 60 minutes. The scoring report software is considered the best route for scoring and interpretation of the test results. The program allows interpretation of results that will generate four types of reports including Interpretive, Clinical, Client, and Statistical.

The WMS-III manuals provide for more extensive data concerning the reliability and validity then the earlier version; however, it still offers only adequate reliability. Although there are some psychometric concerns the WMS-III remains the choice of tests to evaluate memory skills.[1]

\* \* \*

**Title:** Wechsler Memory Scale-Third Edition Abbreviated
**Author:** Wechsler, David
**Purpose:** to screen auditory and visual memory skills
**Acronym:** WMS-III Abbreviated
**Publisher:** PsychCorp, A brand of Harcourt Assessment, Inc.
**Publisher address:** PsychCorp, A brand of Harcourt Assessment, Inc.,

19500 Bulverde Road, San Antonio, TX 78259; Telephone: 800-211-8378; FAX: 800-232-1223; E-mail: customer_care@harcourt.com; Web: www.PsychCorp.com

The Wechsler Memory Scale-Third Edition Abbreviated (WMS-III Abbreviated) is a shorter version of the WMS III. It is a quick way to evaluate visual and auditory memory with only a few subtests. The administration of the four subtests is straightforward and provides a quick screening of memory skills. Depending on the questions being asked in the referral, the clinical decides whether to administer the short or long version of the WMS. This reliable and valid instrument usually only takes 20 minutes to administer. The test manual is often praised for its clarity and usefulness.[1]

**Title:** Wide Range Achievement Test 3
**Author:** Wilkinson, Gary S.
**Purpose:** to screen reading, spelling, and arithmetic skills
**Acronym:** WRAT3
**Publisher:** Psychological Assessment Resources, Inc.
**Publisher address:** Psychological Assessment Resources, Inc., 16204 N. Florida Avenue, Lutz, FL 33549-8119; Telephone: 800-331-8378; FAX: 800-727-9329; E-mail: custsupp@parinc.com; Web: www.parinc.com

The Wide Range Achievement Test 3 (WRAT3) is a very popular test to screen skills in Reading, Spelling, and Arithmetic for individuals aged 5-74 years. The Reading subtest requires  has 42 words that must be pronounced aloud. Spelling subtest requires the individual to write words as they are dictated by the examiner. There are a possible  40 words to be written depending on the level of the examinee. The Arithmetic subtest includes 40 problems to be completed in a designated time frame.

Criticism is abundant in terms of how well each subtest actually assess the subject matter. The Reading does not include any comprehension. The Spelling and Math portions are thought to be inadequate also. Any claim that the WRAT3 covers skills and knowledge related to "general cognitive ability" is not well supported. It also suffers from insufficient evidence of validity or reliability.

In March, 2006, the new and improved version, the WRAT4, will be available. WRAT4 has adding grade-based norms which in fact, increasing the usefulness of the test in grades K-12. The age-based norms have also bee expanded and now extends to age 94 years in order to assess the basic literacy skills of older adults. The WRAT4 has improved and now evaluates in more depth. The improvements are being praised and it appears that the latest version of the WRAT will continue to be a popular test. [1]

# Chapter 23

## Identifying Personal and Family Conflicts

The marriage relationship, family dynamics and personal stressors are important components to be considered when determining placement decisions. Research suggests that a couple's marital satisfaction is one of the best predictors of successful parenting. There are several tests that can be used to evaluate such relationships. Having a comprehensive understanding of family dynamics, personal and interpersonal relationships can offer an agency information that may be the determining factor in whether a couple is approved for placement for foster children or adoptive children.

At times some of the most important data is not readily available through standard screening interviews. Evaluations that explore marriage satisfaction, conflict resolution skills and defense mechanisms can help formulate a more comprehensive profile of the applicants and help professionals make more accurate inferences about possible family dynamics.

Often applicants already have children their home by birth, adoption or foster placement. During the course of screening an array of issues concerning the other children may surface. Due to the importance of having a very clear picture of what goes on in the prospective home environment, a more in-depth assessment may be warranted.

Unfortunately, some couples attempt to bring a child into the marriage as a means of mending a broken relationship. An agency will find valuable answers and good predictive data through a formal assessment to explore specific areas of conflict.

Some of the tests used in marriage and family psychology are summarized below:

**Title:** Balanced Emotional Empathy Scale (The)
**Author:** Mehrabian, Albert
**Purpose:** to measure one's ability to feel the emotional response of others.
**Acronym:** BEES
**Publisher:** Mehrabian, Albert (the author)
**Publisher address:** Albert Mehrabian, Ph.D., 1130 Alta Mesa Road, Monterey, CA 93940; Telephone: 831-649-5710; E-mail: am@kaaj.com; Web: www.kaaj.com/psych/scales

The Balanced Emotional Empathy Scale (BEES) was primarily designed to assess an individual' ability to vicariously or experience the emotional responses of others. The test dos not emphasize the cognitive aspect of "understanding" another's emotions but to "feel their pain."

The manual suggests that the BEES may be helpful gathering data on the examinee's child-rearing practices, altruism, social skills, and interpersonal effectiveness; however, the manual fails to offer the adequate psychometrics to support such claims. Much of the criticism suggests that empathy would be difficult to measure using a paper-and-pencil format , while others support using this test to evaluate the tendency to have empathetic feelings.[1]

\* \* \*

**Title:** Coping Resources Inventory for Stress
**Author:** Matheny, Kenneth B.; Curlette, William L.; Aycock, David W.; Pugh, James L.; Taylor, Harry F.
**Purpose:** to measure coping resources that may be helpful in dealing with stress
**Acronym:** CRIS
**Publisher:** Health Prisms, Inc.

**Publisher address:** Health Prisms, Inc., 130 Pleasant Pointe Way, Fayetteville, GA 30214

The Coping Resources Inventory for Stress (CRIS) is designed to measure a person's coping resources, including personal behaviors, attitudes, and beliefs, in addition to physical being and financial resources. The basis for the test arises from the theory that stress is a product of "inequality between perceived demands and perceived resources." It is that perception that if one has adequate resources to handle life, they can use those resources and the situation will not become stressful. It is a well-known fact that what stresses one person may have little or no stressful effect on another.

This carefully constructed and thoroughly tested inventory consisting of 260 items in a true-false format. The reading level is considered about seventh grade level. There are 15 coping resources scales including: Self-Disclosure, Self-Directedness, Confidence, Acceptance, Social Support, Financial Freedom, Physical Health, Physical Fitness, Stress Monitoring, Tension Control, Structuring, Problem Solving, Cognitive Restructuring, Functional Beliefs, and Social Ease. Scoring is based on the examinee's responses and a global Coping Resource Effectiveness Score is generated.

The CRIS is a popular test that is used in a number of settings, which offers psychometrically sound data to support its claims. In general, the CRIS is a good screening instrument that assess personal coping resources and identifies habits may hinder a healthy lifestyle. Further evaluation can generate "strengths and weaknesses" that may be helpful in determining life change goals.[1]

\* \* \*

**Title:** Defense Mechanisms Inventory [Revised]
**Author:** Ihilevich, David; Gleser, Goldine C.
**Purpose:**   to help predict responses to conflict or threat
**Acronym:** DMI
**Publisher:** Psychological Assessment Resources, Inc.

**Publisher address:** Psychological Assessment Resources, Inc., 16204 N. Florida Avenue, Lutz, FL 33549-8119; Telephone: 800-331-8378; FAX: 800-727-9329; E-mail: custsupp@parinc.com; Web: www.parinc.com

The Defense Mechanisms Inventory [Revised] (DMI) is a measure used to assess ego-defense strategies. This paper-pencil test includes the following scales: Turning Against Object, Projection, Principalization, Turning Against Self, and Reversal. The format is based on 10 popular conflict scenarios related to authority, independence, competition, sexual identity, and situations.

Two of each type of conflict situations is presented in brief narratives. The individual is told to react to the scenarios by reporting their most and least likely behaviors. Further the individual is asked to describe what their fantasy reaction would be and their impulsive reaction may be. They are questioned about their feelings. The scenarios are age and gender appropriate, including youth and the elderly.

It should be noted that the DMI is designed for clinicians that are familiar with theory of defense mechanisms as interpreted in psychoanalytic theory. It is recommended for use with both the clinical and non-clinical populations.

The standard $T$ scores are converted from raw scores and transferred to a profile sheet. Psychometric data is considered adequate for the five defense mechanism scales.[1]

**Title:** Family Assessment Measure Version III
**Author:** Skinner, Harvey A.; Steinhauer, Paul D.; Santa-Barbara, Jack
**Purpose:** to assess indices of family strengths and weaknesses.
**Acronym:** FAM-III
**Publisher:** Multi-Health Systems Inc.
**Publisher address:** Multi-Health Systems, Inc., P.O. Box 950, North Tonawanda, NY 14120-0950; Telephone: 416-492-2627 or 800-456-

3003; FAX: 416-492-3343 or 888-540-4484; E-mail: CUSTOMERSERVICE@MHS.COM; Web: www.mhs.com

The Family Assessment Measure Version III (FAM-III) is a self-report instrument that may be helpful in assessing family strengths and weaknesses. It was primarily designed to provide insight into a family system/s functioning with respect for the past and present. The test tries to integrate family members individually and collectedly. Testing usually takes about an hour, with substantially more depending on the size of the family.

The General scale is derived from 50 forced-choice questions; the Self-Rating and Dyadic scales each have 42 forced-choice questions. After being scored, each family member can compare his or her scores on the profile sheets. Step-by-step guidelines are offered to help reduce misunderstanding and inaccurate interpretations concerning elevations. The FAM-III is considered a good family evaluation test.[1]

\* \* \*

**Title:** Life Roles Inventory
**Author:** Fitzsimmons, George W.; Macnab, Donald; Casserly, Catherine
**Purpose:** To assess life-career values and life roles in Canada
**Acronym:** LRI
**Note:** Test reviewed in the Thirteenth Mental Measurements Yearbook (1998). As of January 2002, publisher advises test is now out of print.
**Publisher:** Psychometrics Canada Ltd. [Canada]
**Publisher address:** Psychometrics Canada Ltd., 7125 - 77 Avenue, Edmonton, Alberta T6B 0B5, Canada; Telephone: 1-800-661-5158; FAX: 780-469-2283; E-mail: info@psychometrics.com; Web: www.psychometrics.com

The Life Roles Inventory (LRI) consists of a two part inventory designed to measure life goals and roles of individuals living in Canada.

The Values Scale and the Salience Inventory part of the LRI have parallel scales developed for use within the United States.

The Value Scale consists of 100-item that measure 20 different values. Each scale has five 4-point items, three of which are common to all countries and two of which are unique to Canada. The item content includes both work and personal values. The U.S. version of the Value Scales contains 21 items, 19 of which are identical to those on the Canadian version.

The Salience Inventory part assesses the relative importance of life roles for individuals as described in the popular life-career rainbow model. Each of five major life roles – Study, Work, Home and Family, Leisure, and Community Service – are evaluated in terms of three aspects of importance – Participation, Commitment, and Value Expectations – to produce a total of 15 scales.

The characteristics of the normative samples are described in some detail in the technical manual; however, it is not clear to what extent the norms are representative of the general Canadian population.

The LRI contributes to the field of vocational and family psychology by providing measures of life roles and values that are more comprehensive than those provided by other instruments. Although viewed primarily as a career inventory, it has utility in life (family) planning. LRI can also be used productively in cross-cultural settings.[1]

✳ ✳ ✳

**Title:** Life Stressors and Social Resources Inventory-Adult Form
**Author:** Moos, Rudolf H.; Moos, Bernice S.
**Purpose:** to evaluated an individual's life stressors and social resources
**Acronym:** LISRES-A
**Publisher:** Psychological Assessment Resources, Inc.
**Publisher address:** Psychological Assessment Resources, Inc., 16204 N. Florida Avenue, Lutz, FL 33549-8119; Telephone: 800-331-8378; FAX: 800-727-9329; E-mail: custsupp@parinc.com; Web: www.parinc.com

The Life Stressors and Social Resources Inventory – Adult Form (LISRES-A) is a test used to evaluate an individual's life stressors and social resources, to look at health and well-being, and provide a comprehensive view of that individual's life situation. The LISRES-A assesses eight life experience domains including: physical health status, housing and neighborhood, finances, work, relationship with spouse or partner, children, extended family, and friends and social group. The test is made up if 200 items representing 16 scales, with 9 representing life stressors and 7 social resources. In general, it helps identify those positive and negative life experiences.

The LISRES-A may be administered as a self-report questionnaire or by a semi-structured interview. The actual administration may be conducted by a papa-professional, however, a trained clinician must supervised the process and make any interpretations. The administration may only take about 30 minutes for the self-report and about 60 minutes for an interview. Templates are used for scoring making that process fairly easy and taking usually about 15 minutes.. About half the questions elicit a yes / no response, with about 40 of the questions leading to further questioning. After raw scores are converted into T scores, they are then assigned to the stressors and resources profiles.

The LISRES-A is a popular test that is considered a valuable tool in assessing the role of stress which can then assist in determining how such stress takes it toll on the individual. The research on how the stressors and resources are related remains a challenge; however, the LISRES-A continues to clearly identity the stressors and resources while the clinician is working with their patient's physical or mental health issues. This inventory still lacks some specificity. At least 50 items are related to partner or child issues, rendering the test less helpful to singles. Some feel that the test should only be administered in the interview format to reach its maximum value.[1]

**Title:** Marital Satisfaction Inventory-Revised
**Author:** Snyder, Douglas K.

274

**Purpose:** Designed to "identify, separately for each partner in a relationship, the nature and extent of distress along several key dimensions of their relationship."

**Acronym:** MSI-R

**Publisher:** Western Psychological Services

**Publisher address:** Western Psychological Services, 12031 Wilshire Blvd., Los Angeles, CA 90025-1251; Telephone: 310-478-2061; FAX: 310-478-7838; Web: www.wpspublish.com

The Marital Satisfaction Inventory-Revised (MSI-R) is a test that evaluates the level of satisfaction or dissatisfaction in relationships. It is primarily designed to assist clinicians that are working with couples in therapy or considering conjoint therapy. It should be noted that the latest version of the test is appropriate to use with a large variety of couples including same-gender couples and couples during courtship or engagement. The format consists of 150 true-false items subdivided into 13 subscales. The higher the scores, the greater the dissatisfaction that is reflected.

The MSI-R is easily administered by a computer or in a paper-and-pencil format. The reading level is considered about sixth grade. It usually takes about 25 minutes to take the test. The MSI-R seems especially well suited for clinical settings; however, it is readily available in the public domain. It remains one of the most used marital satisfaction instruments used. This revision offers even stronger psychometrics. Clinicians praise this test because it also offers a good format for gathering important information including looking at the couple's strengths and weaknesses and assess the home environment for emotionally or behaviorally troubled children.[1]

*   *   *

**Title:** State-Trait Anger Expression Inventory-2

**Author:** Spielberger, Charles D.

**Purpose:** to measure the aspects of anger in adolescents and adults

**Acronym:** STAXI-2

**Publisher:** Psychological Assessment Resources, Inc.
**Publisher address:** Psychological Assessment Resources, Inc., 16204 N. Florida Avenue, Lutz, FL 33549-8119; Telephone: 800-331-8378; FAX: 800-727-9329; E-mail: custsupp@parinc.com; Web: www.parinc.com

The State-Trait Anger Expression Inventory-2 (STAXI-2) is a revised of an earlier version. The new inventory has been expanded from 44 to 57 items. It usually takes about 15 minutes to complete the test. The STAXI-2 was designed to measure the experience, expression, and control of anger for adolescents and adults. The responses are on a 4-point Likert scale and represent six scales including: State Anger, Trait Anger, Anger Expression-Out, Anger Expression- In, Anger Control-Out, Anger Control- In. Beyond the scales the test examines State and Trait subscale areas. The State Anger subscales are: Feeling, Verbal, and Physical. The Trait Anger subscales are: Temperament, and Reaction. There is also an Anger Expression Index.

An experienced examiner is recommended; however, non-clinical personnel can administer and score the inventory after careful review of the manual. Interpretation should be limited to trained and qualified professionals. The STAXI-2 appears to offer valuable information to be used by a trained clinician. Psychometric concerns are focused on the normative sample and the lack of descriptive data concerning the ethnic and cultural make-up of the sample.[1]

\* \* \*

**Title:** Personal Problems Checklist-Adult
**Author:** Schinka, John A.
**Purpose:** to assess an individual's problems as seen from that person's point of view
**Acronym: PPC**
**Publisher:** Psychological Assessment Resources, Inc.

**Publisher address:** Psychological Assessment Resources, Inc., 16204 N. Florida Avenue, Lutz, FL 33549-8119; Telephone: 800-331-8378; FAX: 800-727-9329; E-mail: custsupp@parinc.com; Web: www.parinc.com

The Personal Problems Checklist (PPC) for Adults is an efficient, easy-to-administer survey of problems as seen from the individual's personal perspective. The PPC for Adults is one of a series of similar checklists. It consists of 208 problems divided into 13 specific areas. The instrument is self-explanatory, and no manual is provided.

Only content validation exists for the checklists, but the validation procedures are unspecified for the user. As a organized way of gathering data on a variety of problems, the PPC may be helpful.[1]

✻  ✻  ✻

**Title:** Styles of Conflict Inventory
**Author:** Metz, Michael E.
**Purpose:** to aid in evaluating a couples' conflict
**Acronym:** SCI
**Publisher:** CPP, Inc.
**Publisher address:** CPP, Inc., 3803 East Bayshore Road, Palo Alto, CA 94303; Telephone: 800-624-1765; FAX: 650-623-9273; E-mail: knw@cpp-db.com; Web: www.cpp-db.com

The Styles of Conflict Inventory (SCI) is a test used to help assess conflicts among couples. It has been used primarily to assist in conducting relationship workshops and to help couples clearly understand their conflicts and how each deals with their conflict.

Part I of the SCI is concerned with the partner's perceptions about the general quality of their relationships. The items reflect both cognitive and behavioral styles of dealing with conflict. The SCI also addresses each other's perceptions of their partner's behaviors when dealing with conflicts.

Standardized scores are reported in *T* scores. The test has norms for both heterosexual and homosexual couples. The analysis of reliability and validity is offered is extensive. The SCI takes some time to score and interpret and it should only be used by well-qualified clinicians.[1]

\* \* \*

**The Child Abuse Potential Inventory**
by Joel S. Milner, Ph.D.
**Title:** Child Abuse Potential Inventory, Form VI (The)
**Author:** Milner, Joel S.
**Purpose:** to screen for suspected physical child abuse
**Acronym:** CAP Inventory
**Publisher:** Psytec Inc.
**Publisher address:** Psytec, Inc., P.O. Box 564, DeKalb, IL 60115

The Child Abuse Potential Inventory (CAP) Inventory was originally developed to be used by protective services in its investigative responsibilities of reported child abuse cases. The test is considered helpful in identifying those individuals who are most "at risk" for potential to abuse. The CAP Inventory is a 160 item, self-report inventory in an "agree" or "disagree" format. It is administered to either a male and female parent or primary caregivers who may be suspected of physical child abuse. Within the 10 scales test, the Abuse Scale is sub-divide into 6 factors scales: Distress, Rigidity, Unhappiness, Problems with Child and Self, Problems with Family, and Problems with Others and Total Physical Child Abuse. There are three validity scales: Lie, Random Response and Inconsistency. The test has three response Distortion Indexes including: Faking Good, Faking Bad and Random Response.

The CAP Inventory's validity is paramount due to the test's claim to predict the potential of child abuse. The test manual offers information on content, construct, concurrent predictive and future predictive validity.

It provides interpretive information, scale descriptions, discussion of limitations and related issues.

This test is considered a good standardized instrument for its intended purpose. This, or any such inventory, should never be used in isolation. Results from the CAP Inventory should only be used in conjunction with other comprehensive data used to evaluate the possibility of child abuse potential.[1]

# Chapter 24

## Assessing Parenting Skills

Parenting skills are at the heart of the foster and adoptive placement decision. When an agency makes a referral to a consulting psychologist to determine the possibility of a personality disorder, depression, or substance abuse in a particular family, the primary goal is to determine the extent of the problem and the impact that the problem might have on a child placed in the family.

Not every person who has ever had an emotional or behavioral problem should be automatically excluded as a possible foster or adoptive parent. If agencies only allowed applicants without a blemish of any kind to be approved, few people would be allowed to adopt or foster children. Mental health is seldom a black or white issue.

Methods for assessing actual parenting skills used by psychologists include self-report measures, interviews, and informant reports, along with naturalistic and structured observations. In a typical psychologist's practice, individuals referred for parenting issues usually already have children and the evaluation focuses on problems associated with an identified child.

All of the standard self report measures or informant report assessments reviewed in this chapter are designed for parents who have children already in the home. The adapted use of such instruments may yield some valuable information, even though no standard scoring system has been established for the use of these instruments with couples without children. These instruments ask questions about how the parent handles certain situations, their attitudes about their child, the level of agreement between the couple in disciple, etc. all designed to evaluate a parent-child relationship that is already established. Referrals for such evaluations are typically due to the child exhibiting behavior problems, not to assess an individual's general knowledge of parenting skills.

The naturalistic observations usually take place in the home environment, and they are either videotaped or observed by a trained professional in the home. The structured observation usually takes place in the office, where either specific activities are suggested or a variety of toys are offered and the parent engages in free play with the child while being observed. Modifications of these observation activities may be somewhat useful if the couple has a close relationship with children in the family or close friends that the child could be observed with the applicants. Extreme caution would be advised in interpreting such observation situations since no standardized scoring system has been established for such use.

Many child psychologists, day care workers, teachers and other professionals who provide services to children may fantasize that there should be a test that must be passed in order to have children. When that is actually suggested it is usually done tongue-in-check, but there is no shortage of people who would agree that many couples are often poorly prepared for parenting tasks. A more realistic use of these particular tests would be after a child has been placed, or when children are placed in homes in which there are already other children. Research data clearly suggests that children who are in foster or adoptive situations are just as likely to have adjustment problems as their peers living in their biological homes.

In general, psychologists may approach the assessment of parenting skills for individuals who do not have children in the home by relying heavily on the comprehensive interview, marital satisfaction test data, family history, the client's personal stories, their attachment history and all other applicable tests results.

Well-seasoned examiners will probably gain a lot of insight into a couple's skills through a structured discussion of child rearing topics, such as ways to increase good behavior, appropriate discipline, time-out, natural consequences, noncompliance, expressing feeling, age-appropriate expectations, and a discussion of when a family should seek professional assistance.

**Title:** Parent Awareness Skills Survey
**Author:** Bricklin, Barry
**Purpose:** to assess a parent's sensitivity to typical child care situations
**Acronym:** PASS
**Publisher:** Village Publishing
**Publisher address:** Village Publishing, 73 Valley Drive, Furlong, PA 18925; Telephone: 800-553-7678; FAX: 215-794-3386; E-mail: VP@custody-vp.com; Web: www.custody-vp.com

The Parent Awareness Skills Survey (PASS) is designed to assess parent's awareness of factors important in reacting to and dealing with typical child care problems. The PASS may also be used to identify the strengths and weaknesses of parents. The PASS is designed for use with parents of children of all ages.

The assessment consists of 18 situations that are related to typical child care dilemmas to which the parent is asked to respond. The examiner may probe to get more information on about the parent's response. The probes can increase the scores.

Clinical use of this instrument should be approached with caution due to the lack of information concerning validity and reliability. Until the measure is better substantiated it has limited usefulness for which it has been designed. There are serious limitations to using the PASS beyond in a general information seeking situation.[1]

\*   \*   \*

**Title:** Parenting Stress Index, Third Edition
**Author:** Abidin, Richard R.; PAR Staff; Ona, Noriel
**Purpose:** to identify stressors related to dysfunctional parenting
**Acronym:** PSI
**Publisher:** Psychological Assessment Resources, Inc.

**Publisher address:** Psychological Assessment Resources, Inc., 16204 N. Florida Avenue, Lutz, FL 33549-8119; Telephone: 800-331-8378; FAX: 800-727-9329; E-mail: custsupp@parinc.com; Web: www.parinc.com

The Parenting Stress Index (PSI) is a test designed to identify potentially dysfunctional parent-child relationships. The PSI is a 120-item self-report measure developed to identify stress levels in parent-child systems. It is presented in a 7-page item booklet and in a computerized version. The PSI is praised for its simple and direct format. The PSI takes about 20 minutes to complete how each item best reflects the respondent's feelings on a 5-point Likert scale. The PSI is based on 3 areas: child characteristics, parent characteristics and situational/demographic life stress.

Although the PSI demonstrates good validity, the biggest weakness is its standardization, and its resulting normative data. The sample of 2,633 used was not random nor was it stratified. The PSI will be helpful for anyone interested in the evaluation or assessment of children and parents within a systems context.

The PSI is well grounded in clinical experience and developmental psychology.

It is considered an excellent way for clinicians to help identify important components of family and child adjustments and difficulties. Because so few such instruments exist, it has been utilized extensively. Caution is advised to not use the PSI to make unsupported assumptions about families. The PSI should be used as a screening instrument and only use the global score in considering the dysfunction in the family that may place a child at risk for emotional disturbance.[1]

**Title:** Parent-Child Relationship Inventory
**Author:** Gerard, Anthony B.
**Purpose:** to assess attitudes toward parenting and toward their children

**Acronym:** PCRI

**Publisher:** Western Psychological Services

**Publisher address:** Western Psychological Services, 12031 Wilshire Blvd., Los Angeles, CA 90025-1251; Telephone: 310-478-2061; FAX: 310-478-7838; Web: www.wpspublish.com

The Parent-Child Relationship Inventory (PCRI) assesses parents' attitude toward their children. It is a 78-item self-report questionnaire completed by parents. The parents focus on only one child and respond to items according to a 4-point, Likert scale: strongly agree, agree, disagree, and strongly disagree. Seven content scales yield information about: Parental Support, Satisfaction with Parenting, Involvement, Communication, Limit Setting, and Autonomy.

Raw scores are converted to T-scores and separate norms are provided for mothers and fathers. The development of the PCRI employed sound psychometric procedures and the reliability and validity estimates provided support its utility. In general, the PCRI is considered to be a very useful measure.[1]

\*　\*　\*

**Title:** Parent Behavior Checklist

**Author:** Fox, Robert A.

**Purpose:** Provides an assessment of a family's strengths and needs.

**Acronym:** PBC

**Note:** Test reviewed in the Thirteenth Mental Measurements Yearbook (1998). As of December 2001, publisher advises test is now out of print.

**Publisher:** PRO-ED

**Publisher address:** PRO-ED, 8700 Shoal Creek Blvd., Austin, TX 78757-6897; Telephone: 800-897-3202; FAX: 512-451-8542; E-mail: proedrd2@aol.com; Web: WWW.PROEDINC.COM

The Parent Behavior Checklist (PBC) is a 100-item; self-report questionnaire completed by a parent that helps identify strengths and weaknesses in the parents' behaviors while evaluating a parent's expectations and actual behaviors. The parent must respond to simple statements according to a frequency scale such as: never, sometimes, often, and always. The parent responds to many facets of parenting on a behavioral level.[1]

*   *   *

**Title:** Parenting Alliance Measure
**Author:** Abidin, Richard R.; Konold, Timothy R.
**Purpose**: to evaluate perceived alliance between parents of children
**Acronym:** PAM
**Publisher:** Psychological Assessment Resources, Inc.
**Publisher address:** Psychological Assessment Resources, Inc., 16204 N. Florida Avenue, Lutz, FL 33549-8119; Telephone: 800-331-8378; FAX: 800-727-9329; E-mail: custsupp@parinc.com; Web: www.parinc.com

The Parenting Alliance Measure (PAM) is a simple test using a 20-item paper-and-pencil format that can be administered in about 10 minutes. If the individual being tested has trouble reading the questions it can be read to them. It is written on about a third grade reading level. The PAM is hand-scored and provides information on how well a parent feels they are engaged in a mutually respectful alliance.

Parents respond on a 5 point Likert scale ranging from strongly agree to strongly disagree. Completion of the PAM requires a third-grade reading level. It is permissible to read the PAM items aloud to parents who have difficulty reading.

Although administration is easy, interpretation of the PAM requires graduate training in psychology or related fields. Raw scores are converted into percentile scores and T-scores conversions are provided. Interpretation to the parents is discussed in T scores.

Unfortunately, the Hispanic parents are under represented in the normative sample. No data were provided on ethnic differences in test results.

The PAM significantly negatively correlates with parenting stress and significantly positively correlates with family cohesion, family adaptability, and marital quality as expected.[1]

\* \* \*

**Title:** Parenting Satisfaction Scale(tm)
**Author:** Guidubaldi, John; Cleminshaw, Helen K.
**Purpose:** to assess "parents' attitudes toward parenting"
**Acronym:** PSS
**Publisher:** PsychCorp, A brand of Harcourt Assessment, Inc.
**Publisher address:** PsychCorp, A brand of Harcourt Assessment, Inc., 19500 Bulverde Road, San Antonio, TX 78259; Telephone: 800-211-8378; FAX: 800-232-1223; E-mail: customer_care@harcourt.com; Web: www.PsychCorp.com


The Parenting Satisfaction Scale (PSS) is a test designed to assess parental attitudes toward parenting on three scales: Satisfaction with Spouse/Ex-Spouse Parenting Performance, Satisfaction with the Parent-Child Relationship, and Satisfaction with Parenting Performance. The scale appears to be related to behavioral outcomes. It is considered an excellent tool in helping parents become more aware and in helping promote parenting skills and family healing. The PSS is described as an easy to administer and score. Those taking the test describe it as being easy to understand and quick. The reading level seldom gives parents a problem.

Each parent is asked to describe how he/she feels about the other parent according to parenting skills and their relationship with the children in question. The examinee is also requested to describe his / her own parenting. Each parent is then asked to choose a level of agreement to statements from: strongly agree to strongly disagree. It can be used to evaluate general parenting or the parenting of a specific child. The PSS yields a total satisfaction score as well as scores on three subscales.[1]

*   *   *

**Title:** Home Observation for Measurement of the Environment

**Author:** Caldwell, Betty M.; Bradley, Robert H.

**Purpose:** Screen for sources of potential environmental retardation or risk.

**Acronym:** HOME

**Publisher:** Home Inventory LLC

**Publisher address:** Home Inventory LLC, c/o Lorraine Coulson, 13 Saxony Circle,Little Rock, AR 72209; Telephone: 501-565-7627; E-mail: lrcoulson@ualr.edu; Web: www.ualr.edu/~crtldept/home4.htm

The Home Observation for Measurement of the Environment (HOME) consists of two inventories designed to evaluate a child's home environment. The observations are structured to identity and describe the types of stimulation in the home that fosters cognitive development. During the home visit the observer records data and interviews the parents. Items are scored as to whether or not specific types of stimulation were present in the home or not. The home visit should be when the child is awake and alert. The trained examiner observes interactions between the parent (primary caregiver) and the child. The test time usually takes about an hour.

The HOME Inventory for Families of Infants and Toddlers are appropriate for use with children from birth to age 3 years. The HOME (infant and toddler's version) consists of six subscales. The HOME Inventory for Families of Preschool Age Children is used with children ages 3years to 6 years and has eight subscales.

About one-third of the items are scored through the interview with the parent. These items (stimulations) are considered unlikely to actually occur during the home visit.

The HOME manual is considered well organized and informative for each inventory. After a brief overview, the manual is divided into a detailed description of each of the inventories. The manual offers information on the normative sample; however, it is not representative of a national sample. Replication findings reported good utility of the inventories in predicting cognitive functioning. Predictive validity concerning children in the retarded range and high average range of cognitive functioning is considered good using the Binet IQ scores.

IN general, the HOME inventories are considered useful for its limited purpose. It is considered a fairly well researched test for identifying and understanding stimulation aspects of the home environment. The scores are useful in predicting later cognitive functioning as assessed by traditional IQ measures and achievement tests. The HOME has been described as a "sensitive alternative" to traditional SES indices. Professionals have reported success in including the HOME results in helping to determine necessary interventions. The HOME inventories are highly recommended for use with the population for which it was designed.[1]

\* \* \*

**Title:** Parent As A Teacher Inventory [Revised]
**Author:** Strom, Robert D.
**Purpose:** to identify parenting strengths and needs of preschool and primary grade children
**Acronym:** PAAT
**Publisher:** Scholastic Testing Service, Inc.
**Publisher address:** Scholastic Testing Service, Inc., 480 Meyer Road, Bensenville, IL 60106-1617; Telephone: 1-800-642-6787; FAX: 630-766-8054; E-mail: stesting@email.com; Web: www.ststesting.com

The Parent as a Teacher Inventory (PAAT) is designed to assist parents in understanding the value of their interactions with their children. The PAAT is a 50 item questionnaire that a parent responds on a 4-point yes – no Likert scale. The scale is strong yes, yes, strong no and no. The subscales include: Creativity, Frustration, Control, Play, and Teaching/Learning with 10 items to evaluate each.

The PAAT offers insight into three parent-child interactions including the parent's expectations of the child, how a parent interacts with the child, and how the parent responds to specific behaviors of the child. The PAAT may be administered to groups or individually. The test has been translated into 19 languages.

The manual describes the scoring and offers a scoring key. A score of 4 is desirable down to least desirable score of 1 on each item. A parent would receive five subtest scores and one total score. Each subtest description is given in the manual for the questionnaire. There may be some speculation as to if all subtests are empirically supported. Limited reliability and validity data are reported in the test manual. The test-retest reliability values reported are satisfactorily.

Although some issues are unresolved, the questionnaire is considered to produce some valuable parent information. Some of the more disturbing issues with the tests involve the lack of a clear theoretical bases, the question of content validity, culturally insensitive items and some confusing language.[1]

# ENDNOTES

[i] Adoptions and Safe Families Act of 1997 (H.R. 867), Public Law 105-89.
[ii] Brodzinsky, David M., and Marshall D. Schechter. *The Psychology of Adoption.* New York: Oxford University Press, 1990.
[iii] Ibid.
[iv] Wolins, Martin. *Selection Foster Parents.* New York: Columbia University Press, 1963.
[v] Theis, Sophie Van S. *How Foster Children Turn Out.* New York: State Charities Aid Association, 1924.
[vi] Mass, Henry S., and Richard E. Engler. *Children In Need of Parents.* New York: Columbia University Press, 1954.
[vii] Wolins, Martin. *Selecting Foster Parents.*
[viii] *Ibid.*
[ix] Ibid.
[x] Fanshel, David. *Foster Parenthood: A Role Analysis.* Minneapolis, Minnesota: University of Minnesota Press, 1966.
[xi] Ibid.
[xii] Ibid.
[xiii] Ibid.
[xiv] National Association of Social Workers, 2002.
[xv] American Public Human Services Association (http://icpc.aphsa.org).
[xvi] The Evan B. Donaldson Adoption Institute has published various articles in support of federal legislation to reform the existing ICPC placement process (http://www.adoptioninstitute.org).
[xvii] Kindlon, Dan, and Michael Thompson. *Raising Cain: Protecting the Emotional Life of Boys.* New York: Ballantine Books, 2000.
[xviii] Popenoe, David. *Life Without Father.* New York: Martin Kessler Books/The Free Press,1996.
[xix] Zill, 1985;Kadushin, 1980;Mech, 1973;R. Colburn, 1986.
[xx] Dalby, Fox and Haslam, 1982; Fullerton, Goodrich and Berman, 1986; Kenny, Baldwin and Mackie, 1967; Menlove, 1965; Silver, 1970).
[xxi] Heston, 1966.
[xxii] Loehlin, Willerman and Horn, 1985.
[xxiii] Cadpret. Remi J. "Biologic Perspective of Adoptee Adjustment." *The Psychology of Adoption.*
[xxiv] Brodzinsky, David M. *The Psychology of Adoption.*
[xxv] Dickerson, James. "A Casework Approach to Foster Homes." *Journal of the Ontario Association of Children's Aid Societies* (October 1972).
[xxvi] McLanahan Sara S., and Gary Sandefur. *Growing Up With a Single Parent.* Cambridge, MA: Harvard University Press, 1994.

xxvii Blankenhorn, David. *Fatherless America: Confronting Out Most Urgent Social Problem.* New York: Harper Perennial, 1995.
xxviii Biller, Henry, and Dennis Meredith. *Father Power.* New York: David Mckay Company,1974.
xxix Ban, P. L., and M. Lewis. "*Mothers and Fathers Girls and Boys: Attachment Behavior in the One-Year-Old.* Presented at a meeting of the Eastern Psychological Association, New York.
xxx National Institute of Mental Health, 1988.
xxxi Mendel, 1993.
xxxii Kendler, Kenneth S., et al. Medical College of Virginia Commonwealth University, Archives of General Psychiatry, 2000.
xxxiii *Americal Journal of Public Health,* 1991.
xxxiv Popenoe, David. *Life Without Father.*
xxxv Author interview.
xxxvi Ibid.
xxxvii Ibid.


xxxvii Petty, Richard. *Journal of Personality and Social Psychology* (July 2003).
xxxvii Conniff, Richard. "Reading Faces." *Smithsonian* (January 2004). Ekman, Paul and Wallace Friesen. *Unmasking the Face.* New York: Prentice-Hall, 1975. Eikman, Paul. *Emotions Revealed.* New York: Times Books, 2003.
xxxvii Lundbert, Shelly, and Elaina Rose. *Demography* (May 2005). Partly funded by the National science Foundation.
xxxvii Smith v. OFFER, 1977. U.S. Supreme Court.
xxxvii Festinger, T. *Child Welfare* (1974, number 53).
xxxvii Proch, K. "Foster parents as preferred adoptive parents." Child Welfare (1981, volume 60).
xxxvii Alliance of Five Research Centres on Violence. *Violence Prevention and The Girl Child: Final Report* (research funded by Status of Women Canada, 1999); Dauvergne, Mia, and Holly Johnson. "Children Witnessing Family Violece." Juristat (Canadian Centre for Justice Statistics, Statistics Canada).
xxxvii Research indicates that while about 30 percent of adult sex offenders were found to be sexually abused as children, the percentage of adolescent sex offenders varied widely from 40 to 80 percent. Hunter, R. and Becker, J. "Motivators of Adolescent Sex Offenders and Treatment Perspectives," in J. Shaw (ed.), *Sexual Aggression.* Washington, DC: American Psychiatric Press.
xxxvii Ryckman, Richard M. *Journal of Social and Clinical Psychology* (November 2002).
xxxvii Murray, Sandra, Jl., John G. Holmes, Dale W. Griffin, Gina Bellavia and Dan Dolderman. "Kindred Spirits? The Benefits of Egocentrism in Close Relationships." *Journal of Personality and Social Psychology* (vol. 82, No. 4, 2002).
xxxvii Kantrowitz, Barbara, and Pat Wingert. "Psychology is unlocking the secrets of happy couples." *Newsweek* April 19,1999).

[xxxvii] Farr, Finis. *O'Hara: A Biography.* Boston: Little, Brown and Company, 1973.

[xxxvii] Steele, Brandt. "Proceedings of Conference on Patterns of Parental Behavior Leading to Physical Abuse of Children," unpublished (University of Colorado, School of Medicine, 1966), quoted in D. G. Gill's Violence Against Children.

[xxxvii] Wolins, Martin. *Selecting Foster Parents.*

[xxxvii] The American Psychologist (Vol. 56, No. 2, pages 128 – 165).

[xxxvii] American Psychological Association, "Ethical Principles of Psychologists and Code of Conduct," Washington D.C.: 2002.

[xxxvii] American Educational Research Association, American Psychological Association & National Council on Measurement in Education, "Standards for Educational and Psychological Testing." Washington D.C. 1999.

[xxxvii] "Rights and Responsibilities of Test Takers: Guidelines and Expectations," American Psychological Association, APA On-line Science Directorate, Washington D.C. 2006.

[xxxvii] Ackerman, Marc J. and Kane, Andrew W. Psychological Experts in Divorce, Personal Injury and Other Civil Actions, Second Edition, 106 – 110, Wiley Law Publications, John Wiley & Sons, Inc., New York, New York, 1993.

[xxxvii] Beck Anxiety Inventory by E. Thomas Dowd and Neils G. Waller. Impara, J. C., & Plake, B. S. (Eds.). (1998). The thirteenth mental measurements yearbook. Lincoln, NE: Buros Institute of Mental Measurements.

[xxxvii] Beck Depression Inventory II by Janet T. Carlson and Neils G. Waller.) Plake, B. S., & Impara, J. C. (Eds.). (2001). The fourteenth mental measurements yearbook. Lincoln, NE: Buros Institute of Mental Measurements.

[xxxvii] Beck Hopelessness Scale by Ephrem Fernandez. Impara, J. C., & Plake, B. S. (Eds.). (1998). The thirteenth mental measurements yearbook. Lincoln, NE: Buros Institute of Mental Measurements.

[xxxvii] Beck Scale for Suicide Ideation by Karl R. Hanes and Jay R. Stewart. Impara, J. C., & Plake, B. S. (Eds.). (1998). The thirteenth mental measurements yearbook. Lincoln, NE: Buros Institute of Mental Measurements.

[xxxvii] Plake, B.S., & Impara, J.C. (Eds.). (1998). The thirteenth mental measurements yearbook. Lincoln, NE: Buros Institute of Mental Measurements.

[xxxvii] Impara, J.C. & Plake, B.S. (Eds.). (1998). The thirteenth mental measurements yearbook. Lincoln, NE: Buros Institute of Mental Measurements.

[xxxvii] Reynolds Depression Screening Inventory (RDSI) by Michael H. Campbell and Rosemary Flanagan. Buros, 2001: pp 1023-1027. Plake, B.S., & Impara, J.C. (Eds.). (2001). The fourteenth mental measurements yearbook. Lincoln, NE: Buros Institute of Mental Measurements.

# Bibliography

## BOOKS

Ackerman, Marc J. and Andrew Kane. *Psychological Experts in Divorce, Personal Injury and Other Civil Actions.* New York: Wiley & Sons, 1993.

Ainsworth, M.D. *Patterns of Attachment.* Hillsdale, N.J.: Erlbaun, 1978.

Apgar, V. and J. Beck. *Is My Baby All Right?* New York: Trident, 1973.

Aries, Philippe. *Centuries of Childhood: A Social History of Family Life.* New York: Vintage, 1965.

Bachrach, Arthur J., and Gardner Murphy, eds. *An Outline of Abnormal Psychology.* New York: Modern Library, 1954.

Barron-Cohen, Simon. *The Essential Difference: The Truth About the Male and Female Brain.* New York: Perseus, 2003.

Biddulph, Steve. *Raising Boys.* Berkeley, Calif.: Celestial Arts,

Biller, Henry. *Fathers and Families: Paternal Factors in Child Development.* Westport, Conn.: Auburn House, 1993.

Biller, Henry, and Dennis Meredith. *Father Power.* New York: David McKay, 1974.

Biller, Henry B., and Robert J. Trotter. *The Father Factor: What You Need to Know to Make a Difference.* New York: Pocket Books,

Blankenhorn, David. *Fatherless America: Confonting Our Most Urgent Social Problem.* New York: Harper Perennial, 1995.

Blau, Theodore H. *The Psychologist as Expert Witness.* New York: John Wiley & Sons, 1988.

Bower, T. *Development in Infancy.* San Francisco: Freeman, 1981.

Brazelton, T.B. *The Infant Neonatal Assessment Scale.* Philadelphia: Lippincott, 1984.

Brodzinsky, David M. *The Psychology of Adoption.* New York: Oxford University Press, 1990.

Burns, Ailsa, and Cath Scott. *Mother-Headed Families and Why They Have Increased.* Hillsdale, New Jersey: Lawrence Erlbaum Associates, 1994.


Caldwell, Bettye M., and Henry N. Ricciuti, eds. *Child Development and Social Policy.* Volume 3. Chicago: University of Chicago Press, 1973.

Canfield, Ken R. *The 7 Secrets of Effective Fathers.* Wheaton, Illinois: Tyndale House, 1992.


Daly, Martin and Margo Wilson. "Risk of Maltreatment of Children Living with Stepparents." *Child Abuse and Neglect: Biosocial Dimensions.* Eds. R. Gelles and J. Lancaster. New York: Aldine de Gruyter, 1987.



Ekman, Paul. Emotions Revealed. New York: Henry Holt and Company, 2003.

Eliot, Lise. *What's Going on in there?: How the Brain and Mind Develop in the First Five Years of Life.* New York: Bantam, 1999.

Empfield, Maureen, and Nicholas Bakalar. *Understanding Teenage Depression.* New York: Henry Holt, 1999.

--------------- *Identity and the Life Cycle.* New York: W.W. Norton, reissued 1980.

Erickson, E.H. *Childhood and Society.* New York: W.W. Norton, 1963.


Fahlberg, Vera I. *A Child's Journey Through Placement.* Indianapolis, IN: Perspective Press, 1991.

Fanshel, David. *Foster Parenthood: A Role Analysis.* Minneapolis, Minnesota: University of Minnesota Press, 1966.

Farr, Finis. *John O'Hara: A Biography.* Boston: Little, Brown and Co., 1973.

Foli, Karen J., and John R. Thompson. *The Post-Adoption Blues: Overcoming the Unforeseen Challenges of Adoption.* USA: Rodale, 2004.

Furstenberg, Frank F., and Andrew J. Cherlin. *Divided Families: What Happens to Children When Parents Part.* Cambridge, Mass.: Harvard University Press,

Garfinkel, Irwin and Sara S. McLanahan. *Single Mothers and Their Children.* Washington, DC: The Urban Institute Press, 1986.

Gelles, R. and J. Lancaster, eds. *Child Abuse and Neglect: Biosocial Dimensions.* New York: Aldine de Gruyter, 1987.

Gray, Deborah D. *Attaching in Adoption: Practical Tools for Today's Parents.* Indianapolis, Indiana: Perspectives Press, 2002.

Hetherington, E. Mavis. *For Better or For Worse.* New York: W.W. Norton, 2002.

Ingersoll, Barbara D. and Sam Goldstein. *Lonely, Sad and Angry.* New York: Doubleday, 1995.

Kidman, Antony. *Family Life.* Sydney, Australia: Biochemical and General Services, 1995.

Kindlon, Dan, and Michael Thompson. *Raising Cain: Protecting the Emotional Life of Boys.* New York: Ballantine Books, 2000.

Klaus and J. Kennell. *Maternal-Infant Bonding.* St. Louis: Mosby, 1976.

Lamb, Michael. *The Role of the Father in Child Development.* New York: John Wiley, 1997.

Lamb, Michael and Ann Browns, eds. *Advances in Developmental Psychology.* Hillsdale, N.J.: Erlbaun.

Levine, Mel. *A Mind at a Time.* New York: Simon & Schuster, 2002.

Locke, John. *Some Thoughts Concerning Education.* New York: Oxford University Press, 1999.

McLanahan, Sara, and Gary Sandefur. *Growing Up with a Single Parent.* Cambridge, Mass.: Harvard University Press, 2001.

Macoby, Eleanor. *Social Development, Psychological Growth and Parent-Child Relations.* New York: Harcourt Brace Jovanovich, 1980.
Macoby, Eleanor Emmons and Carol Nagy Jacklin. *The Psychology of Sex Differences.* Stanford, California: Stanford University Press, 1974.
Maddi, Salvatore R. *Personality Theories: A Comparative Analysis.* Homewood, Illinois: Dorsey Press, 1976.
Mass, Henry S., and Richard E. Engler. *Children In Need of Parents.* New York: Columbia University Press, 1954.

Melina, Lois Ruskai. *Raising Adopted Children: Practical Reassuring Advice for Every Adoptive Parent.* New York: Harper Perennial, 1998.
Murphy, James M. *Coping With Teen Suicide.* New York: Rosen Publishing Group, 1999.

Neal, J.H. "Children's Understand of Their Parents' Divorces." In L. Kurdek, ed., *Children and Divorce: New Directions for Child Development.* San Francisco: Jossey-Bass, 1983.

Osofsky, Joy. *Handbook of Infant Development.* New York: John Wiley & Sons, 1987.

Pertman, Adam. *Adoption Nation.* New York: Basic Books, 2000.
Piaget, Jean. *Six Psychological Studies.* New York: Random House, 1967.
---------------- *The Moral Judgment of the Child.* New York: Macmillan, 1932.

Popenoe, David. *Life Without Father.* New York: Martin Kessler Books / Free Press, 1996.

Prokop, Michael S. *Kids' Divorce Workbook.* Warren, Ohio: Alegra House, 1986.

Pruett, Kyle D. *The Nurturing Father: Journey Toward the Complete Man.* New York: Warner Books, 1988.

Rotundo, E. Anthony. *American Manhood.* New York: Basic Books, 1993.

Rousseau, Jean-Jacques. *Emile.* London: Oxford University Press, 1999.

Stolk, Mary Van. *The Battered Child in Canada.* Toronto: McClelland and Stewart, 1972.

Tanner. J. *Education and Physical Growth.* London: Hodder and Stoughton, 1978.

Teyber, Edward. *Helping Children Cope with Divorce.* San Francisco: Jossey-Bass, 1992.

Thomas, M. *Comparing Theories of Child Development.* New York: W.W. Norton, 1996.

Thompson, Clara, Milton Mazer, and Earl Witenberg. *An Outline of Psychoanalysis.* New York: Modern Library, 1955.

Thompson, Michael. *Speaking of Boys.* New York: Ballantine Books, 2000.

Wachtel, Ellen F. *Treating Troubled Children and Their Families.* New York: Guilford Press, 1994.

Wallerstein, Judith, and Sandra Blakeslee. *Second Chances: Men, Women, and Children a Decade After Divorce.* Boston: Houghton Mifflin, 1996.

Wallerstein, Judith, Julie M. Lewis and Sandra Blakeslee. *The Unexpected Legacy of Divorce.* New York: Hyperion, 2000.

Watnik, Webster. *Child Custody Made Simple.* Claremont, Calif.: Single Parent Press, 1997.

Wodrich, David L. *Children's Psychological Testing: A Guide for Nonpsychologists.* Baltimore: Paul H. Brookes Publishing, 1984.

Wolins, Martin. *Selecting Foster Parents.* New York: Columbia University Press, 1963.


## PERIODICALS

Abrahamson, Amy c. and Laura A. Baker. "Rebellious Teens? Genetic and Environmental Influences on the Social Attitudes of Adolescents." *Journal of Personality and Social Psychology,* 2002, (vol. 83, no. 6).

Alessandri, Steven M., and Robert H. Wozniak. "The Child's Awareness of Parental Beliefs concerning the Child: A Developmental Study." Child Development, 1987, volume 58.

Amato, Paul R. "Parental Divorce and Attitudes toward Marriage and Family Life." *Journal of Marriage and the Family,* May 1988.

Amato, Paul R., and Alan Booth. "The Legacy of Parents' Marital Discord: Consequences for Children's Marital Quality." *Journal of Personality and Social Psychology,* October 2001, Vol. 81, No. 4.


Ban, P. L., and M. Lewis. *"Mothers and Fathers Girls and Boys: Attachment Behavior in the One-Year-Old.* Presented at a meeting of the Eastern Psychological Association, New York.


Belsky, Jay. "Parent, Infant, and Social-Contextual Antecendents of Father-Son Attachment Security." *Developmental Psychology,* September 1, 1996, Vol. 32, Issue 5.


Cowley, Geoffrey. "Girls, Boys and Autism." *Newsweek,* September 8, 2003.

Dickerson, James. "A Casework Approach to Foster Homes." *Journal of the Ontario Association of Children's Aid Societies* (October 1972).

Draper, Patricia and Henry Harpending. *Journal of Anthropological Research,* 1982, volume 36, issue 3.

Feigelman, William, and Gordon E. Finley. "Youth Problems Among Adoptees Living in One-Parent Homes: A Comparison With Others From One-Parent Biological Families. *American Journal of Orthopsychiatry,* 2004 (vol. 74, No. 3).

Harris, Judith Rich. "The Outcome of Parenting: What Do We Really Know?" *Journal of Personality,* June 2000.
Hofferth, Sandra L. and Kermyt G. Anderson. "Are All Dads Equal? Biology Versus Marriage as a Basis for Paternal Investment. Journal of Marriage and Family, February 2003.

Jaffee, S.R., T.E. Moffitt, A. Caspi, and A. Taylor. "Life With (or Without) Father: The Benefits of Living with Two Biological Parents Depend on the Father's Antisocial Behavior." *Child Development,* February 1, 2003.

Kerig, Patricia K., Philip A. Cowan and Carolyn Pape Cowan. "Marital Quality and Gender Differences in Parent-Child Interaction." Developmental Psychology, November 1, 1993.
Kroska, Amy. "Investigating Gender Differences in the Meaning of Household Chores and Child Care." *Journal of Marriage and Family,* May 2003.

Loehlin, John C., Lee Willerman, and Jospeh M. Horn. "Personality Resemblance in Adoptive Families: A 10-Year Follow-Up." *Journal of Personality and Social Psychology,* 1987 (vol. 53, no. 5).

Lykken, David. "Factory of Crime." *Psychological Inquiry,* 1997, volume 8.

--------------- "The Causes and Costs of Crime and a Controversial Cure." *Journal of Personality,* 2000, volume 63.


MacKinnon-Lewis, Carol, David Rabiner, and Rebecca Starnes. "Predicting Boys' Social Acceptance and Aggression." *Developmental Psychology,* May 1999, Vol. 35. No. 3.

Martinez, Charles R. "Preventing Problems with Boys' Noncompliance: Effect of a Parent Training Intervention for Divorcing Mothers." *Journal of Consulting and Clinical Psychology,* June 1, 2001, Vol. 69, Issue 3.

Montague, Diane P. F., and Arlene S. Walker-Andrews. "Mothers, Fathers, and Infants: The Role of Person Familiarity and Parental Involvement in Infants' Perception of Emotion Expressions." *Child Development,* September/October 2002.


National Institute of Child Development (NICHD). "Do Children's Attention Processes Mediate the Link Between Family Predictors and School Readiness?" *Developmental Psychology,* May 1, 2003.


Phares, Vicky. "Where's Poppa? A Relative Lack of Attention to the Role of Fathers in Child and Adolescent Psychopathology." *American Psychologist, 1992.*


"Violent Children: Bridging Development, Intervention, and Public Policy." *Developmental Psychology,* March 1, 2003.


Plomin, Robert, John C. Loehlin, and J.C. DeFries. "Genetic and environmental Components of 'Environmental' Influences." *Developmental Psychology,* 1985 (vol. 21, no. 3).

Ross, Emma. "Study Says Broken Homes Harm Kids More." Associated Press, London, Janaury 24, 2003.

Theis, Sophie Van S. *How Foster Children Turn Out.* New York: State Charities Aid Association, 1924.

Walton, G.E., N. J. Bower and T.G. Bower. "Recognition of Familiar Faces by Newborns." *Infant Behavior and Development,* number 15.

www.ingramcontent.com/pod-product-compliance
Lightning Source LLC
Chambersburg PA
CBHW020435130626
46549CB00001B/150